Good Night, Whatever You Are

By Richard Scrivani

Good Night, Whatever You Are
Richard Scrivani
© 2018 Richard Scrivani. All Rights Reserved.
No part of this book may be reproduced in any form or by any means, electronic, mechanical, digital, photocopying or recording, except for the inclusion in a review, without permission in writing from the publisher.

Published in the USA by:
BearManor Media
P. O. Box 71426
Albany, GA 31708
www.bearmanormedia.com

ISBN 978-1-62933-384-7

Printed in the United States of America.
Book design by Robbie Adkins, www.adkinsconsult.com

Dedicated to my father Edward Scrivani, who was amused by my kinship with monsters, and always believed in me.

"Good evening, good evening! Zacherley here! Zacherley here, to tell you that you're now holding the revised edition of this 2006 book by Rich Scrivani, a grand old boy, grand old boy. Ha ha ha ha — ha!"

Table of Contents

A Note from Pat Boone VI
Preface by David Colton VII
Foreword X
Introduction XIII
Chapter 1: Monster Kids Find a Leader 1
Chapter 2: New York-Bound 15
Chapter 3: Switching Channels 30
Chapter 4: Cartoons and New Projects 38
Chapter 5: Coolest Little Monsters 44
Chapter 6: Halloween and the Rolling Stones 54
Chapter 7: A Five O'Clock World 61
Chapter 8: Costume Shows, Groovy Clothes 71
Chapter 9: Ducks and Daydreams 86
Chapter 10: Summer of '66 93
Chapter 11: Clouds, Shadows and Guest Stars 102
Chapter 12: The End of an Era 109
Chapter 13: Radio Days 119
Chapter 14: Timelines Cross: The Disc-O-Teen Reunion 131
Chapter 15: The Chair 140
Chapter 16: The Saga of The Zacherley Archives 144
Chapter 17: Zacherley, Debbie Rochon and a Houseful of Idiots 152
Chapter 18: "Interment for Two" 161
Chapter 19: The Grand Reunion 166
Chapter 20: Excursions 171
Afterword 185
Zach's Final Years 188
Appendix 1 196
Appendix 2 202
Appendix 3 207

A Note from Pat Boone

I'll never forget John Zacherle, the Abe Lincoln of horror. I'm just kidding, of course, because that's what John always did himself!

As he has noted, we "hung out" at ABC, where he was doing a night time show on New York television, and I was doing my *Pat Boone Chevy Showroom* on ABC network television. At that time, folks around the country had no idea who Zacherle was, but I didn't care: I thought he was terrific, he tickled my funny bone, and I insisted that we find ways to include him in my shows from time to time. I'm sure people around the country were scratching their heads, wondering what that was all about, but that made it even funnier to me.

John himself was always friendly and funny and accommodating and he knew I got a kick out of his sense of humor. One of the things I most enjoyed about him was that he literally made fun of "horror." With his

Pat Boone

live schtick, supposedly driving stakes into the hearts of vampires, operating on cauliflower brains and all that, he made all the macabre seem ludicrous, which it certainly is. And his throwaway lines, his muttered observations and comments, always struck me as really funny.

Others, particularly today, keep trying to scare the bejeebers out of little kids, and I wish Zacherle was here to poke holes in all of them. I'll never forget him.

Pat Boone
Los Angeles
June 21, 2006

Preface

By David Colton

Evolutions start slowly, quietly, sometimes subversively and, in Zacherley's case, with an unmistakable laugh.

Most historians say the cultural shift of the '60s began with the assassination of JFK and the anguish of the Vietnam War. But we children of the 1950s know better. We know the '60s really began much earlier.

They began when Mad magazine put Madison Avenue through its merciless, gap-toothed comb; when Jerry Lewis, looking proper in his tuxedo just like a grown-up should, suddenly put a glass into his mouth and clapped hands like a walrus; when kiddie hosts like Chuck McCann and Paul Winchell added just a tiny wink of civil disobedience as they pushed Ovaltine, citizenship ... and Daffy Duck.

No wonder a generation, taught these truths at an early age by Knucklehead Smiff, spilled into the streets.

But most of all, for kids born under the bomb and black-and-white TV; the revolution that was the 1960s began with Zacherley.

Zacherley was a pop phenomenon, as big for a time in Philadelphia, New York City and New Jersey as Davy Crockett, Elvis or hula hoops. He was the Cool Ghoul, after all, a Transylvanian hipster. who was the host of Shock Theater, Drac's best friend, a presidential candidate in 1960, and along with Steve Allen, the hippest man ever to be on television. And we kids all knew it.

Best of all, Zacherley was forbidden. He was every parent's nightmare, appearing on late late TV — on school nights! — and enlisting a growing army of young lab assistants in the eternal struggle to stay up as late as possible.

He showed horror movies on Channel 7 in New York City. Then on Channel 9, Zacherley was our

John Zacherle as Philadelphia's Roland.

introduction to what scared our parents when they were young — Frankenstein, Dracula, the Wolf Man, the Mummy. He did things never done before on television. He'd dress in costume and interrupt the movies in quick cutaways. Sometimes he'd be a villager with a pitchfork. Other times a gravedigger. It was startling, audacious, revolutionary.

Zacherley's late night set was dark and gloomy, with things that moaned and hung on the wall.

His wife, Isobel, lived in a box. She had none of Donna Reed's cheer. Instead, she made eeh-ooh-ah monkey sounds like you'd hear on *Sheena* or

In 1986, Zach hosted the campy direct-to-video filmclip compilation Horrible Horrors. *He poses here with multiple VHS copies. (Photo courtesy John Zacherle.)*

Ramar of the Jungle. When the reception cleared, her box turned out to be a mail cart they found at the station, filled with pulsating amoebas, wind-up toys and all kinds of marvelous electrical contraptions that sparked and arced and sometimes, when things got a little sloppy, even caught fire. And wasn't that exciting!

He was anti-establishment in every way: He'd make fun of the station, or the movie he was showing. He'd get filthy with powder or gook doing experiments. He wasn't very clean, not in that '50s Frigidaire way, and instead was always rubbing his hands on his tattered coat or clapping up dust, live on TV. He was sinister and sly, naughty and wise. And without ever saying it, Zacherley taught every kid watching, every night, that the point of his show, and of life itself, was to enjoy the absurdity of it all.

Zacherley was the real deal. He was television jazz, Lenny Bruce in monster drag, so be-bop perfect that his late-night cameramen, after a long day of jingles and bad weathermen, would laugh at his jokes. They'd laugh so loud that we could hear it at home, a mind-bending break in the Sylvania fourth wall. It was meta to the max. And when kids heard the honesty in the guffaws from these hardboiled union men on the set, well, it just made it even more special to be in on the joke while our parents slept.

And then there was Zach himself, a cadaverous undertaker with hollowed cheeks, white pasty skin, hair parted in the middle like Alfalfa and a delicious and droll delivery that signaled to every kid watching that this indeed was where the underground army would truly begin. "Confound it all," he'd exclaim when something didn't go right. As we said, lessons for life.

Then abruptly, Zach was gone. Well, not gone. But it was clear the Establishment had finally found wolfbane. Even as Soupy Sales arrived to make the joke more direct, Zach turned up on Channel 11, showing *Hercules* cartoons, of all things, in the afternoon. He was still Zach, but like all things undead, even hip ones, something died in the glare of the afternoon light. And we kids knew that, too.

Zach's eviction from the castle was not yet done. Before HDTV, before satellite and cable, before all of that, there was something called UHF, odd channels beyond the usual 2 through 13. And there, on Channel 47 if your TV could pull it in from Jersey, there was Zacherley hosting *Disc-O-Teen*, a Transylvanian bandstand with rock and roll bands, kids dancing to the hits and good ol' Zach changin' with the times.

His transformation was completed a few years later when he turned up on New York's album-format rock station, WNEW-FM. He was John Zacherle by then, a smart and smooth-voiced deejay for the music of a monster-schooled generation. But between the Jefferson Airplane, Doors and

Velvet Underground, we Monster Kids who had gone to college, Woodstock or even Vietnam never doubted for a minute that the man behind the microphone was in greasepaint, wearing a funeral coat and medallion.

Zacherley would rise again — on *Saturday Night Live* in a memorable cameo, in commercials, in taped compilations, at conventions. In many ways, this proud, gentle and wonderful man is as popular now as at his peak in the '60s.

Most biographies and, indeed, most memories, of Zacherley necessarily center on his *Shock Theater* years, his late night shows as Roland in Philadelphia and the Cool Ghoul in New York. But there are few guides to his lost years at *Disc-O-Teen*, his quiet days at WNEW or his comeback years in the 90s and today. And that's where this book comes in, to complete Zacherley's journey from late-night shaman to living, er, undead, legend, his triumphs, his lost years, his setbacks and his 21st century rediscovery and redemption. If one man can be said to have chronicled it all, to have ridden the highs and lows of an icon's remarkable life, it is Zacherley's confidante and sometimes traveling companion, Richard Scrivani. This lifelong fan has unearthed lost footage, videotaped Zacherley in his real-life basement, has traveled with the Cool Ghoul through Jersey and beyond. Indeed, it is his laughter sometimes heard on *The Zacherley Archives*, an essential compilation available on DVD. And it is Richard Scrivani's sure hand who will guide readers through the rest of Zacherley's incredible story.

"Would you like to hear what happened after that?" Mary Shelley asked in *Bride of Frankenstein*.

Well, we pose the same question to you. Whether a long-time fan of "Dinner with Drac" or a newbie wondering how horror hosts began, Richard Scrivani's journey with Zacherley will show how a monster original still echoes in a generation who sat cross-legged in the darkness, all those years ago.

Because in the end, Zacherley's undead celebration of life and revolutionary spirit will always ring true, whatever your politics or, as Zach likes to say, "whatever you are."

David Colton
Arlington, Virginia

David Colton and Zach at WonderFest in 2007.

Foreword

I was at the gym doing my daily workout in the pool when an elderly gentleman named Pat in the next lane said his usual hello and we exchanged the customary familiarities. This time the conversation turned to retirement activities, hobbies and the like, and Pat asked the question that retirees often hear: "What do you do with your time?" I proceeded to list the different interests I have, and mentioned that I was writing a book. "What about?" was, of course, his next question, so I told him it was about a local television celebrity. When he told me he had grown up in Pittsfield, Massachusetts, I said, "Well, you probably don't know about him then. He was popular mostly in the New York area." (Pat was in his seventies, and I also reasoned that he would have been a bit too old to be watching *Shock Theater* even if he had been from the area.) When he told me he had moved to New Jersey in 1959, I took a shot: "Did you ever hear of Zacherley?" His eyes widened, he stood very still in the water and with great excitement said, "Zacherley?! Sure I remember him. He's a legend!"

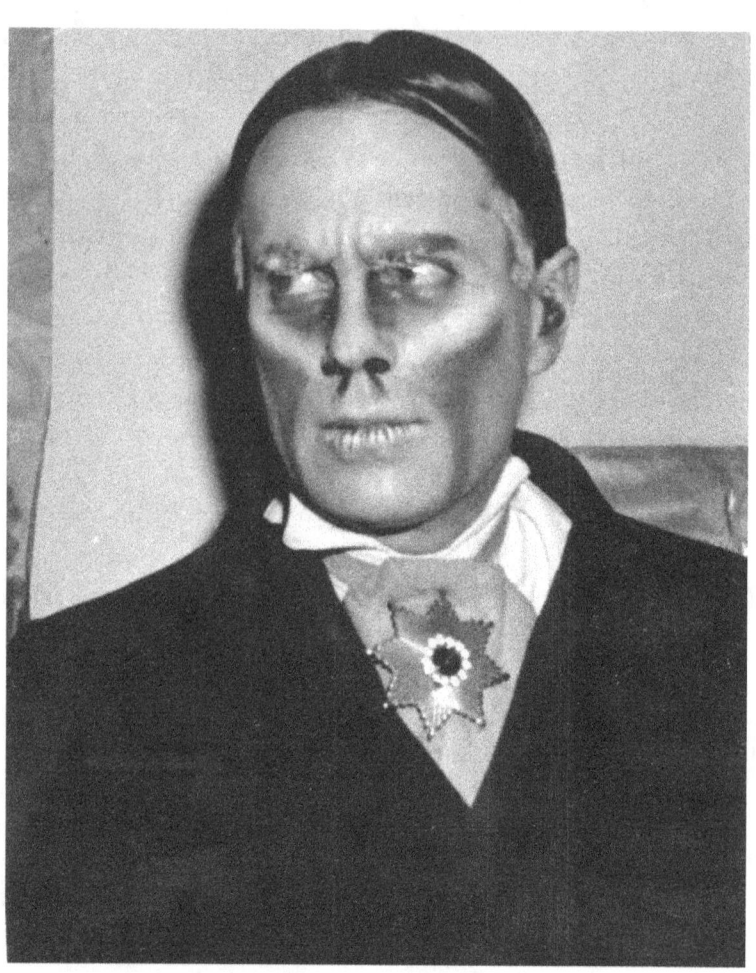

"Zacherley?! He's a legend!" (Photo courtesy John Zacherle.)

Legend. An appellation which the legend himself would acknowledge with a smile but also a shake of his head. We all know it's true, and deep down I'm sure he does too, but if anyone in the world would never take such a compliment seriously, it's John Zacherle.

Many of you who are reading this book may be curious why I decided to write it in the first place.

In October 1998, I was attending Kevin Clement's Chiller Theatre expo at the Sheraton Hotel in Secaucus, New Jersey, waiting outside the small lecture room where Zach was scheduled to hold one of his question-and-answer sessions, when two 40-ish female fans started up a conversation with me. My friends Paul Scrabo, his wife George Ann and I had just co-produced with Zach a video called *The Zacherley Archives*, which had made its debut on VHS at this convention. The buzz it was creating attracted even more than the usual amount of attention Zach's way, and the two women began barraging me with questions about what it was like to know him. I told them about *Disc-O-Teen*, Zach's '60s TV dance show, and how my relationship with him had begun there. "You should write all this down in a book," they said.

I found the idea amusing and flattering, tucking the notion into the nether regions of my brain and promising myself to think about it.

Since that time appeal of the idea began to grow. I did have some stories to tell, and I knew I could supplement them with recollections of other *Disc-O-Teen* "survivors" with whom I was still in touch. I felt it might be interesting to provide a glimpse into the days when I gate-crashed a Zacherley TV show, and what life was like on the set. Since the experience had been energizing for me as a 20-year-old (energizing? It changed my life!), I felt that there were many who could relate to it; hell, John Waters' 1988 movie *Hairspray*, which dealt with life at a 1962 Baltimore dancing program, was a cult favorite and just about to become a Broadway hit. After I caught up with Mr. Zacherle at a 1991 reunion, we remained in contact and began what became a genuine friendship which continued to his death at age 98.

But most importantly, Zach deserves to have a book written about him, so this book is for Zach fans everywhere — and you know who (or what) you are. Here is the man behind the legend; a kind, considerate and giving individual, discerning in the company he keeps, a bit enigmatic at times, but always thoughtful and — rare for a show business figure — non-egocentric. Indeed, the man will turn any conversation with a fan into a discussion about **them**; what his/her childhood was like, where they live, what they do for a living, and so forth. Very seldom will he expound on his own accomplishments, or, more frustrating for someone writing about him, make any lengthy statements about his professional calling in perspective, how he has impacted so many of us, and how much of an icon he has become. He will look back with fondness and a sense of humor about

Right to left, Zach, Debbie Rochon and Mike Thomas as they appeared in 2004's Dr. Horror's "Erotic" House of Idiots, a movie I associate-produced.

career-related events, but never to the point of self-admiration. A famous man with simple likes and dislikes beneath his persona as a living legend, John Zacherle needs to be written about.

Scattered throughout this book are excerpts from recorded conversations with Zach conducted either on the phone or while riding in his car. I've smoothed out some of the rough edges, but I wanted you to feel that you were sitting in on casual conversations as they really were. There are also Zacherle quotes taken from various other sources, but the relaxed talks should be easy to identify.

While I also wanted this memoir to include some biographical elements, I never intended it to be an actual biography. That's for some other ambitious and more enterprising soul to tackle. My goals here are to tell my story — how an adolescent Eisenhower-era monster fan became lucky enough to share time and experiences with his childhood idol; how Mr. Zacherle, funny, hip, ahead of his time as a horror host, began a second career as a "delegate" of the '60s with a teenage dance show; and how, since gaining his friendship, I never need wonder where he is or what he is doing, as I used to as a kid when he disappeared from the airwaves for a year or so. I also wanted to share some of the photos (many previously unpublished) I took with my father's old Polaroid camera on the *Disc-O-Teen* set. I hope Zach's loyal fans have as much fun reading this book as I have had writing it.

No project is ever realized by one person alone, writing a book is always a team effort. I want to acknowledge all the people who generously donated their time, patience, talent and, most significantly, their memories to help bring to life the *Disc-O-Teen* years and also shed some light on the persona of the man you are reading about. With great appreciation I thank: Lou Antonicello, Adrienne Barbeau, Marty Baumann, Pat Boone, John, Ruth, and Michael Brunas, Kevin Clement, David Colton, Arnie DeGaetano, the late Anne Di Dio, Rosemary DiPietra, Christine Domaniecki, Dennis Ferrante, Art Finkelstein, Russell Frost, Mike Furno, Mike and Ruth Gilks, Joe Girardi, Keith Hakala, Barry Landers, Joe LoRé, Richard Heyman of the Doughboys, the late Sharon Lawson, Bob Madison, Joette and Tony Martin, Keith Mirenberg, George Ann Muller, Linda Pace, Vinnie Patanio, Paul Russak, Jeff Samuels, Wende Sasse, Paul Scrabo, Steve, Doug and Joan Scrivani, Steve Shaffer, Ruth and Dona Steinman, the late Mike Thomas, Terry Tousey, "Little Steven" Van Zandt, Tom Weaver and, of course, the late John Zacherle, who gave me unlimited access to his photo collection, records and recollections.

Special thanks to Igor, Phyllis the Amoeba, Isobel, Janos and Gasport.

And if I accomplish nothing else, I want to clear up one important thing: The man's name is spelled *Zacherle*. The ghoul character is *Zacherley*. Let's get that straight once and for all, confound it!

—Richard Scrivani

Introduction

In 1988, Mike Gilks, a 31-year-old musician and guitar teacher, sat with his wife Ruth in an auditorium at Long Island's Dowling College where John Zacherle, the television personality he had enjoyed so much in his youth, was about to make a live appearance. Mike couldn't believe he was going to see one of his childhood idols in person. In the fall of 1963, when Mike was six, he watched a somewhat mediocre cartoon show on New York City's Channel 11: *The Mighty Hercules*. It wasn't the cartoons themselves that prompted him to tune in every day; *Hercules* was the usual semi-animated, cheap fare that TV offered at that time. What had hooked him on the show was its host. What a black-frocked vampire type with slick hair parted down the middle had to do with *Hercules* was anybody's guess. It didn't matter — it was his antics between the cartoons that had Mike laughing so hard he could sometimes hardly catch his breath.

There was Zacherle, made up to look like the living dead, in a coffin-pallor makeup that if played straight might give anyone Mike's age nightmares. But this man wasn't dealing in bad dreams. Instead he played with brains that looked suspiciously like cauliflower, dissected huge, quivering gelatin "amoebas" and conducted experiments guaranteed to slop up his dungeon set so badly it would look unsalvageable by the show's end. Inside a canvas laundry hamper moaned an unseen banshee which every once in awhile needed a wooden stake pounded through her heart to keep her happy. On top of all this, Zacherle would censure the station and the cartoons he was showing, once insisting that he was presenting them "under duress" ("which means I don't like it!" he barked). How did all this have even the remotest connection to a legendary Greek hero? It may have been madness, but it was also magic — pure enchantment. It was Zacherley.

He had heard that John Zacherle was a mild-mannered sort who enjoyed his fans, and this translated in Mike's mind to "approachable." The college appearance show was generally a demonstration of how to dissect a giant Jell-O unicell, followed by a question-and-answer period. The movie *Ghost of Dragstrip Hollow* (1959) was slated to follow the live portion of the show, but the fans overwhelmingly voted to have Zacherley continue; who cared about a movie? During the show a man asked Zach if his records "Spook Along with Zacherley," "Scary Tales" (original tunes with monster lyrics) and "Monster Mash" (ghoulish covers of current hit songs) recorded in the late '50s and early '60s, were available anywhere and was promptly presented with a cassette of some of them from the Cool Ghoul himself. Mike, witnessing this and astonished at the generosity of his hero, had never known about these songs and wished he had been the recipient. After the show, Mike briefly met Zach, who, to his surprise and delight, asked him about himself. Among other things they discussed, Mike was able to work in the fact that he was a working musician. Driving back home to East Quogue, Long Island under a bright full moon, Mike wished the evening had never ended.

A friend provided Zacherle's phone number, and the two began corresponding almost immediately. Mike began sending little joke packages in the mail consisting of nothing more serious than a rubber brain and the like. Eventually the much-coveted tapes of Zach's old records began appearing in Mike's mailbox, and soon after the pair were speaking regularly on the phone. At one point Mike took advantage of an opening in the conversation to ask if Zach had ever considered recording again. The response was encouraging enough for Mike to begin work on a song that

Zacherley on stage with Mike Gilks at a Chiller con.

ry days was the deliriously sexy Elvira, who at the time was making a big splash with adolescent boys by presenting herself as essentially an updated version of the original 1950s West Coast horror hostess Vampira, taking care to accentuate as much as possible her physical attributes. Alluring and tightly dressed, Elvira, on Milwaukee's *Elvira's Movie Macabre* would purr her way through the mid- to late '80s hosting movies like 1971's *Tombs of the Blind Dead* and 1973's *Silent Night, Bloody Night*, making derisive and suggestive remarks about the films while at the same time earning a fortune. It looked like the era of the male horror host was gone forever.

Nothing could have been more disquieting to Zacherley fans than the story that he had placed an ad in *Variety* announcing his availability to perform at children's parties. It seemed that while there was still a loyal fan base somewhere out there, it wasn't enough to provide a decent income for the 72-year-old actor, who also keenly desired to keep active. It was at this point that a spirited Mike Gilks approached Zach at Kevin Clement's first horror expo, Horrorthon '90, and handed him a demo of the song "Zack is Back," an original composition that would ultimately become part of a dream project: a brand new CD collection of Zacherley material.

Despite the enthusiastic reception Zach received at Dowling College and his healthy appearance and buoyant manner, things could have been better for him professionally; his career was more or less at a standstill. There was still a radio gig every Halloween and a few guest appearances on local TV stations, but for the most part John Zacherle felt work was coming too slowly. He had long ago retired from a deejay job on FM radio, and television horror film hosting was largely a thing of the past. In the late '80s, one of the only significant remnants of those glo-

inspired by the lunacy of Zach's old Cameo-Parkway and Electra recordings from 1959 to 1963. About a week later, the day before Halloween, Mike found Zach on the other end of the phone and an agreement was made for the pair to meet in Patchogue, Long Island, at the oddly named "Kno" studios to begin work on the new song.

A short time later, Mike got another phone call with some less happy news: Zach had pulled a hamstring in his leg chasing a kid who was spraying graffiti on the wall of his 96th Street Manhattan apartment building. He had fallen and injured himself so badly that he couldn't walk. To make matters worse, no one had offered to help him and he was reduced to crawling back through the heavy front door and up four flights of stairs to his apartment. The accident had left him in such pain that he was unable to drive, so he apologized that the recording session would have to be postponed. Time passed, but Zach kept in touch.

By the time the next call came, Zach had made a decision that at once confused, disappointed and saddened Mike. Zach still wanted to record, but with a significant modification- he wanted to change the name of the song from "Zack Is Back" to "Drac Is Back." The reason? The song should be about Count Dracula, a character every fan of horror movies knew. Well, Mike thought, that might be true, but why not a song about the famous horror host? The answer that came across the wire from John Zacherle's mouth to Mike's unbelieving ear was, "Because who gives a fuck about me?"

Flash forward — it's the late afternoon of Wednesday, October 29, 2003, and I'm sitting on the carpet in the sunken living room of John Zacherle's apartment trying to make some order out of a pile of photos he has dumped in my lap. It's a small, unpretentious place, in which large portraits of Zacherle ancestors look down upon visitors, a pair of cozy easy chairs face the average-sized TV set, and two antique pull-chain lamps with amber shades and carved, jade-colored glass adorning their stands bathe the place in a gentle, warm light. Except for a few Zacherley-related photos and objects d'art scattered around, I would never suspect that I'm in the home of the legendary Cool Ghoul. We have just returned from Taranto's, a photo gallery on West 19th Street. Zach frequents the place to have new glossy 8x10 photos printed to autograph and sell at Clement's newly named Chiller Theatre expo, then held semi-annually at the Sheraton Hotel in Secaucus, New Jersey. Zach had been the headliner there since October 1990; he was no longer playing to an unseen television audience, but to hundreds of old and new fans who formed long lines to meet him and purchase an autographed picture. Always present to attend to his every need are friends Jeff Samuels and Arnie DeGaetano. It seems an awful lot of people "give a fuck" about John Zacherle these days.

"Here's some more," Zach, says as he dumps another handful of the priceless pictures on the floor. "I've been meaning to get these in order for

quite some time, but they've been sitting here for months." I don't mind; in fact, I'm thrilled to be sharing the day and evening with my former television idol and friend, and being given the privilege to help him get some things squared away. I'm arranging them in little piles and there are all shapes and sizes; 8x10s, 4x8s, color shots from Zach's FM radio days, postcards, stickers announcing "Zacherley for President," snapshots taken off the tube and sent to him by fans, even color photo-booth shots of him in close-up that look so superior to the ones from Woolworth booths in the '50s and '60s that I'm amazed they aren't studio portraits. The ones that interest me the most are the shots from his years at WABC-TV and WOR-TV in New York, and the occasional rare Roland pic from WCAU-TV in Philadelphia.

When I'm done, I must have about a dozen categories neatly in envelopes, clearly marked. "Now you can lay your hands on any phase of your career," I tell him with a smile. I fully realized these are merely the tip of the Zacherley iceberg, that hundreds more were stored away in various drawers, on tabletops, and in the legendary "closet" that Zach is so fond of referencing. In it, waiting in the darkness like some lost Tutankhamun treasure, was the surviving mother lode of mementos and treasures from all stages of his television and radio career. (We would get to those too, when it came time to release the DVD version of *The Zacherley Archives*.)

"How about a little supper?" says Zach, and I'm frankly amazed that I haven't been "dismissed" yet in the classic Zacherle style ("Well, well, well! I guess you're tired, eh? What are you going to do with yourself this evening?"). This is what his best friend Jeff Samuels describes as one of the "very loud signals" Zach gives you when he has had enough company and wishes to be alone, but I have received no such signal this evening and am more than happy to accompany him to dinner. We walk (neither of us very well, Zach having arthritis in his feet and myself with a newly acquired neuropathy) west from his place to Broadway and a fine Italian restaurant named Acqua where he orders a chicken dish and I get simple pasta with tomato sauce. I study his face and his physical appearance, listen to his words — he is downright amazing for a man of 85 years. I think back to my days as a 13-year-old watching him on my parents' black-and-white TV and ask myself, "How on Earth did I get from there to here?"

I enter my mental time machine and step out in the year 1966. Sitting in the top row of bleachers behind a thick glass partition looking down at a UHF television studio in Newark, New Jersey, I'm waiting for something to happen, wondering exactly what's going on in the small office down the darkened hall to my right. In it, John Zacherle is banging out the script to the evening's 8:20 p.m. taping of *Disc-O-Teen*, his answer to Dick Clark's *American Bandstand*. In about a half hour, the office will be packed with teenage kids hoping to get a look at or a few moments of conversation with their idol, the man they used to watch religiously on *Shock Theater*. Recently he had become a kind of Pied Piper to them as they danced to the current Top 40 hits he introduced in this expansive studio atop the Symphony Hall building.

I come here, just like the rest of them, but I'm a bit uncomfortable because I'm older, no longer a teenager, and I've been hanging around here for weeks like something job-wise is about to happen, as if my future is somehow wrapped up in this place. The co-producer, Barry Landers, has taken me under his wing and half-indicated that this might be a starting point for me in television work.

I wait for some of the kids I've gotten to know to show up, and I hope above all that one particular person will be here tonight. But whether she is or not, I'm getting my foot in a very special door, totally oblivious to how exceptional this opportunity will turn out to be. The kids, mainly girls ranging from 14 to 18, are starting to fill the corridors. Another magic night is about to begin, like a movie with that wonderful mid-60s rock music as the soundtrack. Eight years ago I could never have imagined this — eight years; an eternity when you've lived only 20. What was I doing eight years ago?

Chapter 1
Monster Kids Find a Leader

A dinner was served for three at Dracula's House by the Sea.
The hors d'oeuvres were fine, but I choked on my wine
When I found that the main course was me!

—"Dinner with Drac," John Zacherle

"Well, I don't know how many years later, my daughter still can't eat cauliflower because of me watching Zacherley when he was operating on the 'brains.'" (A female fan at the Lead East antique car show in New Jersey, Labor Day weekend, 2004.)

Growing up in my New Jersey neighborhood was very much like living in an episode of *Leave It to Beaver* or *Ozzie and Harriet*. In my home town of Bergenfield, kids typically wore jeans ("dungarees" we called them then) with rolled-up cuffs usually revealing red-plaid lining. Keds sneakers and polo shirts rounded out the ensemble. We kept our hair short, and somewhere around 1955 a buzz-cut sporting a waxed brow line was all the rage. Backyards seemed larger then, and half the lawns in them were rutted away by ongoing stickball or football games, bouts of wrestling and just plain roughhousing. On nice days we'd sail cheap balsa wood airplanes around the neighborhood until a wing or stabilizer would crack and then it was a matter of being patient until you got the 25 cents you needed to run down to the deli that carried them; then you were back in business again until the damned thing got stuck in a tree, 20 feet up. Meanwhile you could fashion homemade bows and arrows and play Robin Hood, or hang out on your front porch reading comic books, or naming the make of each car that would pass by (in 1955 you could do that; all the models looked unique and had a distinct personality). Our world was a profusion of striped shirts, bikes with streamers and fox tails, Davy Crockett caps, baseball cards, Elvis Presley, black-and-white TV, Saturday kiddie matinee movies, bubblegum and Fizzies. Then came October 1957.

They came into my life as suddenly as a bolt of lightning: monsters! Dracula, Frankenstein's Monster, the Mummy, the Wolf Man, the Invisible Man. The deranged denizens of Hollywood's past: the classic Gothic creatures from the musty vaults of Universal Studios. There they were, staring out at me from the pages of *TV Guide*, faces I had never seen before, frightening faces, intriguing faces, forbidden faces. Forbidden to me by my parents, and probably for thousands of other kids around the country who had been bitten by the *Shock Theater* bug. Until that first week in October, I stood a half-decent chance of having a normal life. That was no longer possible after my first glimpse of the incredible fantasy world spread out before me now on late-night television. And even if it were possible that my first flirtation with things monstrous could have faded after the novelty went away, my parents were unwittingly sealing my fate (and theirs) by their rigid stance against my staying up late to see them. It seems strange today, but in the straight-laced, conservative '50s these films, the best of them made in the 1930s by gifted writers, directors and craftsmen, were looked upon as one notch above pornography. And little more than a year previous, the government had slapped a ban of horror comic books with titles like *Tales from the Crypt* and *The Vault of Horror*. It was "unsafe" for things like this to invade the sanctity of the American home; they were trash, dangerous to young minds like mine. For our "safety," the films were broadcast in the middle of the night. The truth is that they were unfairly dismissed by '50s mainstream society and completely misunderstood.

About a year after Screen Gems' *Shock!* package of 52 features was released to local television stations around the country, a new phenomenon arrived. It was announced and heavily promoted in the papers that with the 1958 release of the second horror package, *Son of Shock*, something new would be added: a host to guide us through the films. I didn't think this was all that necessary; the films were entertainment enough. The ghostly disembodied voice that for a week or two preceded the live, in-person debut of New York City's character did, I confess, scare me all over again. The engineers at WABC Channel 7 added a touch of echo to the voice, presumably to make it sound like it might be coming from within a crypt. I was much too old to be affected by such an obvious ploy, so I can't for the life of me fathom why I got the creeps, but I did. I had gotten used to the movies, even regarded them at this point as old friends. It was possibly the implication that this new host would be taking the show to another level—maybe one involving more horrific stuff. Boy, did I have a surprise in store for me. I had been frightened by the voice of someone who would soon earn a reputation as one of the wittiest television personalities ever — John Zacherle!

On a promotional tour for "Dinner with Drac" in Allentown, Pennsylvania, with a lookalike fan. (Photo courtesy John Zacherle.)

I'd already had a bit of exposure to John Zacherle. I had a close friend on the block, Steve Shaffer, who also loved the old horror flicks, belonged to a *Shock Theater* club with me (we were the only members), and even accompanied me on trips around the neighborhood to collect newspapers, under the pretense of being on a Boy Scout paper drive, so we could search through them for the *Shock!* ads and pictures of our favorite monsters. There were as yet no monster magazines in existence; the first issue of Forry Ackerman's *Famous Monsters of Filmland* was months away from publication. The *New York Daily News* was good, it had pictures that were about three inches square; but the prizes we were really in search of could only be found in papers like *The New York Times* and the *New York Journal-American*. Their ads would sprawl across the page some 12x4 inches, one of them, the biggest I ever saw, announcing the New York debut of *Frankenstein* (1931). It ran down the entire length of the page, too large to fit into the scrapbooks that Steve and I had created to hold these "treasures." Besides being a *Shock Theater* compatriot, Steve was always the first on our block to discover anything new that was happening in popular music, which by this time had morphed from Patti Page and Perry Como into Elvis Presley and Chuck Berry. One day we met on the street and he excitedly told me about a new novelty single on the Cameo-Parkway label. It was called "Dinner with Drac," had lyrics about the classic monster characters and was recorded by a man named John Zacherle.*

I had also recently read an article in the March 29, 1958, *TV Guide* entitled "What a Revoltin' Development!" which chronicled the rise of the many television horror hosts around the country, and saw a picture of Philadelphia's Roland (accent on the "land"), played, as everyone knows, by Zacherle. Beneath a photo of the ghostly curator in his crypt, a caption read, "Philadelphia: Roland is hero." Shortly afterward followed the famous *Saturday Evening Post* article "TV's Midnight Madness" with a larger photo of Roland standing next to a six-foot rocket. However, I credit Steve with my very first exposure to the persona of the Cool Ghoul.

Zach celebrates his article in The Saturday Evening Post *with a fan. (Photo courtesy John Zacherle.)*

After being released from the army, John Zacherle had ambiguous feelings as to what type of career to choose. He had had a less than rewarding experience working in a bank, and his higher education culminated in a B.A. in English from the University of Pennsylvania. Not being terribly interested in teaching (most of his days in the schoolroom found him staring out the window, wishing he were "out there, rather than in here"), his life turned a corner one day in the late 1940s when a cousin suggested John might be interested in joining a theater group in Germantown called the Stagecrafters. He became a member, built and painted scenery, and acted. In addition to providing him with new friends, the stint led to some local radio work. Then word started getting out about a new live cowboy show, *Action in the Afternoon*, being broadcast from Philadelphia's CBS affiliate WCAU, Channel 10. In 1953 Zach auditioned, joined the cast and spent the next year as a working actor. But he had to learn one crucial thing: how to ride a horse.

RICH: You tell a story about escaped horses when you were doing *Action in the Afternoon*.

ZACH: In the Philadelphia area, they had riding stables where you could rent horses and go riding in the park. So that was an obvious source for us, I guess there were times we had six or seven horses in the

---

* The song had to be released under the name John Zacherle rather than his then-current Philadelphia TV persona Roland to avoid conflict with his employers at WCAU-TV.

Zach on the live Western TV series Action in the Afternoon.

Zach with another Action in the Afternoon *actor, Johnny D'Armond.*

show and we also had horses that knew how to pull carriages and wagons. So they made a deal with the riding academy to use their horses. But the horses were smart, you know. Usually they'd get a day off, but the weekend was when they worked hard because that's when most people would come in and rent the horses. So during the week, it was usually a slow time for a horse, then suddenly they're working on weekdays too. I think they resented it [*laughs*]!

Nobody knew how to ride a horse, at least the actors didn't. And you had to find out how to ride. So there was one horse who was extra-smart: On weekends when he was rented out to private parties or just walking around the park, he would either dump the person off, or, when the person would get off to take a drink, he'd take off. And instead of going back to the stable to work, he'd come over and hide out in this fake town that we built, behind which we had a fake stable and always some bale of hay sitting around for atmosphere. He was funny. He was a regular, this one horse did it all the time! He'd show up on the weekend. Nobody was there except people who were working in the studio, and they would have to call the stable and say, "Hey, come on, he's over here. If you're lookin' for him, he's over here." Oh, gosh, it got to be a big joke.

One of the factors which prevented Zach from pursuing more and sundry acting roles was his inhibition when it came to memorizing a large amount of lines. He was comfortable with supporting parts, and soon he developed a genuine flair for improvising. In one episode of *Action*, he found himself becoming absorbed in an emotional scene:

> One time, to my amazement, I was playing the part of a rancher who was struggling to make things work at the ranch. He had cattle or whatever he had, but nothing was going right with him, and his wife and

The man behind the makeup, John Zacherle.

Zach in a magazine ad for an adoption agency in the 1950s. (Photo courtesy John Zacherle.)

kids were close to starving. Somehow or another, they struck gold. And I was in one scene there, after halfway through this half-hour show, when the word came down that it wasn't real gold, it was fool's gold. And I'm talkin' to the sheriff and he breaks the news, you know, and I'm talkin' to him and talkin' to him, and to my amazement, this is during rehearsal, I'm cryin'! I'm cryin' all over the place! And I couldn't imagine what was happening. And after the rehearsal was over, the director came down and he says, "That was very good, that was great. We won't change a thing." But from that second on, I thought, "Am I going to be able to do that when we go on the air?" So it comes time for me to do it — I got about two tears, that's all, I managed to do it. I really don't know how those emotions work. I guess actors who really get into acting have experienced that too. But from that point on, I never did any crying. I did a lot of screaming on some of them. But it was a very strange experience that I remember every once in awhile, and I think, "Geez, how did it ever happen?" And the director was so excited, he thought, boy, he really discovered a great actor here or something. But he was wrong, because I never could remember lines!

Nineteen fifty-seven brought Zach another, more significant opportunity. Based on the uniqueness of a character he had played on *Action in the Afternoon*, the station dreamed up a character for him that they believed would be well suited to the actor's talents. WCAU, like many other local TV stations around America, had leased the *Shock!* package and were in search of someone to play host to the films. On *Action*, Zach had portrayed an undertaker who traveled the West selling coffins and had settled for a year in the show's fictional town of Huberle, Montana. Remembering this role, the president of WCAU, Charlie Vanda, called Zach into a meeting with producer Ed White and explained: "Well, Ed here has dreamed up this character called Ro-*land*..."

According to Zach, no one present had the nerve to correct the boss' pronunciation of the name, with his accent on the second syllable, so when the character was created, the appellation stuck. On Monday, October 7, 1957, Roland, the guardian of WCAU's underground crypt, and

One of the first shots of Roland taken on the WCAU set.

prototype for the later "Zacherley," was born. WCAU's makeup man came up with the original look for the character; Zach himself claims that the undertaker's coat he originally wore on *Action in the Afternoon*, which became part of Roland's (and later Zacherley's) costume, came not from the cowboy show but from the little wardrobe room of the Stagecrafters!

The original WCAU ad for the premiere of *The Shock Theatre* announces its first two films, *Frankenstein* (on Monday, October 7) and *Dracula* (Tuesday, October 8), with the lines "For the first time on TV — two of the most terrifying tales to come out of Hollywood" and "Spine-tingling excitement every Monday and Tuesday evening at 11:25 on *The Shock Theatre*." Only one thing is missing: There is no mention of a host. The original Roland, as evidenced by the one existing homemade kinescope and one audiotape recorded right in the WCAU sound booth, was a surlier character than the later Zacherley; although the humor was already there, Roland acted most of the time as if he had either indigestion or a headache, and spewed out his acidic remarks in a somewhat grouchy manner. As has become legend, Roland usually entered while the announcer read a gruesome limerick: He walked down a spiral staircase carrying a basket, dripping blood (chocolate syrup) from an unseen head inside. Vanda wanted his host to be a bit scary and eventually insisted, "If there's a head in that basket, I want to see it!" Zach complied, but only partially, by giving the head a shave one night.

RICH: Did your mother ever watch the show, and if she did, what did she think?

ZACH: She told me one time a little kid came by and wanted to know if I was funny at home. Yes, she enjoyed them. But I don't know that she had said anything about it or if she had even watched it. It was late at night.

RICH: What about your brothers and sister?

ZACH: Yeah, my brother in Philadelphia, he watched it. My cousins watched it. The guy that got me into the Stagecrafters, he watched it, my cousin Bill. He was a big fan, he was great. He also was a big fan of Jean Shepherd. Oh, he loved Jean Shepherd and also W.C. Fields.

I found [a script] the other day from "Roland," I couldn't believe it. I thought, "What's this?" It was like a purple ink, from a mimeograph machine. And there was nothing on it. Apparently the guy who produced the show, Ed White, had written the introductions — "This evening's show is gonna be..." — so on and so on — but there was nothing written down about the intermissions at all! It's very odd.

RICH: Oh, really! You mean about the stuff you did?

ZACH: Yeah! All the experiments, there was nothing there, the intermissions for the night show. I don't know if I was making it up or — we had some props of course, each time, and Jell-O or something to play with, the brains and all.

Roland's original wife was called simply "My Dear"; later, in New York, she was known as Isobel. The only other resident of the ample crypt set was a dangerous-sounding ghoul by the name of Igor, permanently planted behind steel-barred doors (previously used by Ed McMahon, host of another local movie show, as a vault in which the films he was introducing were kept). Igor was known to have a ravenous appetite for mailmen, whom he would stalk down and devour off-camera. One funny bit involving Igor, from the Saturday, April 12, 1958, show, when the film presented was 1935's *WereWolf of London*, had Roland going over to the barred doors and holding out his fists, asking Igor to "guess which hand the goodie's in." When Igor chose, Roland gleefully taunted, "Wrong again!," sending Igor into a rage. The name Igor, by the way, would be used through the years by Zach to address his off-camera floor director.

RICH: Who did the live sound effects when you were in Philadelphia? It wasn't on tape, it seemed as though somebody was doing the noises live.

ZACH: For instance, the wife was done by Ed White, the guy who dreamed up this crazy idea. He knew all about these movies, he'd seen 'em all. I hadn't seen any of them. And I forget how it happened that

(Photo courtesy John Zacherle.)

I had a wife in the box, I don't think it was my idea. It was probably his idea. Oh, and then Igor was off to the left just next to the chair. Through the bars, there was a gate, you know, with bars on it. It would have been Ed White that did all the noises, I don't think they used recordings.

Some *Shock Theater* historians insist that Zach became embroiled in "salary disputes" and was absent from *The Shock Theatre* on Friday, April 18, and Saturday, April 19. According to the story compiled by writer Gerry Wilkinson, "additional duties (for little or no cash) were also part of the dispute. Channel 10 actually announced that Zacherle was off the show and would be replaced by a different actor whom [*sic*] would play the character of Roland." With its "master of scaremonies" gone, Wilkinson claims the show was hosted by My Dear (!) when the movies *Revenge of the Zombies* and *The Mad Ghoul* (both 1943) aired. Apparently the situation was resolved one way or

Zach's office at WCAU. (Photo courtesy John Zacherle.)

another and by the following weekend Zacherle was back, but one can only imagine how Roland's casket-bound "wife," whose only vocalizings consisted of various moans and groans, managed to "host" the show on those two occasions. (I must mention that Zach himself had no recollection of these events, but did volunteer that he received at the time, and still has, a drawing from teenage fan Anne Ambirge, depicting a smiling ghoulish character bearing the message, "You're Back!!!")

RICH: Did you ever have groupies?

ZACH: Groupies? Well, nobody ever followed me home or anything like that, but yeah, there were a couple of girls at the studio, at ABC, that used to come down and look in and hang around. But nothing really — nobody really called me on the phone all the time or anything like that. Never got really pursued. Although there was one girl, what was her name? [*trying to recall*] God Almighty —

RICH: Anne Di Dio?

ZACH: Hmmm? No, no. No, they were just great fans, Anne Di Dio and Ruth Steinman together liked to make things and create songs and stuff. Poetry and pictures and stuff. Ruth was a big fan of the Philadelphia show, and when I moved to New York she was in between signals, she could catch New York stations too. That's why I changed my name (from Roland to Zacherley) when I went to New York, because there was an overlap in the areas where it could be picked up, you could pick up both stations. No, I never really had anybody looking for a date or whatever. Maybe they were scared of me, maybe they thought I really looked like that! There were a lot of followers, a lot of fans, you know, that would send me stuff all the time.

Like Ms. Ambirge, many other young female fans would make the effort to send hand-made gifts to Roland. This unexpected phenomenon surprised the then 39-year-old Zacherle, who was largely unaware of his character's appeal to the opposite sex:

> I saved things (that were sent in) because they were clever. And I must tell you that the most clever of the human race who sent things in were ladies! No kidding. I mean, I was hot and I didn't know it! Really hot! They must have gone crazy when I did a swimming show in that striped bathing suit — I was amazed!

One of the "ladies," artist Rosemary Schroeder, was only 12 when Zach appeared on the New York scene, but found him quite magnetic:

"I was hot and I didn't know it!": Zach had a large female fan base.

My ex-sister-in-law came to my mother's house one day and said to me, "Go to bed early and wake up at midnight. You have to watch this guy on TV, you're gonna love him." I was in school, I was only 12·, so I looked at this program and I said, "Oh, my God, he's fabulous! This guy is great!" I woke up the next day and told my mother, "I'm gonna meet this man, I love this guy." And I did!

When pressed to explain his appeal, Rosemary explained, "I think a lot of women like a guy that makes them laugh. He made me laugh. He was sexy. You could see that behind the make-up·it went beyond the character. I would paint pictures of him. I made a Dracula cape which he immediately showed on his program where he had Isobel's coffin filled with water and he was diving in this striped bathing suit and he said, 'I'm gonna do the "Dracula" dive' or something, and he put on my cape and my mother and I were watching and we're screaming, 'No, don't do it!' And he jumped into Isobel's coffin with my hand-sewing and spangles all over it — all in the water."

Two pieces of art that were sent to Zach. The bottom one was by Rosemary (Schroeder) Tafaro.

Lifelong fan Ruth Steinman, also a friend of Zach's, recalls how they first met:

> My sister told me about Roland. She lived in Sharon Hill, which was a suburb of Philly. I started watching and I was freaked out a bit because everything looked kind of bloody and nasty. But then after she told me that some of her neighbors, teenagers, had met him and he was a nice guy, I thought, "I would like to meet him also." And then there was this "open house" where he was going to make an appearance at WCAU, so my husband and my daughter and I went down and it was a mob scene, and he waved and it was really kind of fun — I almost lost my coat in the mob, but it was neat. After that, I had a neighbor who lived several doors up the street working at WCAU, and I asked him if he could take us on a tour of the building, which he did, and I met Zacherle for the first time. I found him very congenial and we took pictures of him, but alas, the pictures did not turn out too well, so I asked my neighbor for a repeat of the tour, and he took us through again. This time I took a cake, and my sister and I went. It was right before he left for New York.

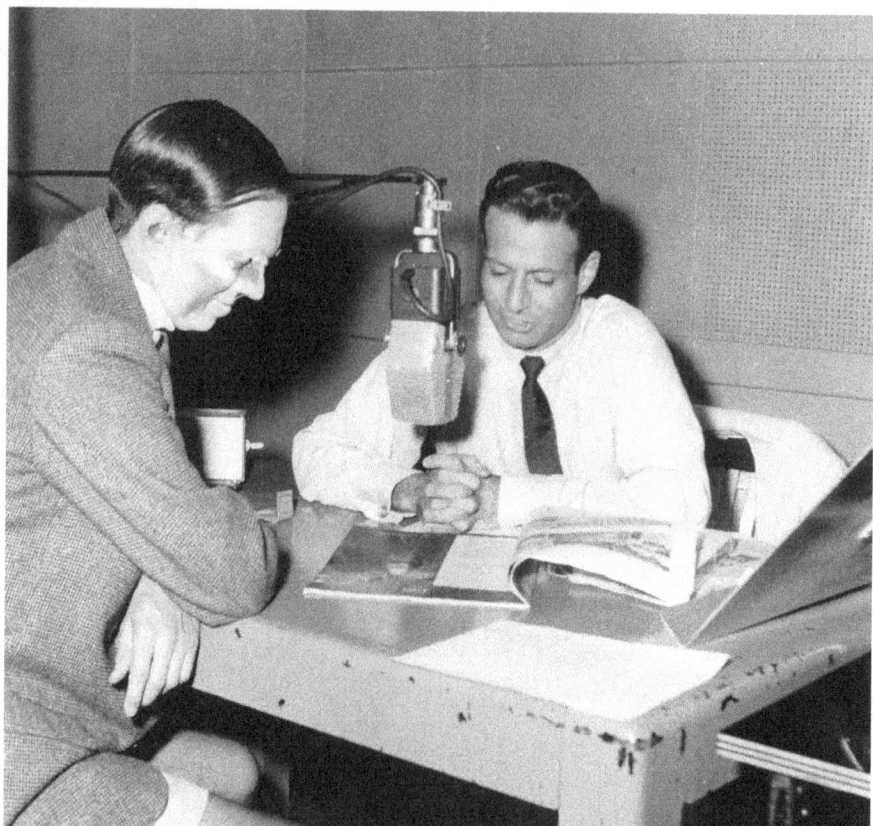

Roland in casual dress for a radio interview. (Photo courtesy John Zacherle.)

By far the most ambitious gift Steinman sent to the show was a huge color map of Transylvania, incredibly detailed, a work of art that Zach has kept through the years. I had the fun of unrolling it (carefully, and with help) on my living room carpet over 40 years after it was created. According to Ruth:

> That didn't come right away, I think the very first thing I sent him was a doll that looked like him. I made one for myself as well, and he wrote a thank you note, which encouraged me to continue making things, and my daughter and I decided to make this big map, and we really took the whole kitchen tabletop to make it. I don't know how long it took, but it became quite detailed, and it was all done in watercolor.

Ruth also won first prize in a unique art competition:

> He had a contest of some sort going on, and people sent things in, and I sent a mummy and a mummy case, and then a standing figure made of pipe cleaners. He sent in return a thank you letter with a silver dollar taped to it with Scotch Tape, and

he said I won first prize in the "mummy case and standing figure" category...*

Ruth actually got friendly enough with Zach that she made visits to the family home in Flourtown, Pennsylvania, to visit his mother:

> I'm not sure how I got to know her, but she was very nice and later I would be driving along with a bunch of flowers and I called from a distance to see whether she would be home or not, and she said, "Yes! Come for lunch!" And I took the flowers and knocked on the door and she says, "Oh! You're not the Ruth I thought—I thought it was another friend of mine, but come in." Later on, I was there for lunch, in fact I was there several times for lunch. One time she had made sandwiches and we sat out back on the sun porch, and we were looking out over the garden, which looked really nice. We each had a sandwich on a plate, Zach was home at the time, he was washing dishes. He came along and took our plates and left our sandwiches on the counter!

One of these visits, this time with another diehard female fan, led to a bit of an adventure:

> I was with Anne Di Dio, a handicapped girl from Brooklyn. She would travel down with her hand-controlled car and visit with me ... and we were out there visiting "Mama Zach" as she called herself, and we all sat in the backyard and Mama Zach fell asleep and Anne said, "Why don't you tiptoe in and take a look at where John sleeps?" So I went in, I thought, "Oh, my God!,"

---

* The map and mummy case with standing figure can be seen in the "Zacherley's Closet" extras chapter on the *Zacherley Archives* DVD.

An original Roland fan club card, front and back.

my heart was pounding, and I found this — either a ladder or a wooden staircase going up to sort of a loft-type room. I went up a couple steps very timidly and saw that it was crammed like a storeroom, I remember paint cans for example, and I quickly ran out back again before Mama Zach woke up. Anne later sent me a paper award and on it, it says, "Award for Courage Beyond the Call of Duty."

Most of Zach's longtime followers have heard about the celebrated "open house" put on by WCAU during which thousands of young fans showed up to meet their hero Roland. Zach recently recalled just what that afternoon was like:

ZACH: The station wanted to find out just how large the audience was, and one of the ways they could do that was by mail — start some kind of a contest or something. The boss decided to have an "open house" to see how many people would show up to see the studio, and I'd be standing in the corner with the lights all on very dramatically, you know, just like the show was on the air. They had a large studio, a big place, and we had one corner of it for a permanent set, and so I stood there, and thousands of people showed up. Somebody said 14,000! They stopped traffic on the main roads outside Philadelphia, which was exciting. The station the next day put out an apology to the people of Philadelphia for the inconvenience that was caused by the amount of people that showed up and stopped traffic on City Line Avenue, which was the big thoroughfare. But nothing came of it. It helped me in a way, because it brought some kind of attention to the people in New York when eventually

With an eight-year-old fan in the summer of 1958.

I had a hit record, to back up their feelings that I should be a big shot in New York! Eventually I took off for New York and they didn't attempt to replace me, they just kept on showing the films, and eventually they got another man on another station who called himself Dr. Shock. Who knows what my life would have been if I'd stayed there?"

RICH: Were the management at WCAU upset that you left?

ZACH: Well, they had something successful and I was walking away from them. They didn't handle it very well. They had a new guy coming in from New York City, I think, and he was gonna put the show on as *The Late, Late Show*. And I had already been talking to a friend who was a writer on the cowboy show, and who was the one that told me who to go see in New York. There'd been the successful 45 record, you know, "Dinner with Drac," and the big crowds that showed up for the open house … It wasn't unpleasant, I was good friends with everybody on the floor and the directors, but the manager never really approached me. Though I was no businessman, I never went to them and said, you know, "I'm thinking of going to New York, can we make a deal?" I never made those kind of statements to anybody anywhere in my whole life [*laughs*]! So I don't really know what those last days were like. It was exciting, you know, to move to New York, I never thought of going to New York in my life.

RICH: And you said you never had a contract in Philadelphia.

ZACH: No, they never approached me with anything. And the pay was terrible. But it was no big deal, I mean, they were paying scale, whatever that scale was, and they never offered to pay more or say, "Look, we'll give you a little bit to stay here."

RICH: I certainly don't want to ask you what you made, but was your New York salary comparable or better than Philadelphia?

ZACH: Well, New York was also scale. I never worked for anything but scale on any of those stations. Because they could always say, "Listen, we can show these movies without anybody," you know.

Chapter 2
New York-Bound

What we were trying to do was be crazy and funny with those old horror movies, the ones that deserved to be "teased." Some of 'em were really classy, the ones like Frankenstein, Dracula *and all that. We didn't want to mess around with them. I asked a lawyer one time, "Is it okay if we jump in and out of these movies and make fun of them?" He said, "Hell, man, we can show them backwards and upside-down with the kind of contract we've got. Do anything you want!"*

— John Zacherle, April 2001

WCAU Channel 10 was originally owned by Philadelphia's *Evening Bulletin* newspaper; there is at least one photo in existence in which the name of the paper can be seen in large graphics on one of the studio cameras. Toward the autumn of 1958, the station was bought by the CBS network and a new boss decided that Roland should move to a new time slot, 90 minutes later than his usual start time, 11:20 p.m. (or thereabouts — the time would change according to the local news broadcast). Zacherle felt this was "a really dumb idea," adding that, upon returning home after his show, all the lights in the surrounding homes seemed to be turned off; everybody was in bed by one a.m. The impending time change was not a good portent for the future of the show, and it seemed like the time had come to move on.

As Philadelphia's Roland began to grow in popularity, the noise was eventually heard as far away as New York, and it was inevitable that overtures would be made for Roland to leave his crypt in the City of Brotherly Love and move his digs to the Big Apple. I had always assumed that the move was just a matter of business; a few papers signed, a lawyer to check it out, and — bingo — Zacherley in New York. This was not the case. In my car parked atop the beautiful Perkins Drive mountain lookout in New York's Harriman State Park on Sunday of Memorial Day weekend, 2004, Zach pulled out a manila folder and dropped it in my lap, announcing that he had been cleaning out his closet and came upon this — a typed record, kept by himself, of his year's experience in Philadelphia and the transition to New York. As I read the sequence of events from 1958, I was shocked — it was anything but a straightforward matter of business; it was a nightmare!

Here's the bare bones of the story: At the recommendation of a friend, Zach took on New York-based Isobel Baker as his agent and left a kinescope of one of his shows with her. On that basis, Baker interested one Ellis Sard in peddling the idea of Zach's hosting movies in New York. A contract was drawn up in which Baker and Sard were to act as "packagers" of John Zacherle, but shortly afterward, Baker had to give up her agency on doctor's orders, leaving Zach with the task of finding a new agent. While Zach put the agent business on the back burner, Baker and Sard came up with a proposed contract from ABC-TV that was "a very tight and tough affair." The journal entry written by Zach himself, relating the details of the proposed contract, can be found in the 2012 BearManor book *The Z Files*.) While the contract was good for 39 weeks, it could be cancelled with four weeks notice and with, according to Zach, "very little chance for financial increase in the meantime." When Zach came to New York to discuss the figures, it was discovered that somehow, working a six-day week, "the package" (Zach) would be left with a salary of $5 a week!

A fight regarding the twisted finances ensued between Baker, Sard and ABC; Zach signed temporarily as an "interested party" while the details were worked out. ABC said it was either "Sign it or no show," according to Zach's notes. As if this wasn't enough of a headache, on the first day working under the contract, Zach was informed that he would be expected to pay the liability insurance for Baker and Sard as producers of the show. Upon legal advice, Zach agreed to pay a third of the cost, causing understandable tension between him and the Baker-Sard team. Zach then went to the William Morris agency whose representative took a meeting with Baker's husband. He insisted that Zach should be "grateful for all they had done," sign as an employee and "get it over with."

Once the show started amongst these complications, Zach was approached directly by a Mr. Stone of ABC-TV and asked to do four nights of

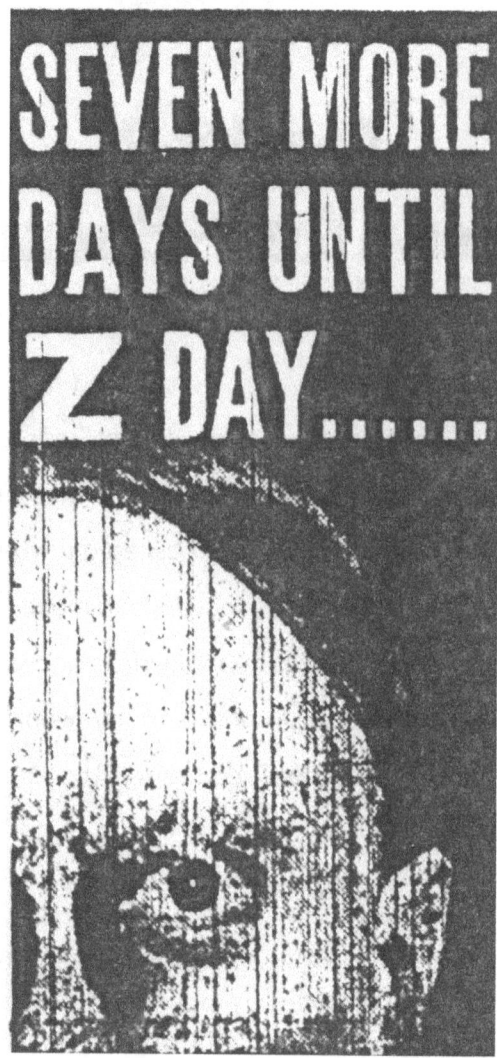

Part of the lead-up to Zacherley's much-publicized New York debut.

voice-over work (as Zacherley) in addition to his two live shows a week. At this point, AFTRA came into the picture to try and straighten out the ongoing contract problems, while Zach was paying out hundreds of dollars in insurance money because Baker and Sard "apparently never had any money to back themselves up." These entanglements kept up all the way through Zach's 39 weeks of *Shock Theater* shows. Meanwhile, Sard departed after the 26th week, leaving Zach to produce, write and perform the show by himself! I worked up the nerve and looked up from the papers to ask Zach if I could include some of this incredible story in this book. His response was disappointing, but not unexpected: "No, this shouldn't go in your book. There's nobody interested in all this except maybe you." Maybe transcribing the entire account would have been a bit much, but I felt that any true fan would be more than interested in the entanglements that 40-year-old John Zacherle found himself caught up in during that fateful year, which, as it seemed, almost put the kibosh on any chance of the Cool Ghoul moving forward into the most important phase of his television career.

It was interesting to read Zach's personal take on the character he was creating at the time it was happening:

> Beginning in October of 1957 with the release of the now familiar *Shock Theater* series of movies, I was employed on a week-to-week basis at WCAU-TV in Philadelphia,

A Zacherley promotion in New York, 1958.

Pa., as a character actor portraying a somewhat nutty mad experimenter...friend of all monsters, etc. The [New York] show has a big following and is basically the same as the show in Philadelphia, though I think the character I portray is somewhat nuttier and there is the added dimension of the ABC musicians... The format has been copied by several stations around the country with their own type of ghoul doing the nonsense at intermission time.

In one of our interviews, Zach told me:
ZACH: When I got to New York, apparently they had better ways of judging the audience and telling who was watching and so on, and we gave the competition some problems with their ratings. I was on *The Jack Paar Show* and he says, "Here's one of my competitors!" [*Laughs*] It was kind of weird to be thought of as a competitor of his kind of a show.

RICH: Tell me the story behind your first really famous publicity picture.

ZACH: We shot them in an airplane hangar. Just hung up a curtain and he did that, and I really wonder, I may have been looking for some publicity pictures because I never had many done. WABC was very good, though, they did make a lot of pictures and I never paid any attention to them. I don't know what happened to them, except the ones that they used. But the ones that I ended up using were the ones that a pilot friend of mine, Pete Gilchrist, did. That was my first shot, the ones that were taken — I don't know who took one in Philadelphia sitting in the chair on the set, which came out very well. That may have been somebody at the studio, shot, you know, for promotion. It's just possible that those shots that Pete took in the airplane hangar were done after I was in New York and I came home for the weekend or something. Wings Field, a small airport, private airport.

Soon after the success of "Dinner with Drac," it was announced that WABC's New York *Shock Theater* was going to kick off its second season with the abovementioned *Son of Shock* package, providing us with further adventures of our favorite monsters, but with a difference: The movies would now be accompanied by a host, a cadaverous character to accompany viewers through the mayhem. Little did I know that the man who rattled off those outrageous lyrics in "Dinner with Drac" and our new midnight host would be one and the same. Arthur Finkelstein, working as a page at WABC at the time, shares this memory of the newly installed horror host:

> I was working at ABC television on 66th Street, and we had been reading in the paper that Channel 7 was bringing up this new personality named Zacherley from Philadelphia to host *Shock Theater*. I had heard about him, but I really didn't know what he looked like. In those days, ABC had a lounge in the basement and there were some studios in the basement, and they had couches down there and soda machines and food machines and all sorts of stuff. I was sitting on the couch eating my sandwich, and I looked up and there's this guy who looked like he was a zombie. He was in full costume and makeup and he was just standing there because there were no seats, and I thought to myself, "That's Zacherley!" And there was this young lady sitting on my right, and she really didn't notice him. And at one point she looked up, saw him and gasped and said, "Oh, I'm sorry, I just got scared, I didn't know you were there!" And Zach said, "I'm sorry I scared you." She said to him, "That's okay, I'll get used to it." And he said, "So did my mother!"

Zacherley's New York City debut, September 22, 1958.

I asked Zach how his relatives felt about the fact that he used the family name "Zacherley" for the character. He replied:

> Well, there weren't many with the same name, we were the only ones that had it. My two brothers had children, but they were very small, and they didn't think anything of it. I was called Roland in Philadelphia, then when I went to New York and began using the family name for the character I never heard any — no feedback from the family at all.

Mystery of Edwin Drood (1935) was the movie being shown on that first night as I sat there in the living room easy chair awaiting the debut of the new "live" host. Visions of enticing quadrants of his face, shown in the *New York Daily News* ads announcing his arrival that week, ran through my head. Making a countdown to "Z" Day, they'd shown only a wide, staring eye one day, the top of a head with the hair parted in the middle the next, and so on. By the time I sat eagerly anticipating this ogre's appearance, I was again unsure, as I had been exactly a year before when the first broadcast of 1932's *The Mummy* hit the airwaves, whether this was a good idea after all. Maybe this guy would creep me out so much that I'd have trouble enjoying the movie.

The time — 11:14 p.m. The last local commercial had run. WABC Channel 7's station ID aired and the screen faded to black. A new *Shock Theater* title card filled the screen and in walked the man I dreaded, wearing a black frock coat, several medallions, that familiar slicked-down hair with the middle part and a face full of sinister shadows. Behind him was a painted stone arch bearing a shelf cluttered with tools, beakers and test tubes. In front was a mysterious worm-eaten wooden box, looking as if it could fall apart at any moment. I was tense, still wondering if I shouldn't click the console TV set off, go to bed, and try again next week.

Then something miraculous happened. The host, who had presented himself as "Zacherley, the curator of *Shock Theater*," introduced the audience to his wife, the resident of the old box, casually produced a mallet and proceeded to drive a stake through her heart. With each "bang" of the wooden stake, the wife, Isobel, gave out a high-pitched "OOOH," lowering in pitch from the second to the third whack, culminating after the fourth in a soft, measured "Ah-h-h-h." She was enjoying it. By Heaven, she *liked* it! It may seem strange now, decades later, but that ten-second "bit" was so incredibly funny, it did such a good job of defining what this fellow was all about, that I began a lifelong mania with the man in the ghostly makeup. This was no spook, someone looking to frighten or alarm me, this was a friend. He was going to laugh with me through the blackness of the midnight hour. We were going to enjoy another macabre film, but damn it, we were also going to have some fun with it.

RICH: How do you feel when people tell you that what you did was absolutely 100 percent original?

ZACH: All I can say is, I watch [the kinescopes] and I think, Jesus, this crazy stuff, I'm playin' around with Jell-O, you know, and brains, cauliflower brains, you know, nobody was doing that, I guess [*laughs*]. I just don't know.

RICH: But I mean, your delivery, your wit and your patterns of speech were unlike anybody else — totally original.

ZACH: Well, I don't know where it came from. And I agree with you, it was kinda weird, and having to cover up when something goes wrong, to quickly make up something to say about it. You've gotta be quick on your feet. I told you I never really watched the shows a lot of the time, I never really saw a WOR show on the air. When I do see things, even watching the old videos that we have, I think, "Gee, why didn't I think of doing something else there," you know? So, when I got tangled up in the ropes, I talked to the camera — It worked.

I had never written a fan letter in my short life of 13 years, but after a few installments of Zacherley's *Shock Theater*, I decided to put pen to paper. This man had me on the floor with his antics, and I was particularly impressed with how far he would go to make the show entertaining. It was enough that he'd break into the films as they were running and have wacky conversations with Boris Karloff or Bela Lugosi, but he seemed to have no compunction about soiling his face, hair and clothes with whatever materials he was using in his outlandish experiments. I remember one night when he wound up covered in some kind of white powder (probably flour) from head to toe. There truly had never been anyone like him on TV, and I had to write to him to let him know, and while I was at it, ask for the usual photograph. To

Zach and Gasport.

my utter surprise, he answered my letter with a handwritten response!

DEAR OLD RICHARD:

GLAD TO HEAR FROM YOU, OLD BOY — EVEN GASPORT [Zacherley's unseen pet creature, which lived in a burlap potato sack; see photo above] GOT A CHARGE OUT OF IT, WHICH IS RARE FOR HIM! THE ONLY PHOTOS AT PRESENT ARE THE CARDS I HAVE ENCLOSED. DON'T SELL THEM, YOU DOG — OR I SHALL NEVER WRITE AGAIN!

ZACHERLEY

The cards were the ones familiar to any collector of Zacherley memorabilia, the famous double image showing Zacherley next to John Zacherle, and the WABC "Shock Club," showing the Cool Ghoul's head to the left of a large spider web.

RICH: Was it you who came up with all these little devices like the Dracula Fizz and bone dust and all that?

ZACH: That could have been Ed White. I remember the amoeba, because I was sitting in a diner, somebody ordered Jell-O and I saw this big plate of Jell-O and how it wiggled, so I told him, I said, "Look, I'm gonna go make this thing and I'll bring it in," and I did, and it was funny, but we didn't have any "skin" on it. It was just a plastic basin that you might wash your socks in, you know, that kind of thing, and I filled it up with Jell-O and so I turned it over and it held its shape! A big rectangle, but it was wobbling, and when they zeroed in on it, it collapsed under its own weight, it split open, and it looked really repulsive. Right in front of the camera on a close shot, it split open, you know, like some ugly, horrible mouth. And, you know, we thought that was hilarious.*

RICH: Is that when you decided to use cheesecloth on it?

ZACH: Somewhere along the line they got the idea of wrapping it up and then I remember Ed White had the idea of making it — we did *The Invisible Man*, so we had the "Invisible Amoeba." And he came in with a leash and a collar, very stiff, and I'd walk around with this like it was a dog. And the "fizz" I remember, he knew about it, I never heard of this stuff, in the drugstores you used to buy little packets of powder and you'd put 'em in water and you'd make a lot of fizz, and you'd drink that for indigestion. So if you used a lot of packets and dumped them into the water, it made a lot of fizz, and just instantly flew all over the

---

* The Jell-O amoeba used in Philadelphia had the peculiar name Thelma. In New York, the creature ("Slobbus Amoebus" was its Latin designation) was named Phyllis, in honor of the wife of an agent friend.

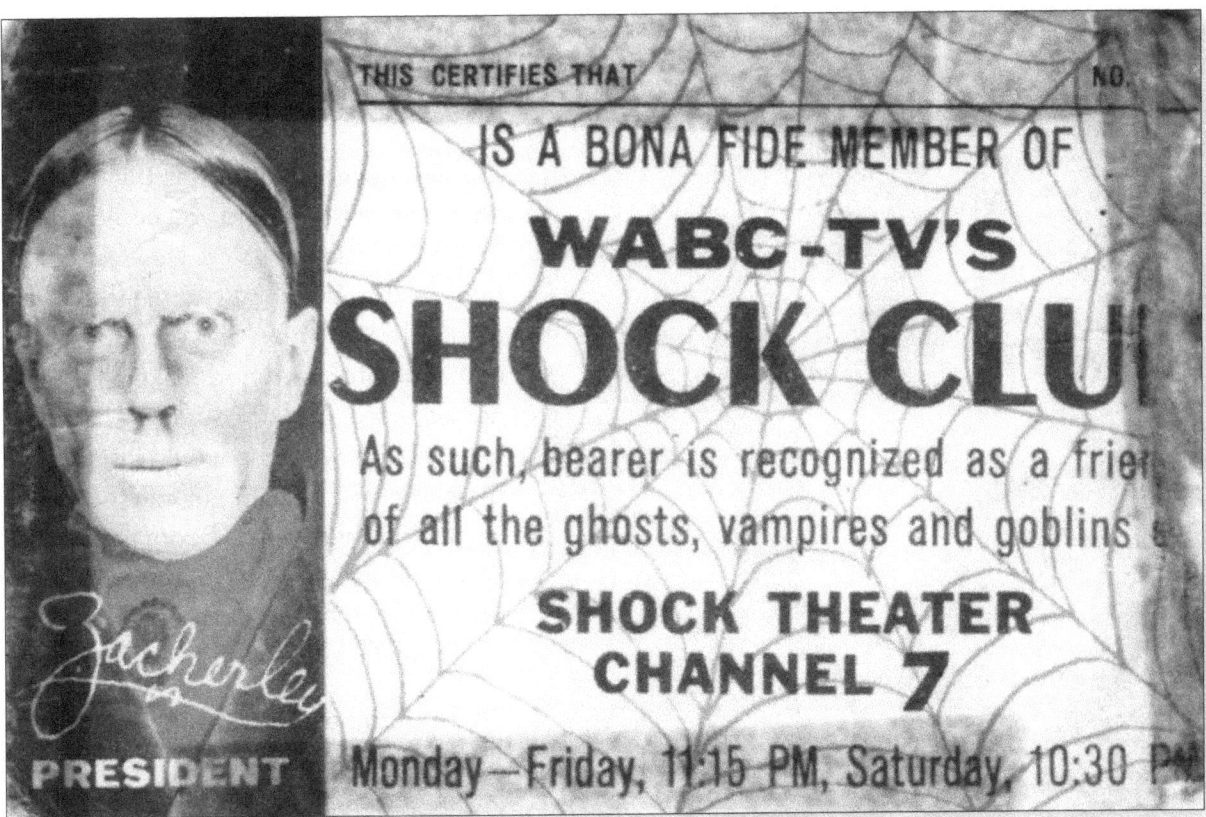

place. That was kind of fun. But that's disappeared from the market, I've never seen that on sale.

RICH: And you said you got a little bit of a hassle from people because of the mess?

ZACH: Yeah, especially at Channel 7 in New York when I first came to New York, and made a mess, of Jell-O or brains or everything else that would be on the floor, and they had to clean up. Stagehands, part of their job is to fix the props. Also, they're the ones that would clean the floor. Well, they didn't mind sweeping, but they didn't like mopping [*laughs*]! And they turned around when I realized what had happened, they told me that the neighborhood kids were all excited about the show. That made them kind of heroes, so they didn't mind later on. Somewhere along the line, they didn't grumble any more. They were nice guys, but they were, you know it's a father and son union, the stagehands' union, and they would disappear, if they were working on a show and the next show they had to work on was two hours later, they would jump on the bus and go down to Broadway and change the signs on the marquees. That was a union job, so they were double-dipping all over the place. When they were being paid by ABC, they would take long lunch hours and go down and make a bundle putting up this week's schedule on the marquees. A lot of movie houses on Broadway at that time.

As a typical *Shock Theater* show progressed and Zacherley became engrossed in some mad experiment, I began to look forward to his "intermissions" almost as much as the rest of the film. More often than not, he would indulge in some operation that would go awry, and in the process leave him looking like a kid who had been playing all day in the mud. His hair, which at the show's opening was always neatly bisected with the trademark middle part, shiny and tightly combed (soap was used to ensure the proper flatness), would by show's end be wildly disheveled, mussed, and flopping down his brow. The

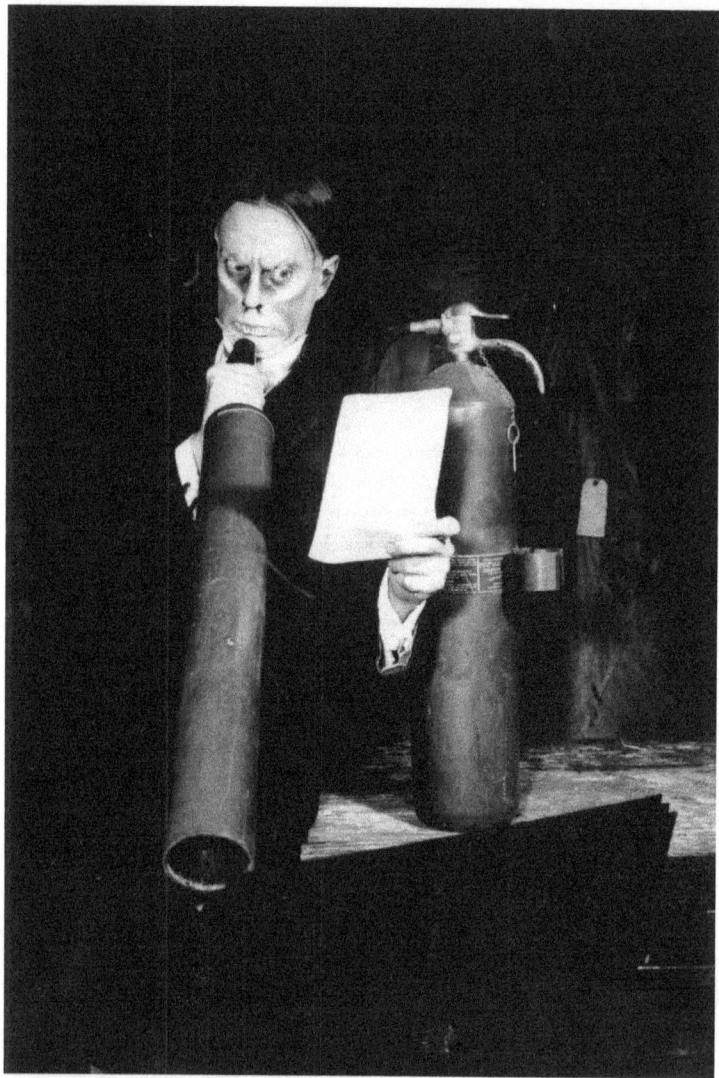

Hanging around at Channel 7 WABC. (Photo courtesy John Zacherle.)

experiments themselves were terrific; cauliflower passed for human brains, and hearts were represented by pieces of calf's liver. Jell-O bound up in cheesecloth served as the mutant giant amoebas, supposedly scooped up in the swamps alongside the Jersey Turnpike. Somewhere along the way, live sound effects, such as the ones Ed White made at WCAU, gave way to the more familiar recorded monkey noises for wife Isobel (named for seldom-seen producer Isobel Baker), and a slowed-down baby's wail for Gasport. These recorded sounds would remain a part of the act for the rest of Zach's TV career. Sound man Bob Prescott did the honors.

RICH: I would hear laughing in the background at times on the kinescopes. Were there many guests allowed in the studio?

ZACH: No, mostly that was the sound effects man there, and you could always hear his particular voice. He was there right next to the camera, he had a turntable, you know, and earphones, and a monitor. And he'd make all those noises there. And of course he had a hearty laugh when he would let go. And the cameraman might get excited and laugh, and there was a boom man — in Philadelphia we used booms, remember booms? I forgot about that, before we had lavalieres.

RICH: But I heard kids laughing in the show where you're digging to the center of the earth.

ZACH: Really? Well, that could be. I don't know who they might be. Occasionally, I guess, some people would come down from the offices if they were around. When we were doing it late at night there weren't too many people there, but during the day there could be somebody wandering in in the background.

RICH: You told me a story about two kids who wormed their way into the WABC studios.

ZACH: That's the guy who's sending us the tape of my performance of "Dinner with Drac" on the 1958 *Dick Clark Show* [originally intended for use in the DVD version of *The Zacherley Archives*]. When he was a kid, he and his friend from high school over in Brooklyn just up and came over, you know, at night and talked their way into the studio. Talked their way past the guard, they got friendly with the guard upstairs at 66th Street. So they often turned up there.

Zach makes a personal appearance at a movie theater in 1958. (Photo courtesy John Zacherle.)

Another kid who'd show up was the guy who eventually did the magazine *Castle of Frankenstein*.

RICH: Oh, Calvin Beck?

ZACH: Calvin Beck and his mother, yeah! I don't know whether they had contacted somebody, but they were occasionally there, not a lot, but sometimes. I guess they must probably have contacted somebody, telling them they had a magazine they ran and wanted to do an interview or something.

RICH: And he had his mother with him all the time, right?

ZACH: Yeah, his mother, and they both were very alike, they looked like Charles Addams people, very strange, they really did. Very strange. They were, visually it was quite a sight to see them, they were both very short and kind of round, and they looked like they just came out of makeup, you know, or wardrobe, and had been made up to look like little weird people.

Film historian Tom Weaver, in his article "Norman, Is That You?" (*Monsters from the Vault* #8), elaborated on just how weird: Calvin Beck's claim to fame, that all fans *know* about, was his magazine *Castle of Frankenstein*, but Beck's *other* achievement, if you want to call it that, is that

he partly inspired the Norman Bates character in Robert Bloch's novel *Psycho*. Bloch's model for the killer half of the character was Ed Gein, the Wisconsin serial killer, but the "normal" half of Norman, the fat, bespectacled momma's boy, was based on Calvin Beck and his mother and their ... kinda grotesque relationship. She was this noisy, dominating old lady who had him under her thumb, went to school with him, went with him to sci-fi cons, went with him when he did interviews for *Castle of Frankenstein* — holy (s)mother love! Bloch observed the both of 'em first-hand, I guess in the late '50s, and based Norman Bates on them — although he, Bloch, didn't like to admit it, and would only tell people after first swearing them to secrecy. Beck knew, and so did some of the people in fandom who were close to him, but until recently it was a pretty well-kept secret otherwise. Everybody knew that Ed Gein was a model, but they didn't know he was only the model for the "Hyde side" of Norman. The "Jekyll" side was Calvin Beck and his mom.

Crazy experiments, jibes at the commercials, cracks about New York Mayor Wagner, the postal service and rival TV shows notwithstanding, my undisputed favorite part of the show were the "break-ins." This was when Zach would appear suddenly within the movie, the set dressed to match (hopefully) the appropriate scene, and make some comment to the actors or add his own "contribution" to the plot. There were hundreds of these, and every fan has his or her favorites. I am no exception; I could fill a chapter with the ones I remember, but the following are a few gems I consider among his best:

> During a screening of *The Black Room* (1935), Boris Karloff is riding in a coach engaged in a conversation with Thurston Hall when suddenly a bullet smashes through the window. Cut to Zach hiding behind a rock, rifle in hand, snapping his fingers as if to say, "Damn! Missed!"

> In *The Raven* (1935), Bela Lugosi as Dr. Vollin ponderously plays his giant pipe organ to the delight of a female guest (Irene Ware). In place of the original soundtrack and the strains of Bach's Tocatta in D Minor filling the room, however, we hear what sounds like a circus calliope playing something like merry-go-round music. The music ends, Bela rises from the organ and turns to face his lovely visitor. She looks up at him admiringly and speaks: "You're not only a great surgeon, but a great musician, too."

> Also from *The Raven*: Bela is on the phone speaking to a doctor colleague. "Who's on the case?" he asks. "Zacherley and Gasport," comes the reply. Bela responds, "Well, I'm satisfied. They can handle it as well as I."

> In the film *The Jungle Captive* (1945), actor Rondo Hatton (known for playing the horror character The Creeper) has just pushed a morgue wagon off a cliff and it bursts into flames. Cut to Zach toasting marshmallows. He ducks, mutters, "Hey, what the heck are you doing up there?!" He sees who it is and waves, "Oh — hiya, Creep!"

> *The Invisible Ray* (1936). One of the members of an African expedition is complaining about the "jungle cuisine": "Antelope stew again! Take it away." We see Zach eating out of a bowl of slop. "Tastes good to me — I like it!" he crows, as he licks his lips.

By this time, local newspapers were turning out feature articles on the phenomenon of the horror films and the people who hosted them. Most were flippantly done, but in the era of the late '50s, when the horror classics were yet to be taken seriously, they really couldn't have turned out any other way. But even though written with tongue planted firmly in cheek, the coverage was surprisingly positive, upbeat, and conveyed a sense of fun. New Jersey's Bergen Record, in a syndicated column titled "TV Key Previews," notorious for its hatred of horror movies, reviewed *Shock Theater* on the evening of Friday,

Zach messes with some kind of glob in a 1959 episode. This shot was snapped by a fan photographing his (her?) (its?) own TV screen at home.

February 20, 1959. In a startlingly generous mood toward the show (if not the film, which was 1944's *The Soul of a Monster*), they recommended: "Forget the film itself; it's terrible. Tonight's star is host and curator, Zacherley, whose delusions of grandeur lead him to attempting all the leading roles in the opera *Faust*, with Earl Wild, a willing accomplice at the piano."

ZACH: Earl Wild is a concert pianist these days. At that time he was the pianist for the ABC orchestra. So he came in and he played in this rinky-tink style, you know, like for old silent movies. He used to do the silent movie music for Sid Caesar on Your Show of Shows. Earl had a great, good time doing this, and we rehearsed maybe ten minutes before the show went on the air!

Looking back today on those old shows, particularly while viewing kinescopes of some of the Channel 7 episodes, Zach tends to get a bit frustrated at what he thinks of as missed opportunities. Instead of immersing himself in the satisfaction of a job well done and truly appreciating the groundbreaking originality he brought to the medium, he'll often say things like, "I wish I'd done this or that," or "It could have been so much better," and so on. Any artist worth his reputation has felt that way at times, it's understandable. But the biggest regret Zach seems to have today is that he or producer Ellis Sard never thought of inviting someone like Boris Karloff on the show for a guest appearance. Karloff, according to Zach, was often in New York at the time and was professionally active and healthy enough to have agreed to appear, but the thought of trying to contact him never crossed anyone's mind. I wonder if any of us enjoying *Shock Theater* at the time would have entertained that notion ourselves? It would be nice to imagine that Dear Boris would have agreed to do it.

RICH: How much rehearsal time did you have at WABC?

ZACH: We didn't have any rehearsal time. We would meet the director of the show just before the show went on the air, and we had this so-called script which said, "Three minutes and ten seconds into the segment," it's the second segment, so-and-so will say something in the film, and you cut to Zach in a make-believe copy of the set, and he will say so and so-and-so, and you cut right back to the film," and that was it. You would describe that to them and hope that would happen. Now with Ellis, Ellis was sitting in the control room, so we would sit down in a little room and watch the movies with the guy who ran the projector. And we would think of things to jump in and say things back — to talk back to the actors and so on. And we'd have to time it with a stopwatch and we'd put that on this working script. Then for the so-called experiments that I did, we'd dream up something based on what was going on in the movie if possible, to show how it really should be done, and the idiot guy in the film didn't know what he was doing. Then we'd sketch that out in little short sentences so that I wouldn't go too far and mess up the whole sequence of the evening. Because there were like, 16 breaks before and after commercials, and also opening and closing for a whole show, so we had to stretch this nonsense out all through the evening without running too far ahead of ourselves. It was a pretty sketchy run-through, our run-through was to stand up and talk about it, that's all."

This WABC publicity photo was used in a TV Guide ad for Zach's show. (Photo courtesy John Zacherle.)

RICH: What was Ellis Sard's role in the New York show?

ZACH: My friend Dick Strome, who was instrumental in that picture book thing that I did ...

RICH: Oh, "Zacherley for President"?

ZACH: Yeah, he must've known him and Isobel Baker, because they were the people I went to see on his suggestion. Ellis Sard did all the work, I never really saw Isobel except occasionally when I first signed up with them, and because I was getting scale,

Fans invade Zach's Channel 7 set in January 1958. (Photo courtesy John Zacherle.)

they weren't allowed to take any money, I think that was part of the rule. But he put a lot of time in on the show for the first half of the year. He was great, he loved doing it. He's the one who dreamed up all those musical things that I did — at WABC, at least. He arranged for the kinescopes to be made because he knew all about television, I didn't know anything about it, I didn't know what a kinescope was. He also was amazing in that he had terrible back trouble. He had a station wagon and he used to come lying down in the back, his wife would drive him to work. Every day she'd drive him to work, with him lying down in pain in the back. Great big guy, great big guy. He'd been in World War II also. He was probably about my age, I guess.

RICH: Could you tell me the story about Dave Garroway calling his wife, or having you call his wife?

ZACH: Yeah, Garroway was a big fan too, and I got on his show too. I must've been on three times altogether, I think. After *The Today Show* was over one morning, he says, "Hey, you know what I want to do is call my wife," he says. "I go around the house imitating you all the time, and so we'll call up and you talk to her and she'll think it's me and we'll just go back and forth there." And I don't remember the whole conversation, but she really did, she kept calling me Dave, and I said [*doing Zacherley voice*], "No-o, it's Zacherley here." [*Laughs*] He was so — he was like a kid.

RICH: And the *Zacherley at Large* show was taken from *Garroway at Large*?

ZACH: Yes. That's when I was at Channel 7, ABC, and either he or some of his friends were watching at night, and halfway through the season we decided to call it *Zacherley at Large*. I don't know if that was the very first title there was on it, I don't think so. So we did that for three or four weeks, then finally they sent us a letter sort of threatening that there would be a lawsuit. I thought it was kind of strange, I mean, *Zacherley at Large*, or anybody ...*At Large*, how could you copyright that expression? But maybe they had!

RICH: But Dave Garroway had nothing to do with that, right? About the complaining?

ZACH: No, no, no! I can't remember whether he mentioned it at all when I saw him.

Garroway was not the only celebrity Zacherley fan at that time. Closer to home, right there in the Channel 7 studios, was a young pop singer who had recently been given his own network show: Pat Boone made Zach a recurring guest on his series, *The Pat Boone Chevy Showroom*.

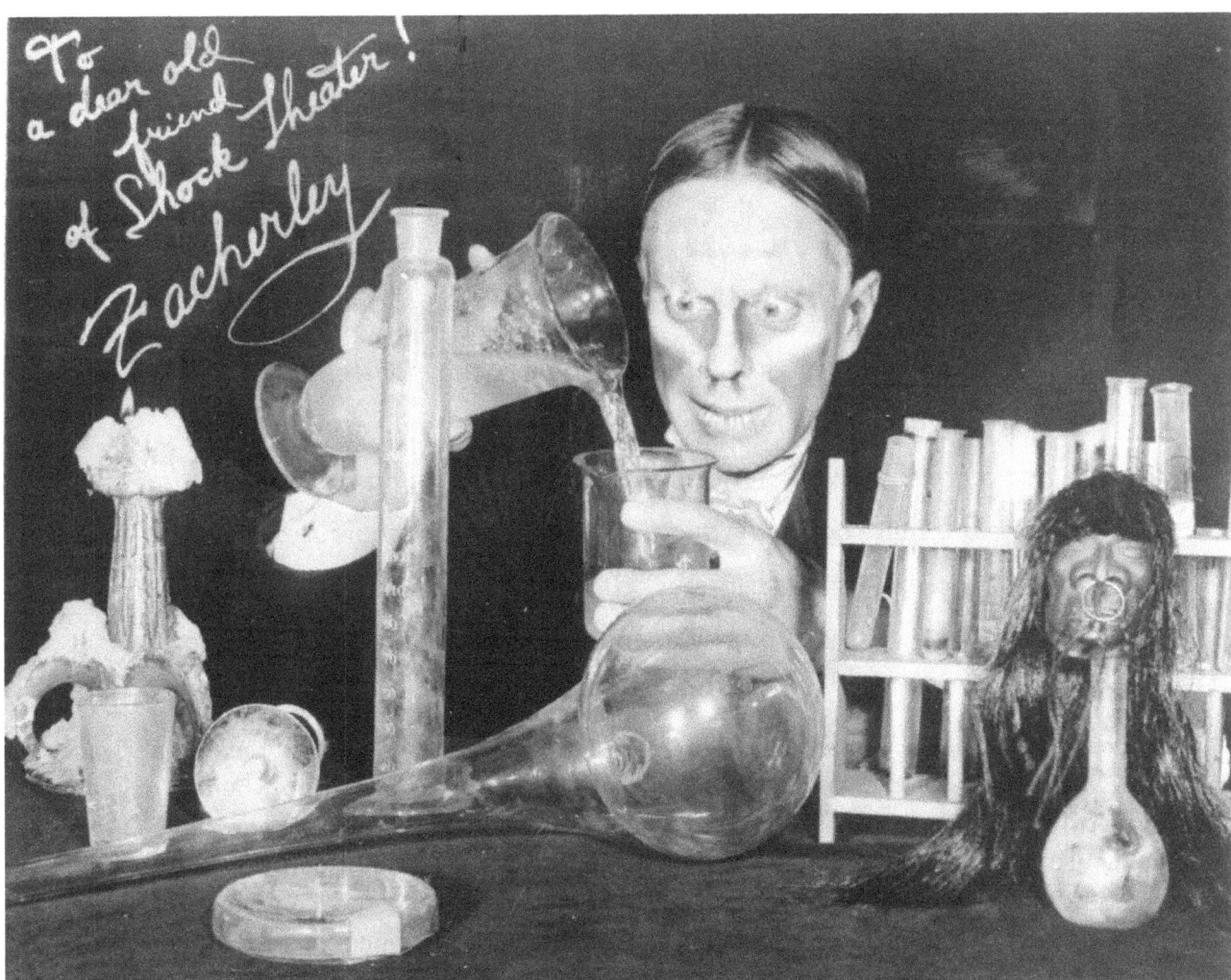

Zach did a series of cameos, often seen leering through a prop window during a "rainstorm" or singing a few bars of a song with monster lyrics. According to Zach,

> I was on two or three times. It was a lot of fun, my first experience with big time TV.

> He was doing a weekly show on the network and he was going to Columbia University at the time. He was a big fan of my show. We shared the same area, there was a whole bunch of dressing rooms there for the network people. They gave me one of 'em to use as an office and a place to get dressed, to get into costume. Once I remember I got bounced from the Boone show because many shows in rehearsal rehearsed more than they could squeeze into the hour, and Jackie Cooper and somebody else were the stars of that show and they had to bounce some section and so they knocked me out — I had a very small part in that particular episode.

> Pat was really a nice guy. Had I known that he was riding around in a flashy car havin' a good time, I might have asked if I could join him, but I didn't. I didn't know about that until later, that he was really having a great time with the money he was making while he was in college! He was a good-time boy. I think it was his agent or somebody I talked to on the set, and I said, "Boy, this is really nice," and he said, "Are you kidding? He'd like to be doing your show!"

Chapter 3
Switching Channels

Zacherley would come into the middle of the monster movie and suddenly appear doing something hilarious, and it was great — he had a great show. He'd have that laboratory going on, and he'd do some bits there and in the middle of the movie he'd show up dancing with a gorilla — it was hilarious.

— Steven Van Zandt, Zacherley fan extraordinaire

Cooper's was a typical suburban deli-magazine-newspaper store of the time, located on the southern end of Hackensack's Main Street near the courthouse where my father worked. It was an old-fashioned place, had been there for years, with its large dark front window and faded maroon awning bearing the store's name in large white letters. After work, Dad was in the habit of picking up the newspaper there, and one day I went along with him. Even though there were plenty of other stores like it, Cooper's became a magical place for me because every time I set foot in there (as I probably prefer to remember it) I found a new monster magazine. This one, an issue of *Famous Monsters of Filmland*, had a feature article on horrordom's new celebrity host, Zacherley. There exists somewhere in Dad's huge stash of 8mm home movies a brief shot of myself and two friends sitting on my front porch, our heads buried in the magazine, staring into the face of the Cool Ghoul.

On Saturday, June 20, 1959, the final *Zacherley at Large* program aired. The movie was 1944's *Weird Woman*. The *TV Guide* caption read: "Zacherley starts his summer vacation tonight. He will return in September." That "vacation" put Zacherle out of a job when WABC's station manager decided not to renew Zach's contract. Ellis Sard, who had been putting in many extra hours producing and co-writing the show with Zach, had quit when his request for a raise was denied. In addition, an efficiency expert (successful at downsizing over at NBC) was brought in to do the same at ABC. But probably the final nail in the coffin (pun intended) was ABC's desire to go up against their NBC competition, *The Jack Paar Show*, with a network variety show of its own: the short-lived *Everything Goes*. The result was that the next season's horror movies, sporadically shown under the umbrella title *The Night Show*, had no live (or undead) host. Zach himself is unclear about what happened then, but at some point in the summer of 1959, he got a call from WOR Channel 9 to begin hosting their mystery movies on a show called *Zacherley at 12*.

On Friday, November 13, 1959, one month after Zach's WOR show debuted, my father drove my friend Keith Hakala and me to the Oritani Theater in Hackensack to see "The Master" (as Keith put it) in person. This was about the time Zach was

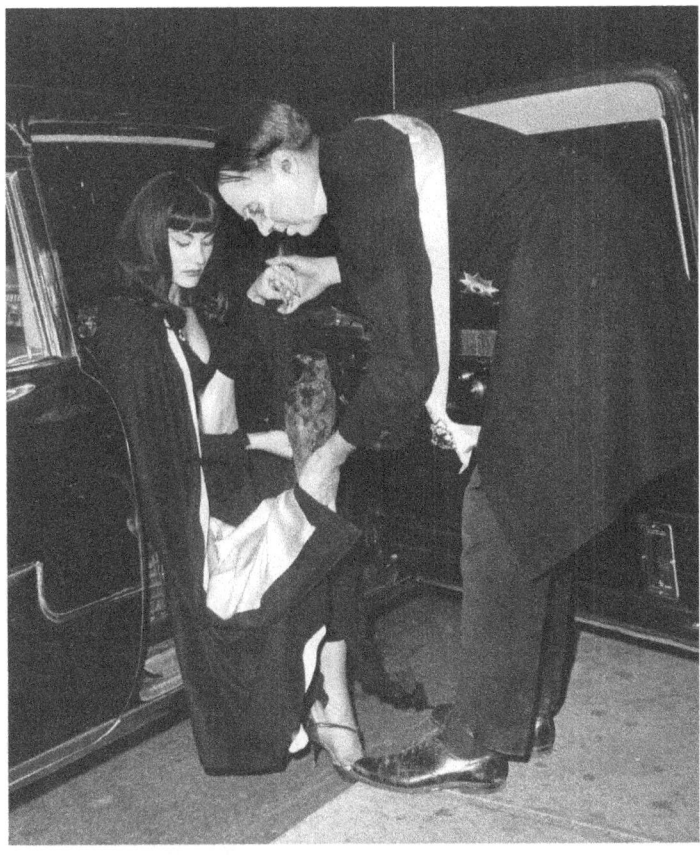

Zach and a Vampira lookalike promote a Spike Jones album. (Photos courtesy John Zacherle.)

putting on a contest to see who could draw the best likeness of his wife, who, since she resided in a coffin, was never seen on the air.

Hackensack's Main Street was unusual in that it had two movie palaces directly across the street from one another, the Oritani and the Fox. We entered the Oritani with high expectations as to what Zach would be doing on stage that night. We found seats, the lights darkened, and — a movie started. "Oh, that's right, we have to sit through a movie first," I thought, somewhat annoyed. As it turned out, the movie, *The Haunted Strangler* with Boris Karloff, wasn't bad at all, and all subsequent viewings of it have transported me back to that magical night when I first laid eyes on a three-dimensional, full-color Zacherley.

The film ended, the lights went up, and a voice introduced "The Cool Ghoul, ZACH-ERLEY!" Out on the stage ran that familiar figure, his feet clad in tan hush puppies, presumably to give better traction than his usual black leather-soled shoes. It looked kind of funny, this vampire-like figure with that familiar makeup, dressed in black frock coat and trousers, wearing tan suede casuals on his feet. He pulled out some familiar props, including the famous "brain," at which time a portion of the audience, in a sincere and mature attempt to show their appreciation of the act, yelled out, "THAT'S CAULIFLOW-ER!" Similar caterwauling accompanied Zach's other attempts at recreating the spirit of his show, so much that, when he got around to experimenting with a "human heart," he confessed, "This is actually a calf's liver, you know!" It made me feel bad for him, although I'm sure this was just part of the game in his eyes. It was another rite of passage for me: my first experience with hecklers. The show was rounded out with a costume contest, some wolf howls and his signature line "Good night, whatever you are!" Zach ran off the stage, but seconds later, reappeared from stage right and made a mad dash across the

Zach on the WOR Channel 9 set. Notice the chalk outlines for walls!

footlights. The only thing marring this final, frenzied moment was a barrage of spitballs and crumpled paper thrown at the stage, with Zach doing his best to duck them. But despite the goons in the audience, we had a great night.

By the early 2000s, I had gotten to know Richard Gordon, the man whose production company had made *The Haunted Strangler*. Zach and I had been close friends for over ten years at that point and were both invited to a dinner party at the apartment of writer Bob Madison. Among the other guests were Mr. Gordon, authors John and Michael Brunas and Tom Weaver. I told the story of that night at the Oritani and how the show was comprised of Zach's personal appearance *and* Mr. Gordon's movie. I said that that night at the Oritani now felt to me like an omen, foreshadowing a future relationship with both of them, but I'm afraid I was the only one there who found the story interesting!

RICH: I went to one of your shows, when you used to do the live shows, at the Oritani Theater in Hackensack in 1959.

ZACH: Oh! That was tough, all those shows were tough, because as much as they ballyhooed them and all, nobody showed up for them. And it was a little unnerving because there were occasions when a lot of people showed up, but they didn't really show up at those movie houses. Whether time had passed for special events at movies on Saturday afternoon, I don't know.

RICH: This was a special show with you. In the newspaper ad, it was just you.

ZACH: I did that great big Stanley Theater in Jersey City, and I don't recall that there were many people there. The guy that put the show on, he said, "We had Jackie Gleason out here," and he said that's the first time that Jackie Gleason said: "Boy!" He looked out the dressing room window behind the stage and he saw the crowds of people, and he said, "That's when I realized the power of television, when I saw that." Lines of people, you know, just jammed, not a single line, but jam-packed, four or five abreast, coming all the way around the corner.

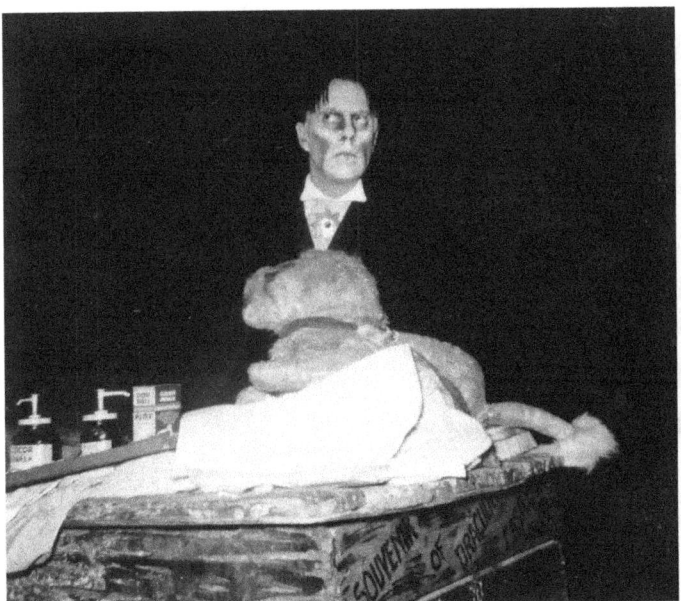

Another bizarre experiment at Channel 9. Note the Cocoa Marsh jar! (Photo courtesy John Zacherle.)

Zach lurking at WOR. (Photo courtesy John Zacherle.)

RICH: You didn't get that idea in Philadelphia when they did that open house?

ZACH: Well, yes, that's true too. Somebody should have gotten in touch with me and said, "Let's make a cheap movie" or something, because that was a big event, it really was, that was almost scary, there were so many people.

The WOR studio in New York was much larger than the cramped quarters that served as home at WABC. The new "crypt" appeared less detailed than the previous one, with a background of what looked like white chalk lines to serve as a suggestion of a stone wall. The worm-eaten casket was back, as were all the by-now-familiar unseen cast and their accompanying sound effects. Zach even continued putting on his beloved operettas. But in place of live music contributed by WABC staff musicians, public domain recordings had to do.

RICH: Who wrote all the lyrics to all the operatic stuff you did on WOR in New York?

ZACH: I had to do it myself. There was nobody over there. I didn't have any help at WOR except for Chris Steinbrunner, who ended up as the film buyer for WOR. He knew all about the movies, and occasionally he would sit down and we'd watch movies together. He also wrote several books about mystery films. When you have to make up the lyrics, you just do it, that's all. I told you that we had a good man in the music library who knew where there were a lot of records of instrumental versions of old songs. That's what we used.

But though the studio was bigger, the quality of the film fare was lower. No longer available were horror classics of the stature of 1931's *Dracula* and *Frankenstein*; instead Zach had to make do with films from the RKO library. While the programming sometimes offered bona-fide horror titles (1943's *The Return of the Vampire*, 1944's *Cry of the Werewolf* and 1948's *Unknown Island*), the more standard affairs were grade-B mysteries, and sometimes barely that. The station even threw in a Western or two! The more prestigious titles were out of bounds for Zach, the station hesitant to have him "playing" with them.

RICH: I always felt you didn't enjoy Channel 9 as much as WABC.

(Photo courtesy John Zacherle.)

ZACH: Well, it was difficult because, you know, the setup was weird. The tape machine was like on the 24th floor, the studio was on the first floor, the film chain was in the Empire State Building, and they didn't have enough tape machines. If I was taping, they'd have to stop and take my stuff off so they could play a tape commercial over the air at that time. My show was always taped for replay later on. I don't know what — I forget — how many shows did we do for WOR a week?

RICH: It would play three times.

ZACH: Just one show, and they'd do it on Friday, Saturday and Sunday?

RICH: Two nights, one show would play Friday and Saturday, I think Saturday afternoon, like midday, then Saturday night.

ZACH: But it was just one a week?

RICH: One show a week, but played three times.

ZACH: Yeah, yeah. Wow.

RICH: You made a big deal about that, the first show was like, "You're gonna have to suffer through this three times, this awful movie!" That kind of thing.

ZACH: A lot of them were just very bad detective movies with —

RICH: Yeah, murder mystery.

ZACH: Jimmy Gleason and — what was her name? Great old actress.

RICH: Edna May Oliver.

ZACH: Edna May Oliver. Bingo!

RICH: I remember one of the movies. I have a good memory. *The Penguin Pool Murder* [1932].

Fifteen-year-old WOR contest winner John Panitz in Isobel's coffin (wearing a Dracula cape) as Zach and crew "All hail!" (Photo courtesy John Zacherle.)

ZACH: Ah — terrible. It was embarrassing. They wouldn't give me their big movies, they were saving them for the *Million Dollar Movie* series. We couldn't get *King Kong*, but we did get *Mighty Joe Young* eventually.

Zach also did a unique thing at both WABC and WOR. Having run through the usual gamut of ideas and wacky experiments, he filled Isobel's coffin with water, donned a turn-of-the-century style orange-and-black striped bathing suit and demonstrated "diving" techniques in that cramped little space. I asked him how the box was able to hold gallons of water, and he told me that the carpenters at the station had to construct a more substantial box out of heavier wood because the original (collapsible and stored at the station), used at both WABC and WOR, would bulge dangerously after having been half-filled. The bathing suit reappeared on the *Disc-O-Teen* show in 1966, and again in the extra features of the *Zacherley Archives* DVD.

Among the most memorable things about Channel 7's *Shock Theater* and Channel 9's *Zacherley at 12* were the openings. The former program would open with a piece of unsettling music in which the predominant instrument was a sinister bassoon. The music would build to a shrieking climax, stop abruptly, and then a voice would scream, "*Give me some light!*" It always had a bizarre effect on me, because all I could picture was some wretched soul screeching from some dark and slimy prison cell or dungeon. It actually was a portion of the soundtrack from the 1948 Laurence Olivier production *Hamlet*. The music was composed by William Walton and the actor in misery, Basil Sydney, played the

King of Denmark. Whoever chose this particular piece of audio certainly had imagination — it was appropriate but strangely off-kilter. The following year, Zach chose to open his WOR show with something similar, but with new music (a few bars from Bela Bartok's impressionistic "Concerto for Orchestra") and himself hollering *"Let me out of h-e-e-e-r-e!"* On WXRK-FM's New York Halloween show (1992), Zach explained the origin of the line to co-host Maria Milito:

> How that came about was, we used to open the show with that, with the old horror movies, and that was from way back in my dim past when I was in the Army — I don't know why! Sometimes I wonder what side I was on! At any rate, they had this big camp over in Africa somewhere, where all these poor guys were sitting waiting to be moved on to some other group, and it was just a big replacement place and lots of guys were just wandering around there, some for weeks and weeks and weeks. They never got assigned to any other unit, you know, and it got on their nerves! And in the moonlight there, one guy would come out of his tent and he'd holler, *"Get me outta h-e-e-e-e-e-e-r-r-e!"* and everybody would scream back and answer him, *"Go to Hell!"*

Zach once told me that he used to bring the films home and screen them himself:

> ZACH: I did that at WOR when I lived in a hotel on the West Side. They gave me a projector and I guess they had no time to give me anybody to run it, and so they allowed me to take the films and see them at my leisure, you know?
>
> RICH: And you said every once in awhile you'd have a little accident?
>
> ZACH: Yeah [*laughs*]. You'd stop the projector from moving, but the light is still on, right? I would stop it to write something down, and then I'd look up and think, "Oh my God, burned the film again!" It was a great effect, it reminded me of the effects that I saw later on at the Fillmore East [a Manhattan rock venue] in the light shows.

Zach's WOR tenure only lasted another six months or so, and, as happened at WABC, he simply vanished, coming out at the end of his final installment sans makeup (as he had also done at WABC) for his last "goodbye." At some point during the WOR season, and as happened at Channel 7 the year before, a man in a white coat appeared, spent some time enjoying Zach's hijinks with him (I seem to remember the two of them playing "leapfrog" with a dummy known as the Cardiff Giant), then the white-coat guy grew serious and led him out of the crypt to his second (or possibly third, as you'll find out later) stay at the funny farm. But there was always something strange, to my mind, about this man's disappearance from the air. Other live hosts had come and gone through the years without my giving them a second thought. In Zach's case, I always kept my eyes peeled for any indication of his return, wondering where he was, what he was doing, and why the local TV channels weren't scrambling to pick him up again. Didn't they see how unique he was, how original? Zach transcended his colleagues in the business, but more to the point he transcended his time. He was one of the first TV hosts to tell it like it was, even if it meant lashing out at the film fare that was his bread and butter. He was also just plain hip. In the Eisenhower era, at a time when conservatism was the order of the day, he punctured the barriers, pushed the envelope, spoke his mind. He was successful at it because it was so consistent with the character he was playing, and when he'd take a jab at the New York postal system or even the mayor, all he'd have to do is follow it up with his famous laugh and it was all cool. He could get away with kidding anything and anybody the same way Groucho Marx did, because, as with Groucho, it became an honor to become the target of one of his barbs. He didn't speak like other people, always had a well-honed wit, and delivered it with that wonderfully resonant voice coupled with his most important ingredient: a touch of class. When Zach left the television scene, there was a gaping hole that needed to be filled. What I wasn't consciously aware of at the time, however, was the familiarity of his persona; the way he spoke, the gentle dry bite of his humor, the twinkle in his eye. All of this was for me very familiar. Later I'd realize what it was: He reminded me of my father.

Chapter 4
Cartoons and New Projects

RICH: How did your two paperback story collections, *Zacherley's Midnight Snacks* and *Zacherley's Vulture Stew*, come about?

ZACH: We had at one time a guy, Sid Rubin, who was a merchandiser, I guess you'd say, with ideas to make things, and he made up that "Zacherley for President" kit and, you know, buttons and things to sell. I don't think he was ever highly successful at it, but he also got in touch with Ballantine Books. I had an agent there for awhile, from Ashley-Steiner, named Harold Cohen, and he may have arranged that. And they wanted to put out a book of scary stories, you know. They handed me all these pulp magazines, and I was so busy I didn't have time to read 'em, and I thought, well, I'd better read one of them and see which — they wanted me to pick out the best ones and they would say that I was the one that edited it, you know. And I read a couple of them and they were really, some of them were homosexual stories, and I thought, "Oh, God, I can't have this in here."

So I had to read them all and pick them out. I don't know how many they sold, or whether any money came in or not, I have no idea. But they made those two books, and it was kind of fun to have done that. Luckily I learned that I'd better read this stuff before it gets printed, or chosen as something that I had approved.

RICH: So you did actually read all the stories that were in the books?

ZACH: Yeah, yeah, had to. After I found that first one about a bunch of sailors, and the sailors were having sex and all this stuff, and I'd think, "Oh, my God!" [*Laughs*]

RICH: Whose idea was the *Zacherley for President* book?

ZACH: It was during the 1960 presidential campaign. Dick Strome, a real nice guy, was a copywriter for a big advertising agency and dreamed that up. That type of book was popular in those days. They used to have books with pictures of animals that had funny captions under them. Dick's bald head even made an appearance in one of the pictures! Books with pictures were very big back then, but not that one, that didn't make it. It was too big for the racks — it was the wrong size! [*Laughs*]

It was a creative period for Zach, as fans would soon discover. In 1960, "Spook Along with Zacherley," his first album of original tunes on the Electra label, appeared in music stores. The album's title was a takeoff on the then-popular "Sing Along with Mitch" records. Zach was in fine voice on the collection of 11 novelty songs, and confided to me that during recording, he had given the first two songs such energy that he nearly lost his voice. A few tea and honeys later, he was ready to continue singing.

RICH: Who offered you the chance to do your first LP, "Spook Along with Zacherley"?

ZACH: The guy that wrote the songs, he was watching the show and he saw the opportunity. His big claim to fame was he wrote that big standard in those days called "Sunday Kind of Love." His name was Stan Rhodes, and he approached us about it. He may first have gone to record companies and he made a deal with Elektra Records. In those days, Jac Holzman was doing folk singers, and he was peddling his records from a bicycle, riding around the Village getting his records in stores. This was the first big deal that he had, or was more than just a folk singer in a studio with a guitar, because we had a nice little orchestra in a big studio. He was the one who arranged all that. He got Jerry Adler, a Broadway musical director, to do the scoring of the songs, and I think Stanley Rhodes was really a lyricist. I've never seen a copy of "Sunday Kind of Love," as to whether he did the words and music, I don't know. [Rhodes shares writing credit on "Sunday Kind of Love" with Barbara Belle, Anita Leonard and Louis Prima.]

Nineteen sixty-one came and went without so much as a hint of any potential new show starring my favorite horror host. He did make a guest appearance on the Halloween episode of NBC's *1 2 3 Go!*, hosted by a very young Richard Thomas, who in the 1970s found fame as John-Boy on the popular TV series *The Waltons*. Zach, in makeup and costume, explored the history of Halloween, guiding Thomas around a haunted house (the exteriors were taped at an abandoned old house in Long Island) and, at the end of the show, bantering with Jack "Lescoulie the Ghoulie." In 1962, I managed to discover a new album called "Monster Mash," with Zach doing a cover of the recent hit by Bobby "Boris" Pickett, plus wacky versions of a dozen other Cameo-Parkway hits of the time, and it satisfied my appetite for new Zacherley material. Okay, it wasn't a TV show, but it was the next best thing as he ad-libbed his way through "The Pistol Stomp," "Weird Watusi," "The Bat" and "Hurry, Bury Baby." For the most part the songs were spoken rather than sung, and the result was very much like listening to audio from the old horror days. "Monster Mash" was followed in 1963 by a third LP, "Scary Tales," containing an odd assortment of tunes: "Happy Halloween," "Clementine," "Surfboard 109," "I Was a Teenage Caveman" and "Little Red Riding Hood." We expected novelty albums from him, but what very few of us knew was that in 1962, during his hiatus from television, John Zacherle had been cast in a stage musical called *La Belle*. He recalled:

> It was the story of Helen of Troy set to the music of Offenbach. And Joan Diener was in it, Menasha Skulnik was in it, George Segal and Howard DaSilva. It would have been George Segal's first play on Broadway, but it didn't make it to Broadway. We rehearsed it in a theater down on 45th Street somewhere, and we took it to Philadelphia and that's where it died — very quickly!

Things were not all wonderful during this period: By the summer of 1962 my father had been battling Hodgkin's Disease (lymph cancer) for about a year, and finally succumbed that July, a few weeks before his 56th birthday. The loss was shared by my mother and three brothers. Largely due to my immersion in film and fantasy, I got through it fairly easily. What I didn't know was how much I would have valued his advice a few years down the line. Zacherley had been absent also — from television for over two years, and at that point I really could also have used the diversion of his comedy and wit. One afternoon in the late summer of 1963, I was watching an afternoon program on WPIX Channel 11, when there he was, the Cool Ghoul himself (an appellation bestowed upon him by Dick Clark following the release of "Dinner with Drac" in 1958), reading from what appeared to be an old piece of parchment that announced his imminent return to television as host of the cartoon show *The Mighty Hercules*.

Before he could finish reading, the paper, held too close to a nearby candle, burst into flame. My vigil was coming to an end; my friend was coming back in the fall. He would be part of a new live lineup of after-school kid shows that included some old and new personalities, and he would be introduced to a man who would be responsible for the next phase of his career. That man's name was Barry Friedlander, professionally known as Barry Landers.

Allow me to jump forward a few decades: In the 1980s, there had been rumors circulating for some time that Landers, so much a part of the second half of John Zacherle's television career, was dead of a heart attack. But Barry has (so far) "enjoyed" the distinction of having died not only once, but twice! In 1990, I spoke to him on the phone (he lived in Arizona) after the first rumor was dispelled; then by 2004 it had started all over again. His second "demise," happily, turned out to be another whole cloth fantasy, and to this day no one is sure how these stories got started. I finally reached him in March 2005, still living in Arizona, and was able to interview him — the last link in the Zacherley chain.

> BARRY LANDERS: I got into Channel 11 on a lie. They were looking for a writer, and I said I was a writer. I had come from radio. I actually went in to visit a friend of mine who was a cameraman there, and I met Terry Bennett. Terry said they were looking for a writer and I said, "I'm a writer." "Well, can you write blackout skits?" I said, "Oh, sure!" I didn't even know what the hell a blackout skit was! So he gave me the format for the Clay Cole dance show and I said, "Oh, I can do that." Then he said to me, "Well, you're a lousy writer, but you work hard, so we'll keep you for another two weeks," and that lasted four and a half years! Everything Chuck McCann did, I did. I was Chuck's writer and we would sit there with Paul Ashley, who was one of the great puppeteers in the world for hand puppets.

Chuck was doing a show called *Laurel and Hardy and Chuck*, and we would write skits for that and we had Laurel and Hardy puppets. Chuck would do the voices and Paul Ashley would be behind the set working the puppets. They had the children's market pretty much sewed up — Channel 5 was their only competitor. Actually, Channel 9 did a couple of things too. Chuck was a holy terror to work with because he was so intense, so very, very intense. He never let up. Even in his lighter moments, he was very critical. But even the stuff he didn't like, he played to the hilt. He was a complete entertainer.

I asked Zach what Barry Landers did at Channel 11:

ZACH: When I first met Barry, he was the floor director, the guy who stands with the earphones. I don't know what other shows he did, he must have done other things besides *Disc-O-Teen* or my show at Channel 11, but I'm not aware of which ones he did. I'm sure he had an eight-hour schedule and he just did one show right after another. I don't know who else had that job there, he's the only one I ever saw on the floor when I was working. And the director was Marvin Long.

RICH: The director of your show?

ZACH: Yeah. But that's where I met him. And his idea was, they were in competition with Channel 9 and Channel 5. They all had kiddie shows, I think, in the afternoon, showing cartoons and things, and they were all in competition to get the commercials. If you got a lot of commercials, you got good ratings. Or if you didn't get any commercials, or else you got cheap commercials. Whatever. So the program manager approached the people at Channel 11 on a lineup of people for the afternoon. They had picked up that cartoon of *Hercules*, which was like a limited animation, which I thought was terrible, I'd never seen one like that, where nothing moves on the figure except maybe the jaw, [*wagging his jaw*] "wawawawawa," you know? [*Laughs*] Very weird. Chet Dowling must have talked me up to the managers at Channel 11, and I had this afternoon show, the 4:30 time slot. And I met "Officer Joe" Bolton there, he was doing the Three Stooges, "Captain Jack" McCarthy was ahead of me doing Popeye cartoons, and somewhere in there was the guy, "Beachcomber Bill," or somebody, remember him? He's the one who had the parrot that Chuck McCann taught to say "Fuck you." He claims he put a continuous loop tape next to the parrot, which was sharing his dressing room, and taught the parrot to say "Fuck you." When everybody went home, the parrot would hear "Fuck you" for an hour or however long the thing lasted, and eventually Chuck claimed the parrot said it on the air when Beachcomber Bill had it on his shoulder [*laughs*]. He makes a great story out of it. Anyway, at the end of the year Barry approached me and I guess he's the one that told me that they were gonna drop this thing that I was doing and maybe, I don't know, maybe somebody else — I think they hired a guy as a fireman — "Fireman Bob" or somebody. ["Fireman" Todd Russell.]

RICH: Did you ever hang out with Chuck McCann socially?

ZACH: Yes, he was a good friend of Earl Doud's[*] too, he lived right across the street from him. Yes, we did, he and his mother, he had a wonderful old mother who lived across the street from him, and she used to work for Ripley, the Believe It or Not guy.

---

[*] Comedy writer Earl Doud wrote for Jack Paar, among others. In 1962, he produced the hugely successful comedy album *The First Family* which featured Vaughn Meader and lampooned the John F. Kennedy administration.

RICH: Oh, yeah!

ZACH: And Chuck McCann I think also lived across the street with his wife, and he was often in there too, so that's when I really got to know him. A lot of good times there. Earl unfortunately died last year, he never really knew how to handle his money. He earned a lot of money on that first album *The First Family*. He tried a follow-up album and it sold a little bit. I don't know how well it did, but every other presidential election he would make another presidential comedy album, but they never really were as funny as the first one. When he ran out of money, he snuck out of town. He called me up and said, "Say, Zach, I'm leavin' for California, don't tell anybody where I'm goin', okay?" So he went to California and he worked again with Chuck McCann on some projects, survived out there but not too well, then his wife died. She was great. She was a Playboy bunny originally, though I never saw her costume. She was really nice, and they had two nice boys, but... Anyway, this afternoon thing kind of fell apart. It didn't win a lot of ratings, I guess. Chuck McCann was still there and so was Captain Jack and Officer Joe.

According to Barry Landers,

Zach with Chuck McCann at WPIX in 1963 and at a Chiller con decades later.

Joe Bolton was one of the nicest, sweetest guys you ever met in your life. He always had the attitude that no matter what they told him to do, he was gonna do it. We'd sit in the announcer's lounge and he'd spin these great stories about the Three Stooges, because he got to know them real well. When I first met

John Zacherle, he was not in costume. He was a very easygoing, jolly guy. He would go into the dressing room and put makeup on and he became Zacherley, and I was just in complete awe of this man. This was the character I got to know from the TV show *Chiller Theatre*. The John Zacherle I knew was not "Zacherley."

Even in the office, when we shared an office together, as soon as that makeup went on, "Zacherley" came out. He just amazed me, he always amazed me. And he was probably one of the kindest people you ever met. But he was intense — he took everything so seriously, as it should have been.

The Mighty Hercules, broadcast five days a week on WPIX from 4:30 to 5:00 p.m., hit the airwaves on Monday, September 2, 1963, and finished on Friday, November 16, 1963. Zach then hosted WPIX's *The Three Stooges Show* from Monday, January 6, 1964, until Friday, January 31, 1964. The remainder of the season found him back at more familiar duties as host of *Chiller Theatre* on Saturday nights, hosting low-budget '50s sci-fi and horror films such as *Attack of the 50 Foot Woman* (1958), *Plan 9 from Outer Space* (1958), *The Neanderthal Man* (1953) and *Attack of the Crab Monsters* (1957).

Things in those early years of the '60s seemed to be sailing along familiarly, not far from the sensibilities of the previous decade. Then came the Big Change, not only for all of us fans, not just for John Zacherle, but for popular culture as well.

Chapter 5
Coolest Little Monsters

I spent the winter of 1963 in a haze of melancholy. The world had just experienced the assassination of President John F. Kennedy, an event unthinkable to an impressionable young mind like mine. In its wake, and through the perspective of years, I realized that what I was going through was a rite of passage, a sort of forced growth spurt, a byproduct of which was the realization that unimaginable things can indeed happen. I needed, the *whole country* needed, a diversion — something to foster new enthusiasms and help us to look forward to the future as something worth living for. In my case, it came in the form of four English musicians.

I had a younger brother, Doug. With friends Kurt Meyers and Doug Shaffer, Doug, like many Baby Boomer kids, had started a rock'n'roll band called Herald Square. On the evening of Sunday, February 9, 1964, 16-year-old Doug and I sat in our dining room in the Bergenfield house, the small Admiral TV set tuned to Channel 2, anxiously awaiting the evening's edition of *The Ed Sullivan Show*. A brand-new phenomenon had taken hold in England and was poised on the periphery of the United States, ready to rip away the chilly conservatism of the black-and-white 1950s and hurl us headlong into the Technicolor glory of the '60s. Ladies and gentlemen, the Beatles!

What we saw that night changed the course of Doug's life and altered the way I listened to pop music. Transfixed with the startling new look of the performers on stage, and delightedly attuned to the music, I asked him, "What is it that makes them so special?" He answered immediately: "Are you kidding? They write their own music and play their own instruments!" Like I should have known.

I wasn't aware that, with a few exceptions, popular music at that time was largely the product of Tin Pan Alley songwriters, many of them working out of New York's Brill Building: names not yet well known to the general public, among them Jerry Goffin, Carole King, Jeff Barry, Ellie Greenwich and Neil Diamond. These and many more would regularly pump out material for agents to match with the right artists, and *voila* — hit records! Most were backed up by the best studio musicians, and the singer's job was only to lay down the vocals. Any performer who took on the task of writing the material, playing the instruments, and in some cases (for example, Brian Wilson of the Beach Boys) producing the records, well, they were pretty special, at least in my brother's eyes. My older brother Steve, less impressed, only had one reaction to the Fab Four: "The rest of them look okay, but that Ringo! Ugh! He looks like he's on drugs!"

For some time to come, monsters took a temporary back seat to the Beatles and this new musical invasion. Not that I ever lost my love for the movies, but these were new feelings, emotions that felt something like "growing up." (I should be honest and admit that in the midst of all this "growing up," I was busy with a group of friends filming an 8mm movie I had written. It was tentatively titled *Frankenstein Meets the Mummy*.) In the spring of 1965, some of Herald Square's band members and I went to my first rock concert. Held at the Paramount Theater in New York City, it featured a smorgasbord of acts that had had hit records. On the bill: the Hullabaloos (a one-hit English band with really long hair — very cool), King Curtis and his Orchestra, Little Richard (with backup guitarist Jimmy James, soon to be known as superstar Jimi Hendrix), the Hollies, Shirley Ellis ("The Name Game"), the Exciters ("Tell Him") and the Detergents ("Leader of the Laundromat"). The headliner was Soupy Sales, whose WNEW Channel 5 show was enormously popular then, but his stage time was dwarfed by all the rock'n'roll acts!

Herald Square took a serious approach to what they were doing, how they appeared on stage, and what music they played. More than that, they took the time to develop their musical skills and lined up a selection of songs that not every garden variety suburban garage band was doing: A mix of Motown soul, current hits, some original material and new arrangements of a few oldies rounded out their repertoire. It wasn't long before they attracted a bit of attention, found a manager, and scraped some money together to record a few demos at Karew Records, a local home recording studio. Their first was "Learnin' the Hard Way," an original song written by Doug Shaffer, the band's bass player. The summer of '65 was a busy one for them, with lots of performing, the usual block dances, high school proms and "band battles." Then followed a series of events that led them to cross paths with an unlikely individual: John Zacherle.

Some time in the spring or early summer, Doug and some friends began tuning in to *Disc-O-Teen*, a new TV show aimed at the teen market. It featured not only dancing, but performances by local high school bands competing against one another for the chance to win a recording contract. One afternoon in the early summer, they were watching the show when something unexpected happened. That afternoon's band had failed to show up, and the host asked if there might be anyone in the studio who could fill in for them. Doug couldn't believe his eyes when up on the stage hopped two members of Herald Square, rhythm guitarist Dave Meyers and lead singer Frank Youngblood! I was immediately told about this for two reasons: first, because two of our friends had appeared from out of nowhere on a TV show, and second because the show's host was none other than — Zacherley!

A unique turn of events had propelled the Cool Ghoul headlong into the world of pop music. Zach's run as host of WPIX's *Chiller Theatre* had ended and both he and Barry Landers were out of work. Zach took a short break while Barry got in touch with some people he knew from Channel 13 who had pooled their money and invested in starting up WNJU, Channel 47. Their goal was to do things the New York stations weren't doing: present a mix of shows that included bullfights (which I found so disturbing as to be unwatchable), wrestling, a social awareness show with folk singer Pete Seeger, and programs in Spanish and other languages. Barry convinced the owners that a teenage dancing show would be a big hit, recalling Dick Clark's *American Bandstand* as an example.

Barry Landers on leaving Channel 11:

> Zach got fired and I got fired. There was a vice-president there named Hank Boorham who was a complete, total ass. He would hold meetings after every show in Chuck McCann's office, which would drive Chuck nuts. And he wanted to get rid of Zach, he never really cared for anything that Zach did. He just played favorites, that's all. After four and a half years, he let me go, I remember the day vividly because it was cold and I was walking up Park Avenue without a job and I was just devastated. But then I heard about or read somewhere about Fred Sayles putting together Channel 47 and that's when I drove down there and got the idea to talk to him.

I got the story of the genesis of *Disc-O-Teen* right from Zach:

> ZACH: Well, Barry had already found a new job at Channel 47. And Barry found that they were opening up a new studio in Newark, New Jersey, that had formerly been for Channel 13, the PBS station. And

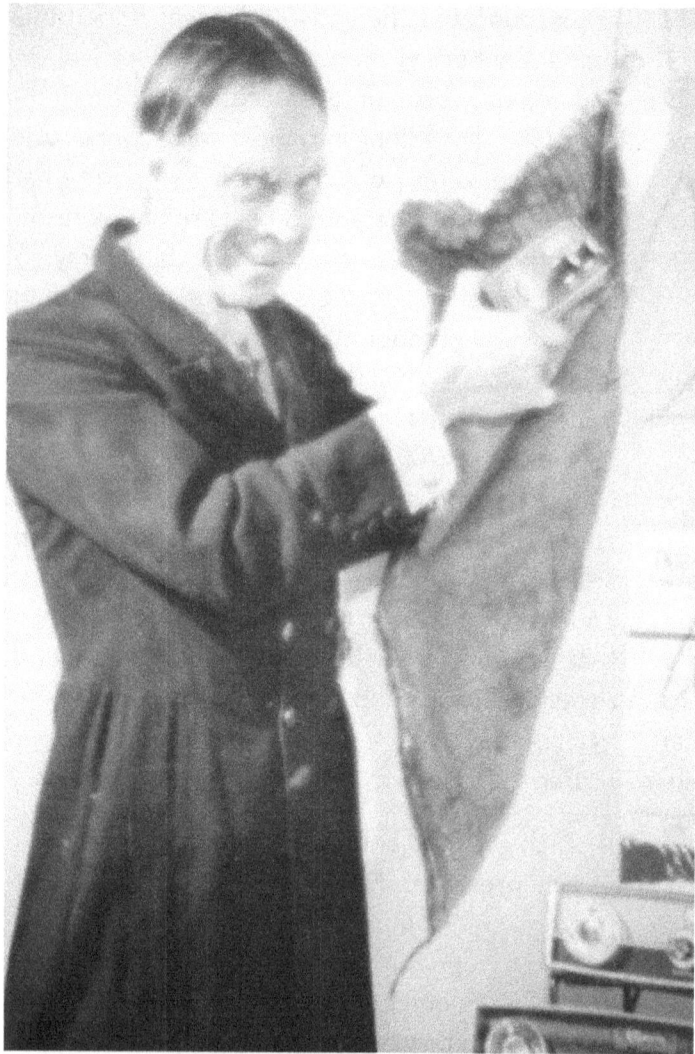

Zach promoting UHF converter boxes in 1965. (Photo courtesy John Zacherle.)

PBS had moved most of their production to New York City, but they maintained a station in Newark, which at that time was the only television station in the state of New Jersey, as I recall. And he got himself a job there and he talked them up about me doing a dancing show. They were looking for any kind of counter-programming so they could get a niche — this was UHF, before there was cable. So you had to have a little box to pick it up, or else you had to have an old-fashioned radio-style dial on the TV, not the "click-click-click," but one you moved silently, and with that you could pick up this new station. So I never knew how many people actually could see the show.

RICH: There are photos of you promoting those UHF boxes.

ZACH: Really!

RICH: I have it, one of those pictures you gave me, there's one of you holding them, yeah.

ZACH: No kidding! Well, maybe people, because they had foreign-language on there, maybe a lot of people did that because the other stations were not producing, as I recall, any foreign-language programs. And so they ended up with bullfighting and wrestling and interviews and things and a certain amount of English programming, and that's what we did, we did a dancing show because nobody in the whole New York area was doing a teenage dancing show. Barry got himself a job there as the floor director, and he probably worked his butt off there too, because they certainly didn't have a surplus of anybody, certainly not a surplus of floor directors.

Among the fans watching Zacherley during his Channel 9 days was a pretty little blonde-haired girl who would one day be indirectly responsible for enlisting Zach in Channel 47's most popular program. Wende Sasse, daughter of Fred Sayles, Channel 13's "Uncle Fred" on *Junior Frolics*, the very first TV show I regularly watched, remembers her first exposure to Zach:

My brother and I used to watch Zach on WOR, and my father used to come home from playing golf and he would sit down and watch with us, and we just used to die laughing. You know, those ridiculous kind of "B" horror movies, we just loved it. That's how I first remember seeing Zach. My father would come in, ask, "What are you doing?," and we'd say, "Wait 'til you see, wait, wait, wait," and then Zach would come on and my father was like, "What is that?"

Zach and Barry's office at Channel 47 with unknown staff member at bottom.

We would just explain to him how Zach would come in and make fun of whatever scene, and then the movie would cut to him doing sort of a parody of what we had just seen, and we just had such a good time.

Disc-O-Teen was impossible to receive on many TV sets unless you had that UHF (ultra high frequency) tuner, which one of our sets did. And even if you could pull it in, half the time the reception would be so snowy that you could hardly make out what was going on. There were lots of days, however, when reception in our house was just fine, and in between the black-and-white images of kids dancing to the latest hit records, the camera would dolly over to a corner shrouded in string and cheesecloth spider webs, a Gothic chair, settee and hand-drawn monster posters sent in by fans, to reveal the familiar and most welcome face of the Cool Ghoul, once again doing his act but combining it with the emceeing chores of a Dick Clark or Clay Cole. The makeup was still the same, and when pop music wasn't pulsing forth from the speakers it seemed pretty much like Zacherley's old days at WABC or WOR. I couldn't stop wondering, "How did Zach go from hosting horror movies to *this*?"

WENDE (SAYLES) SASSE: I think Ed Cooperstein, Herb Greene and my father got together and brought some investors, my dad was an investor, my uncle Manny Berlinrut, Will Becton, the guy from Becton Dickinson [Company] was a big investor, probably the biggest money guy. They got together and started the station, and I remember the first night they went on the air. There was a big, huge party launching the station, big gala thing, and they all got up and spoke, my father spoke, and it was for the investors and I think for the press. My father was program director, so he was in charge of finding programs that they could run. One of the things they decided they wanted to do was have some sort of a teen show. That's when my father had decided after seeing Zach with us, that Zach would be funny and could be an interesting person, and the next thing I knew, Zach was on the air!

BARRY LANDERS: Fred asked, "Can you get a hold of Zacherley?" and I said, "Yeah, I think so." And I called Zach and we got together for lunch in New York and talked over this concept, and you know the rest of the story, it's history. There were quite a few shows, *Hootenanny* was one of them, there was one that I think Bruce Morrow wanted to do, later on he finally did it, he stole a lot of stuff from us. We were innovators. Zach was an innovator. He took a lot of the stuff that he did over at Channel 11 and brought it over to 47. They were open to a lot of things, especially bringing Zach over, because Zach was such a name, and they figured getting him was a coup. And I was not supposed to be a director, I was supposed to be just the associate producer. And they said, "No, you be a director too, so that you can get into the union and your job will be secure," which it was for the whole time I was there.

WEEK OF MAY 10, 1965

According to a May 10, 1965, news item:

"The Cool Ghoul" — John Zacherle — known in the New York area for his appearances on various Charles Addams-type shows on New York TV stations, will host *Disco Teen* [sic] on WNJU-TV (Channel 47) which signs on this week. The teen dance show will, from time to time, cover more serious topics like dropping out of school.

Barry Landers doesn't recall wanting to add "serious topics" to *Disc-O-Teen*: "No, I never thought of that, not that I remember. I did it on my show, *Up and Coming*, I took that part of it and it was called 'Rap Session' and we did talk about teen problems. I never thought of it for *Disc-O-Teen*. Not that I remember."

Between that exciting day when Dave and Frank popped up in front of the cameras performing an impromptu version of the Drifters' 1963 hit "On Broadway" and the middle of the summer, the Herald Square members contacted *Disc-O-Teen* and set up a date for their own appearance on the show. The drill was that the band would bring along as many classmates from their schools as they could to fill the dance floor and they would frug-jerk-monkey-swim-twist to canned music until the band made its appearance, perform two songs live, after which they'd pony-stroll-stomp-watusi to a few more songs. Zach would talk to the band and some lucky audience members, do a live commercial or two, say "Good night, whatever you are!" and fade to black. Pretty simple. On the hot, humid afternoon of Tuesday, August 17, 1965, my red-and-white 1957 Chevy Bel Air was part of a car caravan headed down Jersey's Garden State Parkway to exit 143A through Newark's grubby merchant area and the Mosque Theater, Ground Zero. While I was happy for my brother, I was thrilled for myself more, because I was about to meet a man who was my hero.

Upon entering the Mosque, you'd be ushered one floor up in a rickety antique elevator and you'd walk into a long hallway full of noise and teenagers. We were told to sit in rows of bleachers which faced the huge glass windows that looked down on Studio "A" and wait for our warm-up, which was eventually delivered by Barry (who reminded me of a college graduate student, good-looking with his slightly balding short haircut and youthful, nononsense face). After some tepid cracks about waiting for the giant ape to get off the top of the Empire State Building where he was interfering with the station's transmitter, we were led down a flight of stairs into another hallway, this one sporting thick, maple-colored wooden doors with small diamond-shaped windows. These opened into the spacious studio, where I would get my first close-up view of John Zacherle. I also got a slight thrill out of standing next to a tall, sexy blonde with typical '60s false eyelashes, dressed in clinging white jeans and revealing matching mod top. Her name was Patti Nash. From watching the show, we all knew her as one of the regular crowd of girls who showed up practically every day to dance. It struck me how that kind of familiarity, the sort gotten on TV, could elevate one into a kind of mini-stardom and provide a measure of genuine celebrity through repeated public exposure.

Christine Domaniecki, a regular dancer on the show from its start, remembers Patti as

> very tall and gorgeous, having blonde hair and always having a tan. She was the typical California blonde living in New Jersey, she was so unlike anyone else on the show, because all of us had either black hair or strawberry blonde hair. She had really blonde hair and she stood out. I know a lot of people would write in to see her, and the show sent in a team to do a makeover on her. ...They had a hair stylist come in, a makeup artist, and they transformed her, they put clothes on her, and I think they gave her all kinds of gift certificates. She seemed to have vanished from the show probably by the end of that year.

It was at about this time that I first became aware of a group of about eight such girls, accurately dubbed the "regulars." Prominent in one group shot I took on the set were recurring dancers Linda Pace, sisters Patti and Linda Nash, "Big" Sue Mercedante, "Little" Sue Parinello, Diane Topolewski, Joette Wrubel and Christine, the latter sporting a "Cleopatra" sweatshirt, an enthusiastic smile, jet black hair and an uncanny resemblance to actress Barbara Feldon from the TV show *Get Smart*. (I met Christine again years after *Disc-O'Teen*'s demise, and we remain friends to this day.)

On the very first show, the set was far from impressive as Christine set eyes on it:

> They had nothing. It was up where the old Channel 13 used to be, on the second floor. When we walked in, the set was straight ahead, it had a small curtain and a very, very tiny area to make it look like it was crowded. Then they played recorded songs and we just danced. Barry interviewed everyone, stuck a microphone into your face and asked your name, your age and what high school you attended. Then in between dances he would ask other questions like "Who are your favorite groups?" and that was it, just dancing and prerecorded music. Meeting Zach took place that Monday after school. It was great, he was dressed up in his Zacherley paraphernalia and we just had a great time. The show really exploded and by the time September rolled around, that place was jumping.

> BARRY LANDERS: It was a question of getting the studio ready. What you don't realize was that whole studio was sprayed with asbestos. We worked in that. I was their first employee. There were no lights, no grid, nothing. It was sprayed. There was nothing there. Bare walls. Wooden floor. And I watched them put the pipes up, watched them put the grid up, hang the lights and spray, and the second person there was director Jack Wilson.

I asked Zach who came up with the idea for the set and how it should look:

ZACH: Oh, I remember saying that it was kind of gloomy, just leave it looking weird and ugly, there was nothing you could do with it. It was dark, so you didn't see much of the background anyway. And then we convinced them to have some boxes for the kids to get up higher and make it more interesting. It's a wonder some of 'em didn't fall off those boxes, they weren't terribly big, especially when two people got up on 'em. But they enjoyed doing that. And we needed a little stage, too, for the bands to play. It was probably Barry's idea to get the high school kids to bring the bands along. He was a go-getter, he really was, he was full of enthusiasm and he kept his hands off those little girls [laughs]. That always concerned me the whole time I was there. The cameramen, you know, they had their favorites that they would — I thought, oh God, I don't want any trouble here. Because Dick Clark got his job because the guy ahead of him [Bob Horn], who was doing a dance show, got carried away and had the girls come out to his little estate of some kind he had, with a swimming pool, and I don't know if they were taking pictures or what, but he was arrested, so Dick got his job. I'd been on Dick's show when he got going.

RICH: Did you do a lot of listening to pick out the songs, or was that Barry's job?

ZACH: No, we both did that. I'm sorry now that I didn't get more input from the kids. I think they did ask us, sure, I'm sure they did ask us to play certain songs, and we'd do that. We knew what the big hits were, but we had to make sure that they were really danceable, upbeat stuff. Slow songs we kind of avoided, 'cause we always had more girls than boys anyway on the show, so it made sense not to do slow dances.

According to Barry Landers,

We would ask the kids what the hit records were, and we went out and bought them. We would ask them, "What's the record? What do you like to dance to?" We had no concept at all as to what was a hit. None whatsoever. They would come to us and say "You've gotta play this, you've gotta play that. This is what we like, this is the hot one." They choreographed a lot of the dances. The kids made the show. And Zach just had this great love for them, you know, and they loved him, they just adored him. And the crew did too.

Barry tells a story of the first few shows as Zach hosted them, but as to the accuracy of his memories, the jury is still out: "For the show originally, Zach was not in costume. He wanted to do the show as John Zacherle. He was Zacherley's 'brother'! And it just never played! We did about three or four shows and it was just dull ... It was like rope, it was like watching rope!"

(This recollection seemed to be vivid in Barry's mind, but Zach himself has no memory of it, and insists that Barry must have been drinking "silly juice" or, as he put it, wondering what he might have been smoking: "Is Barry living near the Mexican border?" The story sounds plausible to me, has a ring of truth, but for now I must relate it as having possibly been obscured by the passage of 39 years. The truth of it will probably never be known.)

I walked into the studio and saw Zach in full makeup and costume. He was tall, thin and surprisingly handsome even in his coffin-pallor makeup with the famous cheek-shadows. There was that famous black hair slickly parted down the middle, invented back in 1957 when he was known as Roland. I had seen him in person only on that one occasion in 1959 at the Oritani Theater and he looked as though he hadn't aged a day since then. He was busy attending to the business of the day's program, but you could just tell he was accessible.

Scrivani Meets Zacherley: Our very first encounter, August 1965.

Linda "Pach" Pace describes her first days there:

> I remember first meeting Zach — I think the first time was actually when he was in full costume, and then meeting him after, I was so impressed, first of all by what a handsome man he was, but at how personable he was. He was always so caring, and always made you feel that he was concerned about you. He was like that with everybody, whether you knew him for a while or whether he was just meeting you. He was magnetic.

WENDE SASSE: My father asked me if I wanted to go down with him and see the show and I did, and I started just going down and dancing on the show, taking the bus down to Newark down Bloomfield Avenue, and then he would wait for me and take me home at night. I think I was there very close to the beginning of Zach's show. Becton's daughter Elizabeth, I think she did a weather show. And then they had the bullfights. Hysterical! *Disc-O-Teen* seemed to me, for a live show, very easygoing, the way they were able to put things together. These people were pulling off shows as if it was no problem at all. The whole group that worked on it was fantastic. Barry was a lot of fun, and I think he brought his children to the show a couple of times. My father was very close with him, but my father was sort of like his boss, so — they were always nice to me, you know — "The boss' daughter's here!" I was treated very well.

I mentioned to Zach the 8mm movie I was in the midst of completing (which, by the way, I stayed in the midst of and never finished). He *acted* interested as I described the makeup with which I had managed to transform myself into the Frankenstein Monster, and my dance partner Sami Hovis talked about a Dracula's Daughter outfit she was making for Halloween. Not knowing then that Zach had not the slightest interest in horror movies and that his career as a ghoul was simply a job, we thought our conversation was of immense interest to him. It may not have been, but it was providential that we brought it up. Indeed, it was the springboard into the aforementioned new phase of my life.

It was god-awful hot inside that studio. The temperature was in the high 80s outside, and the lights inside must have brought that reading up at least ten degrees. I couldn't believe that a modern television studio didn't even have air conditioning, just a huge standup fan to one side which only succeeded in moving the hot air around. The sweat was dripping off us all, but at our age it wasn't half the bother it could have been. I was lucky enough to have the beautiful, raven-haired Sami, girlfriend of Herald Square rhythm guitarist Dave, as my dance partner. We had hit it off that summer as friends, as I had no girlfriend at the time, being shy by nature. Sami had been persistent enough to get me to drop my inhibitions at a Herald Square block dance and, against my will, she made me have a wonderful time. This day on *Disc-O-Teen* she was performing the same service, and I was grateful.

The show began with Zach, on a stepladder high in the rafters, his head protruding from between two steel girders, introducing the first song with his trademark maniacal laugh. "Reelin' and Rockin'" by the Dave Clark Five blasted through the studio, followed by the Beach Boys' current smash "California Girls." In the corner of my eye, I could see the studio monitor, and every chance the cameramen got, there was Sami on the screen. Since she had caught the eyes of the guys in the control room (and eventually Zach's), they never missed an opportunity to focus in on her. Anyone would have done the same thing — she was easily the best-looking girl in the studio that day. Since I was dancing with her, the cameras couldn't help but pick me up at times, so I enjoyed my 15 minutes of instant celebrity too. The music stopped and lucky for us, Zach headed right for Sami and some between-dancing chat:

ZACH [*referring to the heat*]: I'll speak to you now, because you may be dead later on.

SAMI: I might be!

ZACH: It looked like some kind of athletic exercise you were doing there, my dear. What was that called, that little step there?

SAMI: It's a "criss-cross" or something like that.

ZACH: Certainly was. Make sure this big oaf doesn't give you the double-cross [*laughs*]! (Thanks, Zach.)

ZACH [*after finding out our names*]: Sami, I think you have a fan club already, you're dancing marvelously there, and we appreciate it very much.

The Beatles' new single "Help!" came blasting out of the studio speakers and sent Sami off into a dancing frenzy, with Zach screaming out, "Oh, there she goes — there she goes! Look at her, there she goes!" A commercial, and then it's Herald Square's big moment. They launched into "Second to None" by Billy J. Kramer and the Dakotas, followed by Otis Redding's "Midnight Hour." Zach joined them on the stage to explain the rules of a contest they were involved in: At the end of the first round, they would wind up with four quarter-finalists who would then compete for the top prize of a recording contract with World Artist Records. (To this day, the only thing I know about World Artist Records is that it was run by the Jerome brothers, and they owned a label called Smash. A year later, a group known as the Left Banke had the Smash hit "Walk Away

Renee.") While going over the terms of the contest, Zach got a bit sidetracked, much to Sami's delight and mine:

> ZACH: Now, what will happen is, that here at the Mosque Theater there's going to be a great big show on Halloween. Hey, hey, that's for you, come here, my dear! Halloween, will you come?
>
> SAMI: I sure will!
>
> ZACH: Step right over here, my dear. You step over here, Frankenstein. They promised that they would come dressed up as Frankenstein and Lady Drac, right? So it'll be a Halloween show here. So you can forget about Murray the K and all those idiots, we'll have the show right here. You don't have to go to Brooklyn and get massacred, you can come over to Newark and get massacred! And stepped on and tromped on, you know, and kicked in the lobby and all that.

Zach mentioned a big show he was to be a part of down at Asbury Park's Convention Hall. The show was to feature Sonny and Cher.

> ZACH: That's on the fourth of September, Labor Day weekend, that'll be a marvelous day, we'll be down there with Sonny and Cher. You dig them, do you?
>
> SAMI: Oh, yeah.
>
> ZACH: They're wild, are they not?
>
> SAMI: Oh, *wild*!
>
> ZACH: I may kidnap this girl before the day's over.

World Artists representative Steve Jerome and his assistant confer with Zach.

Needless to say, Sami and I were stunned and excited. Another chance to appear with Zach — and as a featured act! Even then, though, I had no illusions as to why we were asked back; it was Sami that Zach wanted to have on the show again. Our mention of my movie, the Frankenstein makeup, etc. may have helped it along, but I knew he was being tactful and diplomatic by including me because it appeared that Sami and I were together. You have no idea how little that mattered to me. Another visit to this show was a gift I never anticipated, and I didn't care how it came about, only that it was going to happen. I drove home with a car full of excited band members, singing along with the radio which was playing the Beatles' "I Should Have Known Better" — my friend Bill Curtis' voice was the loudest. It was one of those moments when, if you're lucky, you live in the moment and realize that it doesn't get any better than this. It was the '60s in full swing. It was euphoric

Chapter 6
Halloween and the Rolling Stones

Through the nauseous night I'll soar through the pools of rancid gore, through the sewer pipes I'll crawl To the Horror Hall
—"Happy Halloween," John Zacherle

The Big Day came on Friday, October 29, 1965. Excited was not the word to describe my state of mind that morning. Make it more like — single-mindedly obsessed. I was attending classes at the Teaneck campus of Fairleigh Dickinson University and all I could think about was what I was going to do that evening. I couldn't study, and due to the nervous condition of my stomach, I didn't feel well at all. I did make it home, though, and good old "Countess Zaleska" Sami arrived and we both excitedly donned our respective monster outfits. Mine was the Frankenstein Monster costume and head left over from our 8mm film. Sami's was a simple dyed-black sheet and heavy eye makeup, topped by a cheap black wig. Voila! Frankenstein's Monster and Dracula's Daughter!

Right to left, Zach, Sami and I posed for this photo just prior to taping the 1965 Halloween show.

I check the optics at Channel 47.

When you're 20, walking the streets of Newark dressed as the Monster is not a lot of fun. I loved monster movies and was ecstatic over the idea of appearing on TV with the Cool Ghoul himself, but being an introvert, I was easily embarrassed by the laughing of passersby. My older brother Steve helped out by driving us there and shooting a roll of color slides to commemorate the event. I thought I was embarrassed outside the building; it was ten times worse inside. Upon entering the Channel 47 studios I was immediately struck by the age of the kids in costume, mostly girls, who would populate the dance floor that night. Young. Extremely young. They acted like elementary school kids as they ran up and down the halls screaming and giggling. For a few disappointing minutes I actually regretted taking part in this if Junior High School was going to be the order of the day. Sami didn't seem to mind, she was just going with the flow. There was also the extra bonus of Zach seemingly having a little "thing" for her. It would be hard not to, as Sami was quite a beauty.

Amid the tumult and confusion (there had to be a couple hundred kids there), we had a chance to talk to Zach and ask him how he got involved in, of all things, a teenage dance show. He explained quickly about his transition from hosting horror films at WPIX in New York to his new job being the brainstorm of Barry Landers. I asked him if he really liked rock and roll, as it was still referred to then, and he made it clear that he loved the music, especially since the Beatles changed the face of it, but couldn't stand the incessant chatter of the disc jockeys! There were no FM rock stations in 1965, with their trademark soft-spoken hosts, and wouldn't be until the following year. Until then we had to endure the likes of Cousin Brucie (Bruce Morrow), Charlie Greer, Gary Stevens and a host of other screaming hyenas as they introduced the latest hits from the Top 40. It could easily get on your nerves, and apparently got on Zach's big time. *Disc-O-Teen's* Halloween Ball was being taped on a Friday, so we asked Zach if he went back to his apartment in New York City after the taping. "No, no," he replied, "I go back to Philadelphia for the weekend. I've got an ancient mother to take care of."

The show got underway and I was surprised and amused by how little preparation seemed to go into it. Zach had a rough script, but the taping was very haphazard and our segment came off as almost a throwaway. I realized later that to do five live shows a week, Monday through Friday, and in addition on Friday evening an hour-long taping for Saturday, some "looseness" must have been necessary.

All of a sudden, about halfway through the show, Zach told everyone to sit on the floor and the Frankenstein Monster and Dracula's Daughter were led down the "aisle" (to the accompaniment of taped thunder) to be married, as they had been every year for many years, as Zach explained, "to appease the family." Zach lip-synched the official wedding song, "A Wicked Thought Will Pull You Through" (from the "Spook Along" album), pronounced us "monster and wife," and feigned embarrassment as I reached out to kiss the bride. He began yelling, "Oh, no, no! That comes later — later — later on! Ha ha ha ha — *ha*!" It was actually a pretty funny moment as we watched the show on TV the following afternoon. My only other on-camera moment was during a short sketch with Zach imploring his wife to exit her casket (a canvas laundry hamper) and make her first public appearance. While he was pleading with her, ("You can't do this to me. You've been promising all week to come out!") Barry whispered to me, "Go over there and start banging on the casket." I did, and Zach (in character) went berserk: "No, *no*! No, my boy, don't you pound! *No*!" I was having the time of my life.

November 1965 rolled around and I had found my way into a part-time job ushering at the local movie palace, appropriately called the Palace Theater. Since the '50s it had been the Saturday afternoon hangout for myself and scores of friends, as we excitedly took in selected shorts, 10 color cartoons and usually a double feature. With me the film fare was overwhelmingly science-fiction and/or horror, and within the Palace's popcorn-scented walls I had been scared to death by titles like *Revenge of the Creature* (I'll always remember a little girl meeting her mother outside the theater afterward, saying: "Mommy, you should have seen the monster — he had no nose!"), *The War of the Worlds*, *Creature with the Atom Brain*, *Earth vs. the Flying Saucers*, *The Werewolf*, *Invaders from Mars* — the list goes on and on. In the early '60s, my visits there were for titles like *The Time Machine*, *Mysterious Island*, *The Innocents*, *Black Sunday* and the Roger Corman-Vincent Price Poe pictures.

At the end of 1965, I wondered where all the fantasy fare had gone, as I ushered my way through showing after showing of *Ship of Fools* (too heavy for me at the time), *The Hallelujah Trail* (long and dull), *Dear Brigitte* (cute fluff), *Sands of the Kalahari* (adventure — better), *Bunny Lake Is Missing* (even better) and Bette Davis in *The Nanny* (even *more* better). Being a movie buff, it wasn't a bad job; hey, at least I was getting paid to watch movies even if I wasn't particularly impassioned by all the mainstream titles. What was eating at me on one particular day in November was that I was there instead of seeing the Rolling Stones.

Yeah, I thought that would grab you. How did Mick and company get into the picture? Simple enough: During the fall, Herald Square had been notified that they were in the running to win the *Disc-O-Teen* band contest and were to be on the show again for the final face-off against three other quarter-finalists. The band's musical lineup this time included a cover of the Stones' version of "Have Mercy," Tom Jones' "It's Not Unusual" and an up tempo version of "A Summer Place"(!). Besides the crowd filling the studio being a bit more sparse than the previous August, two things stick out in my mind about our third visit to the Channel 47 studios: Dave Meyers "playing" rhythm guitar while lying on his back as he had seen Jimmy James (later Jimi Hendrix) do at the Soupy Sales stage show in New York, and Sami and I dancing in the wrestling ring adjacent to the *Disc-O-Teen* set.

ZACH: Live wrestling! Live wrestling is when I got the crabs! Have you ever had the crabs?

RICH: No, I can honestly say I never—

ZACH: Well, you were there. You must have never gone to the bathroom.

RICH: I did! Many times. I guess I was lucky.

ZACH [*laughs*]: Ha, yeah, if you want to call it that. It was exciting! I didn't know what they were, I'd never heard of them. I must have made the mistake of getting dressed somewhere and dropping my trousers on the floor or something and putting them on, I don't really remember. I don't know how else. But anyway, I remember sitting home and I was itching all the time and I couldn't figure out what it was, and then bathing myself in alcohol and all kinds of things, you know, and one day I was sitting there on a hot summer day in my birthday suit at home, reading the paper and scratching myself, and I scratch and I'm looking and — what the hell is that? There's this little thing crawling around my — that's how you discover you got 'em. And you can get rid of 'em overnight once you know what you've got.

It was decided by the show that, in addition to the "recording contract," the four finalists would have the privilege of being opening acts for the Rolling Stones concert scheduled to be held at the Mosque on Sunday, November 7. You have to remember that at that time the Stones were achieving a level of popularity (and notoriety) that threatened to eclipse the Beatles! This was no small thing — appearing on the same stage with

Herald Square setting up at the Stones show

the Stones would be an event not easily matched in the short life of an average homegrown rock group.

I still can't really fathom my mental processes the day I announced to my boss that my brother was going to play in the same show with the Rolling Stones and asked for the afternoon off. The old Hungarian manager launched into a tirade I hadn't theretofore experienced — ending in a resounding "*No!*" I was not yet a big fan of the Stones; I was more in the Beatles' camp, but I knew that this group was important and that this was to be a special occasion. Also, since jobs much better than ushering in a movie theater were so plentiful then, why did I cave in to this old tyrant's rantings? The only explanation is my misplaced sense of responsibility at age 20. I simply felt that if you didn't get the boss' blessing, you shouldn't do it. I still regret that decision and feel that I cheated myself out of an afternoon I would have remembered the rest of my life. The sad thing is that I can't even remember what movie I watched at that malodorous old theater on that Sunday in November 1965.

I can at least share with you, compliments of my brother Doug, what happened on that day. Herald Square arrived early and met Zach and

Barry backstage. Also present were some of the *Disc-O-Teen* "regulars," the more strikingly attractive girls. Dressed in flapper-fringed "go-go" outfits of varied bright colors, their job as dancers was to open the show in the fashion of *Hullabaloo*, one of the hottest TV shows at the time. As Doug and some of the band members watched from large iron-barred windows, a huge limo bearing the Stones pulled up to the side of the building. Doug was immediately reminded of a scene out of A Hard Day's Night as teenage girls mobbed the car, lunging for whichever Stone they imagined they could grab. As the super-group fought its way inside and climbed the stairs to the backstage area, Doug felt like he was watching an album cover come to life as the famous faces paraded past and into the dressing room.

Herald Square occupied the same room, at least for the moment. Keith Richards promptly strapped on his guitar and started tuning up, and it wasn't long before the lowly bunch of mortals called Herald Square were asked to leave — after all, the Stones had shared the air with these peons long enough and needed their privacy. Outside in the less special air back of the stage, hoping to take home a souvenir, Herald Square drummer Kurt Meyers asked Stones drummer Charlie Watts if he would consider trading drumsticks. Watts tried Kurt's sticks out, paused, then asked with a quizzical look, "Does he *use* them?" Apparently Kurt's drumsticks were very heavy. Doug then asked a grubby-looking, unshaven man he later realized must have been the Stones' road manager (probably Ian Stewart, former keyboard-playing member of the Stones) what a particular

Rolling Stones bass player Bill Wyman is met by a flurry of flashbulbs at the Mosque Theater.

At the Mosque, WMCA deejay Gary Stevens and Disc-O-Teen crew members pose with Bill Wyman.

Vox amp he was setting up was used for, as he had never seen one so large. "You mean you've never seen a fookin' base amp before?" came the terse reply. All in all, not the lightest rapport between a local band and one of legend.

Eventually the concert began, "Cousin Brucie" Morrow of WABC Radio introducing the acts. All quarter-finalists in the *Disc-O-Teen* contest got to play, starting with Herald Square. Since they only got to perform one number, they chose to do another original penned by bassist Doug Shaffer, "You're Not Me." Frank Youngblood usually performed lead singing chores, but couldn't on this day due to damage done to his voice by singing without a vocal coach. Nodes had begun to grow in his throat and he had to learn to use his voice in a different manner when his condition improved. My brother Doug nervously inherited the lead vocal duties. This was the first time he had ever sung lead, but he managed — he had to. The other backing acts for the Stones were the Vibrations and Patti LaBelle and the Bluebelles, one of the Bluebelles being Cindy Birdsong, later to join the Supremes. Apparently LaBelle was a smash that day, as she rendered a fantastically moving rendition of Rodgers and Hammerstein's "You'll Never Walk Alone." The backup band for any act that needed them was the Rockin' Ramrods. During one of the opening acts, Frank worked up enough nerve to approach Mick Jagger, who was quietly watching the show backstage, and after a few moments, walked back to Doug, saying, "He's been drinking, man."

Then it was time for the Stones. The energy in the crowd was palpable as Cousin Brucie made a show of peering behind the curtain and taunting the girls with "Brian's got red pants on!" The Stones exploded onto the stage, and immediately the entire audience stood on their seats. Their opening song was Solomon Burke's "Everybody Needs Somebody to Love," Mick reducing the girls to ear-piercing screaming machines as he growled, "I need you, you, you," while pointing to selected adolescent females in the audience. It was pandemonium. Backstage, a disappointed John Zacherle listened, not only to the music he was beginning to love so much, but to a clamor of screeching that, for the moment, put him off from the enjoyment of live rock performances.

RICH: When the Stones did their live concert at the Mosque Theater, you were there.

ZACH: Yeah.

RICH: My brother Doug's band played on the same stage before them because they were quarter-finalists in a Battle of the Bands contest on *Disc-O-Teen*.

ZACH: The Stones' management objected to that—they didn't like the idea that an amateur band was playing as an opening act. But they were so late getting there, I was glad somebody was there to do it. And, they played, right?

RICH: Yeah. You had said to me one time you didn't care back then for live concerts, you'd rather hear the records. I was wondering, was it so noisy at the Stones concert that you couldn't really hear them play?

ZACH: Well, I guess, I don't know why I would've said that because I really like live music. I don't think that I had been to many concerts at that time. It wasn't 'til radio that I got into concerts. I remember being backstage when they finally got in there, and eventually I wandered up to the very back of the auditorium, up top and in back of the balcony and watched the whole scene. You couldn't hear anything, the girls were all screeching through the whole performance.

RICH: Any other memories of that concert?

ZACH: Well, we were all very upset because the Stones were so late getting there, and the kids were getting nervous and upset, you know, and restless. It was the first time I realized that rock'n'roll groups don't always get there when they're supposed to. The concerts don't always start when they're supposed to.

Wende Sasse reminisces:

I was there for the Rolling Stones. "The boss' daughter" — my father gave me like eight tickets or something, so we went into the Mosque and they brought us down to the very front where they had put special seats in front of the front row, and I was in the front of the front and I was so nervous, I was like looking up Mick Jagger's nostrils. It freaked me out! I went backstage, I met the Stones. I was afraid to meet them. I was a nervous wreck. I was a little kid, and I was scared to death. My friends came backstage with me and they just couldn't believe the whole thing was going on. I think Cousin Brucie was there too, wasn't he? He was really nice. He grabbed my hand and put "F.S.D.," for Fred Sayles' Daughter, on it with a magic marker.

I finally remembered what the movie was that day I was ushering at the Palace Theater. Who cared about what was going on at the Mosque Theater when I was lucky enough to be watching *First Spaceship on Venus*?!

Chapter 7
A Five O'Clock World

It's a five o'clock world when the whistle blows,
No one owns a piece of my time.
And there's a long-haired girl who waits, I know
To ease my troubled mind.
— "Five O'Clock World," The Vogues

RICH: Christine [Domaniecki] always said that if you wanted to clear out the office, you would threaten the kids with "These Boots Are Made for Walkin'."

ZACH [*laughs*]: That's right, oh yeah, there were songs on the hit parade — in those days Top 40 included things like that!

Tuesday, December 28, 1965: I found myself driving down Springfield Avenue in Newark with Keith Hakala, my old buddy from the 1959 Zacherley Oritani appearance, telling him what a nice guy Zach was and how glad I was that Keith was going to meet him. I had met Keith in 1957 at Trinity Lutheran Church when we were both 12 years old, just about the time that WABC Channel 7 started running the classic Universal horror films, and, since I wasn't allowed to stay up late to see them and he was, Keith became a sort of intermediary between me and the films. I'd ask him to describe *Dracula* scene by scene, and what kind of a creature Karloff's Monster was. By the time I'd convinced my parents to allow horror films into my life, the third film, *The Mummy*, was airing in New York. The concept of reincarnation was beyond me at that time, so Keith offered up a beautifully mystical explanation of the film's plot. He became my monster mentor, and a friendship was struck on the basis of this mutual interest.

Over the years, Keith's interests grew further away from mine, as I hung firm in the monster movie camp while he prepared himself for a life in the Merchant Marine. I was, however, able to reel him back in one more time to play Kharis, the mummy, in the 8mm film project I had begun in 1963. Keith — serious, often melancholy and a too-heavy thinker (even as a preteen) — was long gone from the Monster Kid world that I still inhabited, but was always ready to take part in a creative project. He played Kharis willingly, and even had a good time. But once he was attending the U.S. Merchant Marine Academy in Maine, he never dreamed he'd see that mummy costume again. Little did he know what the ride to Newark on that cold December evening would entail.

A New Jersey group I'd never heard of, the Young Rascals, was on the radio, holding forth with their first Top 10 hit, "I Ain't Gonna Eat Out My Heart Anymore." God, they sounded good. Keith was home on holiday leave from the Academy, where he spent as long as six months at a time shipping out. I'm not sure that it wasn't just politeness that had him in the car with me now, passing through a squalid section of the city, heading once again for the Mosque Theater to visit the *Disc-O-Teen* show. It certainly wouldn't have been his idea of a way to pass an evening on leave, and he probably would have been much happier had I said, "Hey, let's head upstate to a bar where we might get lucky!" All the kids from my neighborhood seemed to know how to "hang out," an interesting term, either at Phil's Pizza on the main drag in Bergenfield, or, if experiencing wanderlust, at an upstate New York tavern called Scotty's, where 18 was the legal age to get drunk and cruise girls. Zacherley show or no Zacherley show, I had never understood what made that kind of activity so interesting. I understand now, but not then. No, to me a visit to a television studio (an exciting place and a prospect for possible employment at some point) where my childhood hero worked had far more allure.

We parked at the abandoned-looking Kinney parking lot just around the corner from the Mosque and walked toward the building with the huge glass dome above the sidewalk. There was something so impressive about the Mosque Theater as you approached it — it had an aura of importance and excitement. As my friend Keith Mirenberg said to me the following summer, it always felt like you were approaching the set of the railway station in the opening scenes of *A Hard Day's Night*. We entered without a problem; a mood-swinging police officer known as John the Cop was stationed there and would decide, seemingly based on his current disposition, whether he would let you slip by without a ticket or brusquely turn you away. Once inside, we decided to stay out of the way by sitting in one of the many rows of bleachers that looked down on Channel 47's Studio "A" through the thick, slanted glass windows. The bleachers were at catwalk-level, on an eye-line with the huge studio arc lights. It wasn't a bad place to perch and watch the show, because you could see and hear everything clearly. But that wasn't even an option for me as six o'clock approached; as far as I was concerned, the only place for my friend and me was down on the studio floor.

It was just the dinnertime show that Zach did live five days a week, so there was no "theme" or special antics going on, just a lot of talking to the kids, an amateur rock band hoping to win first prize in the current contest, some of the singers sounding abysmally underprepared and off-key. Also, the vocals weren't amplified, only the guitars and drums, so the vocalists couldn't hear themselves when they were singing. The show's frantic pace afforded no extra time for rehearsal and a decent sound check, so what went out on the air at times sounded like a pack of hungry wolves with a guitar backup. As Zach often said, he always depended on the expert ear of their youngest engineer, 19-year-old Joe Loré, if he happened to be working that evening, to get the best audio mix they could. That evening, Zach played with his new pet, a snowy-white female duck (on the show in honor of Jackie Lee's current hit song, "The Duck"), and cavorted in his wife's laundry hamper-casket for most of that evening's 30 minutes. A packed floor of over a hundred kids danced to the latest hits: "Rescue Me" by Fontella Bass, "Kara-lin" by the Strangeloves, "Get Off of My Cloud" by the Stones. At 6:30 p.m. the show ended, and this was the time to make a beeline for the office, where you always hung around until either you felt like going or Zach started to turn off the lights.

Barry Landers: "Oh! That office was a sight to behold!"

The office was a show in itself. Decorated with painted portraits of Zach, Frankenstein's

Monster, an awesome pose of the actor Max Schreck in 1922's *Nosferatu,* a huge, stuffed hanging banana (presumably snatched from King Kong), bats on strings, and other artwork from fans, it resembled some kind of demented college dorm. As you entered, Zach's large gray desk would be slightly off to the right, a small record player next to it. Piled next to that would be umpteen deejay copies of the newest top 100 releases, some well-known, some soon to be hits, but the majority destined for the trash bin. On the wall behind Zach hung two large handmade pennants, one reading "Transylvania University," the other "Bedlam Tech." To the left near the far wall was Barry's desk, in front of it a shelf littered with dozens of "Pianola" player piano rolls that went with a player piano that Barry had acquired and installed in the studio. Thumb-tacked to the adjacent wall were several 8x10 photos from various Laurel and Hardy movies. The room looked as though it hadn't been painted for 40 years.

Real eye-catchers were a pair of "portraits" of the Cool Ghoul in different settings that showed remarkable talent. They were the work of long-time fan Rosemary Schroeder, a long-haired Cher type who often came to the show dressed as a vampire. She had done many of these paintings, and you'd often walk into the office and see a new one hanging in place of another from the previous week. Many of the times I'd visit, the office would be packed with kids, most of whom danced regularly on the show, but also intruders like myself who just wanted to share the same space with a man who made them a little less frightened of horror films, but more importantly, made them laugh along with them. How Zach put up with this mass intrusion night after night amazed me; however, it didn't stop me.

Somehow I managed to introduce Keith to Zach, who was congenial as always, but also showed a genuine interest in him when he learned he was in the Merchant Marine. This marked the first time I noticed how Zach would be truly engaged by the stories of other people, usually not members of show business, and how he would question them and listen with rapt attention. So he did with Keith, a sailor whose job was to toil for the U.S. military on a transport ship, and sat listening to Keith's stories when he could have been on his way home. I recalled from reading about Zach that he had seen service as a captain in the Army during World War II and had traveled through Italy and North Africa, setting up the camps for the many infantry who would be active there. It seemed to me that he and Keith were trading "war stories."

Before we left, Zach mentioned that there was to be another big costume party the following Friday night to be taped for air on Saturday. With that, a klieg light snapped on in my personal thought bubble. I thought of the 8mm monster movie and the fact that I still had not only my Frankenstein costume, but the painstakingly made Kharis mummy suit. And who wore it in the movie but Keith, who was right here with me! "Zach, we have these great costumes. How would it be if we came on New Year's Eve all decked out?" I couldn't believe the unprecedented nerve I was demonstrating as I, very uncharacteristically, invited myself and Keith onto the show. Any reserve of chutzpah buried in the recesses of my psyche seemed to come out that night. Trust me, I was always very shy and would *never* pushed myself on anyone, but something about Zach's easygoing manner made me feel comfortable about it, even if he were to say no. He didn't say no, and like it or not, Keith, my stoic, no-nonsense friend, was going to appear three days later on *Disc-O-Teen* swathed in filthy bandages and a mummy mask. Just what he always wanted.

Friday evening, December 31, 1965: At Channel 47 again, waiting behind a heavy black curtain in full Frankenstein makeup, I again wondered, "How did I get here?" as Zach introduced a professional band, the Revengers, to open the New Year's Eve costume ball. I wondered what was going through Keith's mind as he sat covered by a mass of wrappings inside an upright wooden crate, a clay and latex mask covering his face and dressed in his mummy suit. Another harebrained idea from his friend who refused to grow up? "Oh well, might as well go along with it, it'll all be over in an hour." Actually, Keith had shown remarkable interest in this wacky adventure once we got into makeup, even trying to talk Zach into a rather elaborate "unveiling" of the mummy. His idea was for Zach to open the box only to discover all sorts of packing material inside. As he'd start removing the excelsior bit by bit, he'd expose a finger, a hand, finally an arm, then finally he'd unveil a face, and

slowly the mummy would come to life.

Disappointingly, but typical for *Disc-O-Teen*, there wasn't the time or interest on Zach's part for such an elaborate plan. When the Revengers finished their set, Zach informed the audience that he had a special guest behind the curtain, "One of the 'Frank' boys." He led me out, then had me yank the cloth away from the front of the crate that housed the mummy and help him out of it. So much for Keith's cool idea. In full makeup, we danced with a bevy of cute girls. The strains of James Brown's "I Feel Good" and the Vogues' "Five O'Clock World" blared from the overhead speakers as I had fun and Keith, I'm sure, must have been wondering how the hell he let himself be talked into this nonsense. In spite of any misgivings, he joined in the spirit of things, even adding a touch of comedy by manually helping his left leg move by dragging it along the dance floor with his free hand. (The mummy, as you remember, had one paralyzed arm and leg.)

Later, in the dressing room, Keith asked Barry if Zach had any plans to bring back Phyllis the Amoeba, the quivering creature made of Jell-O and covered with cheesecloth, to the show. The giant unicell had been a regular feature of the old horror film days, usually serving as laboratory fodder as Zach operated on it, eventually spilling its insides all over the studio floor while Zach probed the poor creature's "nervous system." Still in mummy makeup, Keith said, "I wish he'd bring it back, I really love that amoeba." Barry broke out in laughter and Keith asked him what was so funny. Convulsed, Barry said, "It's just the sight of this mummy sitting there saying, 'I love that amoeba!'"*

Keith recalls:

It was just fun to go down there, being in the studio and talking to Zacherley. It was something that you don't expect to do. I remember being in the box. And I went from a curled position to a moving position, and one little girl actually goes, "A-h-h-h!" That I remember. The costume fit perfectly. It had mobility and everything else. I remember when we went up on the little bandstand there, both of us, we had taken some of the instruments and we were pretending like we were playing them. I always wondered whether the cameras caught that. I thought that was a funny bit. I remember we were moving around and making motions, and our makeup wasn't professional makeup. So all of a sudden Zach comes up behind me like this and he says, "Your ear's falling off!" And of course my thought was, "That's sort of appropriate for a mummy."

---

* I had not had any contact with Keith for a full 20 years prior to the writing of this book. After tracking him down at his current home in Jacksonville Beach, Florida, and telling him that I was attempting to write a book about Zacherley and *Disc-O-Teen*, the very first thing out of his mouth in response was, "Oh! I loved that amoeba!"

We picked the winner of the night's costume contest (who turned out to be Pach) and, after the taping, cleaned up and went up to the office to say good night. Zach thanked us up and down for our contribution to the madness and wished Keith best of luck with his career. As we were leaving, a small group, obviously personal friends, entered the office and asked Zach how he was planning to usher in the New Year. Obviously hoping he'd join them for the night, Zach indicated he was just going home. "You're spending it alone again?" a nicely dressed woman in her 40s asked. I left with the image of Zach preferring a quiet evening on his own, while I always assumed that anyone in the business would prefer to be either the center of attention or at some high-profile club partying. It surprised me, but somehow seemed to fit his profile. With this visit, and the unexpected bonus of appearing on his show again, there was no reason to ever return to the Channel 47 studios. I was sure that I had seen the last of John Zacherle.

Poor Keith never saw the playback of that show the next day. He mused, "When I went back to the Academy, I was gone — literally. It was a 24/7 job. I never got a chance to see the show. I didn't even know it was on the next day. If the guys at the Academy ever got wind that I dressed up as a mummy and went on the Zacherley show, I would have heard nothing else throughout the next four years!" Keith would have been happy to learn that the very next week, Phyllis the Amoeba returned to delight *Disc-O-Teen*'s audience. Possibly Zach took a cue from Keith's fondness for the oversized unicell and resurrected her over the weekend!

By about mid-January, I had made *Disc-O-Teen* a part of my weekly routine. Friday afternoon after leaving my new job at *Parents Magazine*'s subscription department, I'd rush home, take a quick bath, change and jump into the Chevy in time to make it down to Newark a little past six o'clock. Once there, I'd camp myself upstairs from the studio, where from the glass window I'd watch the remainder of the live show.

By this time I had enough confidence to bring along with me an 8mm movie camera in addition to a beat-up old Polaroid Land camera, both of which had belonged to my father. Since his death in 1962, the torch had been passed to me to continue the tradition of documenting family activities via home movies, a hobby he had started in the late 1930s, resulting in literally miles of color Kodachrome footage. I had been using this very same piece of equipment to make my monster movie, and also to fool around with its special feature of exposing one frame at a time, concocting short animated films in my basement. Now I had found a new and better use for it — to grab some shots of Zacherley, in full color, right in the studio! Anyone with any knowledge of the television business, particularly of unions, would have been much more discreet than I was about to be with this little toy, but no one said "boo" to me about it, so I proceeded to expose as much film

"Hail, Transylvania!": I meet my hero again.

as I could, hoping to compile a few shots of Zach at work. I came out with six minutes of footage. I would expand that to 40 minutes within the next three months.

It was a strange feeling for me, hanging out during the production of a very busy TV show by myself. Up until this week I had visited sporadically with different friends, selling them on the notion of meeting the famous ex-horror host and tasting the excitement of live television. This was the first time I'd been there alone, so I had more of a chance to talk to some of the girls who danced on the show. Generally, after the 6:00 show on Friday, everyone would hightail it across Broad Street to Nick's, a little greasy spoon on the corner. It was the perfect place to kill an hour and grab a bite. I never ate at Nick's, I stayed in the Mosque, so at this point there were just a few people hanging around the bleachers. One particularly friendly girl started a conversation with me as we waited for the 8:45 p.m. taping to begin. She was thin, with long black hair, attractive angular features, beautiful cheekbones, and wore a black- and red-striped shirt. She told me she was 20 years old, married, and had been a devoted Zacherley fan for years. I asked her if her husband was there, and she indicated that he wasn't, but he didn't mind at all her dancing on the show. We joked and laughed, and I finally felt accepted socially by someone in the "dance crowd." I had met Rosemary Schroeder (then Tafaro), a lifelong Zach fan, who had painted those amazing fantasy portraits of Zach.

RICH: Tell me something about Rosemary Schroeder, she was always doing the artwork.

ZACH: She started, yeah, sure. She and her brother were big fans. He was a really nice guy, he would bring her to the show when I was at Channel 7, and I remember visiting them at their house. It seems to me the house was very much like a Charles Addams house in Brooklyn. Their grandmother was there, and everybody, and she kept in touch when I went from one station to another. I found some of her pictures yesterday and said, "Oh boy, I forgot about these." She painted these big pictures, stylized portraits of me and my wife and my son, who was back from Transylvania University, that kind of stuff. I took pictures of her portraits before I gave them back to her.

Zach applies his makeup in his Disc-O-Teen *office.*

Sometimes *Disc-O-Teen* would actually have professional groups show up, sometimes to promo a record they had coming out, which was the case this night with the Critters, a Jersey band known to Barry and recording on the Kapp label, a subsidiary of Kama Sutra. No one had yet heard of them, but they lip-synched to their single "Children and Flowers," written by Jackie DeShannon, which they were hopeful would be their first hit. It wasn't, but it would be only a few months before their next one, "Younger Girl," written by John Sebastian of the Lovin' Spoonful, reached #2 in the New York charts. They became very loyal to Zach and Barry for giving them their "start."

RICH: There was a band called the Critters, who were on your show before they had a hit record.

ZACH: Yeah, okay, yep. They were Kama Sutra people, that's probably where I got to know Kama Sutra, I guess. They were doing songs by the Lovin' Spoonful, am I right?

RICH: Yeah, "Younger Girl," a John Sebastian song. The Critters rearranged it quite a bit.

ZACH: Yeah, yeah. But they had access to a library of all the Kama Sutra hits.

RICH: They had about five records that made the charts. The only other one that ever charted seriously was one called "Mr. Dieingly Sad" [written by lead singer Don Ciccone], which became the follow-up to "Younger Girl."

ZACH: I don't know where they recorded. Kama Sutra's office was in an office building, it wasn't a recording studio, so they probably used the same place for both. Anyway, they were nice kids and they tried hard. And one of them is manager of the Bitter End.

Chips & Co.

RICH: Oh, really? It wouldn't be Ken Gorka, would it?

ZACH: Ken Gorka, indeed. "Kenny Critter" I call him.

RICH: Jim Ryan wound up playing guitar in Carly Simon's back-up band.

ZACH: That's right, yeah, yeah. I don't know what's happened with all the musicians by this time.

According to Barry Landers,

Once we were established, I broke my tail getting publicity out, I mean, everywhere I could possibly think of . I pulled every stop out I knew. Cousin Brucie, everybody. The show became popular because Zach and I broke our necks making it public. We formed a camaraderie with Kama Sutra. Eddie Levine — I hung out in that office on Sixth Avenue almost every day, and I got to be a real pain in the neck. But they finally gave me the logo that was on the door and we hung that in the studio. Eddie Levine, who later went on to Columbia Records, loved Zach and anything he could send us he would send us.

JOETTE MARTIN (dancer): Kama Sutra gave us a big hanging logo of the goddess with the arms and they had it hanging there, which was a great filler, it was very picturesque, and I remember Zach getting a letter from someone who was in the war or something and he said, "Well, I know what that means, and you shouldn't have that on with kids, it's a terrible thing, and kids shouldn't know about that, and how dare you do that!"

The studio was particularly crowded that January evening, playing host to Port Richmond High School, their huge school banner Zach hung within camera range over the heads of the dancers. Also present for the taping was a pair of young Hispanic twins, Danny and Diego, who were there to promo a very catchy new release of theirs called "Glitter and Gold," which I assumed had at least charted because it had "hit" written all over it. I never heard of them again, but I still have the 45 RPM recording of that song. Chips & Co. was another band Zach would invite back many times. They had cut a single with a Beatles-style sound, "You're You." Chips' lead singer Dennis Ferrante, now working in the engineering end of the music business, remembers:

We performed on the same shows in concert with the Rascals, the Doors, the Royal Guardsmen, the Lovin' Spoonful, and the Blues Magoos. Zach's show was very hip for that time because he was taking local bands and getting them before they became stars. He was very ahead of the curve. *Disc-O-Teen* became like the benchmark of new acts. We used to come downstairs at the end of the show and people would be waiting outside for autographs and everything, and we felt pretty cool.

Another special guest returned to the show the night of January 14 — Phyllis the Amoeba.

JOETTE MARTIN: I remember when we made the amoebas upstairs. Zach had a great big cake tin, probably 16 by 20-something, and he had a big bag of surgical gauze and would lay it out nicely in the cake pan, and I remember it was orange Jell-O. He put boiling water in it, put it in there, and it only had a limited life under the lights, because Jell-O would start to melt. He would pull up the edges of the gauze, tie them and turn the whole thing out onto a board on top of Isobel's laundry basket "coffin."

Zach was the lifeguard at the beach party.

Along with my two cameras, I also managed to haul my Concord reel-to-reel tape recorder down the noisy Newark streets and deposit it in Zach's office, hoping to use it later that night. If I were thrown out of the place and never saw it again, at least I'd have proof of my visits — I'd have movies, pictures, what's left? A recording of Zach's voice, maybe with me on it! What I recorded still exists today, sounding every bit as good as it did 40 years ago. Pandemonium—girls with thick Jersey accents shouting, "Anybody got change of a dollah-h?" Barry yells, "We have to leave the office! I have to lock the office!" Well, there goes my chance of recording Zach, I thought. With amazing speed the office did clear out, so that it was only myself, my brass testicles and a few long hair-and-bangs teenyboppers remaining. One of them was an

After the beach party taping (January 21, 1966). Patti Nash is the blonde at top.

attractive doe-eyed nymphet in a red and white sweater, one of the regulars I had always noticed whenever I watched the show at home and whom I thought was particularly cute. Besides seeing Zach, she was soon to become one of the prime motivations for continued visits to the show. Finally Zach showed up and announced: "Thank you all very much, and I have to ask you all to leave because the men are coming up to hear the music, and we'll never make it!"

The Critters were coming in to hear how they sounded on the show. I grabbed my last chance to leave with the ultimate souvenir and shoved the mike in front of Zach, asking for a few words. He sounded a bit annoyed, rightfully so: "Well, wait'll I put the duck away. He's had a hard day's night, this duck." He produced the white duck from a cardboard box and dumped him gently into a large pan of water. Again he thanked the girls and politely asked them to leave, and I could have kissed the one who said, indicating my tape recorder, "Just give us one of your great big laughs, Zach!"

RICH: Yeah, just one laugh.

ZACH: Is that all you want? Is it working? Oh, it's running! You didn't tell me the thing was going, my boy! (followed by that wonderful laugh, loud and long, pushing the needle off the meter) We've gotta get ready, my boy, gotta get ready! We can't just stand here — eating crackers and things, we've gotta get ready! Don't know what we're getting ready for, but we're getting ready!

RICH: Any time you have another costume show, just let me know.

ZACH: Let you know, eh? Well, we're having a beach party, maybe you should be a Creature from the Black Lagoon and come up out of the sea or something.

RICH: I have a whole Creature from the Black Lagoon outfit — [The girls, excitedly — "Oh, then, come on!"]

ZACH: You *do*? Oh, my word, my word. You never should've said that [*laughs*].

[More talk about my enjoying a canned ham that Zach had given me as a gift after the New Year's Eve show, along with a copy of the record album "Live from the L.B.J. Ranch," another Earl Doud production, featuring comedian Vaughn Meader.]

ZACH: Oh, yes, it's a good record, a fine record. A lot of good laughs there! [more loud Zacherley Laughter]

RICH: That was an exclusive interview with Zach, and now we've gotta get out of here —

ZACH [*singing*]: "We've Gotta Get Outta This Place—"

GIRLS: 'Bye!

ZACH: Bye bye! Whatever you are! [*Zach performs his wolf howl*]

I left that night, tape recorder in hand, feeling I was carrying the Hope Diamond.

Chapter 8
Costume Shows, Groovy Clothes

Have you seen her all in gold? Like a queen in days of old?
She shoots colors all around, like a sunset going down.
Have you seen a lady fairer?
—"She's a Rainbow," The Rolling Stones

The following week, on January 21, I was back again, this time with only the battered Polaroid in hand. Zach had started devoting the Saturday shows to special themes, and he thought the idea of a beach party in the dead of winter would be amusing. I didn't bring my Creature costume for the simple reason that I really didn't have one. The Channel 47 main studio was at that time the second largest broadcast facility on the East Coast, the largest being NBC's Studio 8H in Manhattan, where the teen show *Hullabaloo* was being taped, and nine years down the road would become the home of NBC's *Saturday Night Live*. *Disc-O-Teen* always had plenty of room for hundreds of kids to dance if necessary, and for this show a huge lifeguard's platform had been erected for Zach to oversee the "beach." He did this wearing his turn-of-the-century orange and black-striped bathing suit, an incongruous get-up in combination with his coffin-pallor makeup. He had worn this outfit at various times through the *Shock Theater* and Channel 9 years, and on more than one memorable show had Isobel's casket filled with water and used it to demonstrate some diving techniques. Ironically, Zach once told me that he had never learned how to swim!

RICH: The different costume shows you used to do — whose ideas were they, were they mainly thought up by yourself?

ZACH: Well, we had to get a theme, like, you know, something about going to the beach in the middle of winter, and get dressed up at Halloween, of course. I had an old bathing suit that I wore on the midnight show, but I don't know that that'd be a reason to build a show around it.

By the end of January, I was even more aware of the big-eyed teen nymphet I had met in Zach's office a few weeks earlier. To avoid embarrassing anyone, I'll call her Donna, a girl of Polish and Italian descent who made me feel that there could be no sexier gene pool on earth than the one of which she was a product. During the Friday, January 28, taping for the Saturday show, I started noticing that wherever I went in the studio or upstairs, she would be nearby. What was particularly cute to me was the outfit she was wearing under the hot lights that Friday evening — a white sweat shirt with **DISC-O-TEEN** embroidered on the front and **ZACHERLEY** on the back. She had brought along an autograph book, and, having

The infamous Zap Machine!

remembered my "performance" as the Frankenstein Monster on New Year's Eve, asked me to sign it. I still remember what I wrote: "Always be the great little dancer you are. *Disc-O-Teen* would be nothing without you." Zach had invited as his guest WABC radio deejay Charlie Greer, whom he kept "prisoner" in a large crate, with instructions to keep quiet during the show. To ensure Greer's cooperation, Zach had his Zap Machine (a pseudo-scientific Tesla coil that generated an electrical arc) at the ready along with the killer white duck. At various moments during the show, he would allow Greer to say "hello" to the audience, but only for a few seconds. Any longer than that and the Zap Machine would be activated, effectively drowning out the prattling record-spinner. "Confounded disc jockeys, talk all day long, they do!" was Zach's assessment of these AM radio chatterers.

Chips & Co. singer Dennis Ferrante had his own experience with the Zap Machine: One time I went on the show and I had a cold. And Zach says to me, "Well, I've got something that'll cure it. Wait'll we go back after the commercial." And he brings out this thing he used to have with the two poles on either side and like an electric bolt would go across it. Well, I used to see this thing being used. I know a lot about electronics, and I know there's voltage going across that, I don't know how much, but to create a spark like that it's gotta be pretty much! And he says, "Well, here, put your hand in here," and he's trying to pull my hand in, and I'm pulling my hand out and I'm saying, "No, no, no, no — it's okay! That's not necessary! I'll be fine!" And he's saying, "No, no, no, this'll clear you right up!" and I said, "Yeah, that's what I'm afraid of!" And he says, "Look, I'll prove to you it's harmless," and he takes a marshmallow and he puts it in and it went *z-z-z-p!* and all that was left was ash! And I just looked at him like, "And you wanted me to put my hand in there?" And then he laughed. After the show was over, I went over and said, "You're an insane person. You need psychiatric care!" He said, "I wouldn't have let you do it." I said, "Well, I was almost stupid enough to put my hand in it!"

One of *Disc-O-Teen*'s loyal sponsors was a local TV repair shop, Angelo's. Each day Zach would hold up a small black card with his handwritten white lettering on one side, "Angelo's TV—Sales and Service," and on the flip side, the shop's phone number. I took the opportunity one day to sit down and draw a picture of the Frankenstein Monster holding up a TV set with the Angelo ad on the screen and the phone number on the back. I guess I was hoping Zach would make use of it at some point, but was I surprised when he announced on the air to Charlie Greer that he was going to tear up his old sign and use this new one done by "Richard the Scrivani!" On that show and for the next few months, my new sign was the one Zach would use whenever he did an Angelo's commercial.

The following Friday evening, February 4, was host to another costume show. Joette Martin says, "We had a hillbilly show, I remember that one. A couple of people with the appropriate bodies did the 'Daisy Mae' thing. I remember I had jeans which I tied with rope, and like someone's old plaid shirt, and I dug up a straw beach hat or something."

The hillbilly show taping marked the second appearance of the Critters, still two months short of their first Top 10 hit, "Younger Girl." They performed live again to a studio full of girls dressed to look like characters in Al Capp's *LI'l Abner* comic strip. Donna was there, resplendent in cutoff jeans, her hair tied back in double ponytails, her face done up with painted freckles. The only other notable thing about this show, for me anyway, was that for some reason all my photos came out blurry. And while I'm speaking of photos, I should mention that in those days black-and-white Polaroid pictures had to be swiped with a chemical fixative or they'd fade within a few days. During the show I'd have taken at least a dozen shots, then spread them out on Barry's desk in the office (Barry was hardly ever in there). Then I'd apply a thick coat of fixative to each one and wait for them to dry. The odor from this was hard to describe, but one day Zach came into the office, noticed the smell and asked if someone had opened a bottle of wine! I never would have likened the obnoxious smell of that chemical to that of the grape.

By the February 11 show, I had had three full weeks to indulge in what had become my favorite hobby: obsessing and being depressed about Donna. I had found out, to my shock and dismay,

Zach welcomes back the Critters.

that despite her older appearance she was barely in her teens. I knew full well that she was much too young for me to think of as someone to ask out, but that fact only made me think about her more. There seems to be no greater pain than the pain of youthful heartache; I had never dealt with these feelings before. I was also ruefully coming to terms with the old bromide "You always want what you can't have." I could think of nothing but this adorable, bouncy girl with the long hair and big hazel eyes, pained to accept how young she was, and would stare at her picture incessantly, usually while listening to songs on my stereo that reminded me of *Disc-O-Teen*. Two of the biggies were Lou Christie's "Lightnin' Strikes" and Herman's Hermits' "Listen, People." If you want to know what the exquisite mixture of bliss and pain was like for me during that vibrant time, a lyric from the Mamas and Papas 1967 single, "Glad to Be Unhappy," sums it up pretty well: "Unrequited love's a bore, and I've got it pretty bad. But for someone you adore, it's a pleasure to be sad."

The weeks were becoming longer now, and I was beginning to live for Friday afternoons when I'd jump in the car and hightail it down to Newark, which by now seemed to be the home of all the things that made me happy. I wasn't fully aware of it then, but there was a void in my life. Since the death of my father four years earlier I was missing a male role model with whom I could discuss these new feelings. One Friday evening I was sitting in the bleachers upstairs overlooking the studio, when I felt a pair of arms suddenly grab me around the neck, followed by laughing and a very exuberant "hello.'" The night was complete — Donna had arrived. Wearing a lime-green sweater, matching pants and black boots, she was a knockout, and seemed genuinely excited to see me. I started thinking along the lines of waiting and being patient, waiting until she was a few years older, when we'd be able to actually date. My immaturity for my age was surprising and embarrassing. But I was slowly, and painfully, growing up.

On the following Friday, February 18, my original dance partner Sami decided to come with me to another costume show, the "Vampire's Ball." When I told Zach she would be coming (and in costume), he immediately decided to feature her again as Dracula's Daughter, the honored guest. Zach seemed to have a little "thing" for Sami, and was visibly excited at her return to the show. I even wore an appropriate outfit: a black coat of my mother's (!) turned inside out made an acceptable cape, and I had darkened my face with black greasepaint (which immediately melted away in rivulets of sweat under the hot lights, creating a cool "streaking" effect). Donna was there of course, dressed for the occasion as her version of Lily Munster, complete with bright red cape, glitter and gray-streaked hair. I didn't get much of a chance to talk to her, probably due to being there with Sami, but you can bet that I knew where she was at every moment and who she was dancing with.

"Countess Sami" was introduced to that week's guest, WABC jock Chuck Leonard, who was all decked out in a loaned Dracula cape, looking as if he felt very much out of place. Sami had asked me if I thought she should go out with "Zachyerley" (as she pronounced it) if he ever asked her; I thought, "Why not?" She was 20, he was 47, they were both adults. I fully expected Zach to ask her, but to the best of my knowledge he never did. I think, among other reasons, he never wanted to be suspected of "untoward behavior" with any of the girls who danced on his show.

RICH: How did you regulate who danced, especially if they were like overweight, or, you know?

ZACH [*sigh*]: A-h-h, well, some of the cameramen had their favorites, and there were two very large Puerto Rican girls that they were friendly with and they would zoom in on these girls all the time and they were pretty gross. But cameramen were not supposed to do anything unless they were told to do it by the director. And we got 'em to pick their own shots and make 'em happier. They did that, and did a very good job, really. But one of the cameramen was Puerto Rican and he was always going after these two girls who looked a little older than — they must've been seniors at least, and they were big. And he liked to zoom in on them.

According to Barry Landers, "They'd line up in the vestibule and I used to go downstairs and weed them out, or I would tell Hector or Artie or whoever was on camera to stay off them. Stay off them! Boy, they used to fight to dance on those boxes! Boy, did they fight to get on them."

JOETTE MARTIN [*imitating Barry*]: "You can't go up on the risers because you're too (ahem!) short." He threw me off the beach show because I wasn't wearing a bathing suit, I was wearing a beach cover-up. "Don't touch the props!", that I remember, he would slap our wrists constantly for touching the props. He called everyone "sweetheart" — he was the first person I knew who really did that in real life.

As with any social situation populated by dozens of teenagers, there are those who find their own group or clique. In what I like to call the "second tier" of regulars, three girls stood out, and to protect the innocent I'll only use their first names: Gail, Dawn and Andrea. They were cousins, and each shared something in common — height and beauty. Gail was dark-skinned and sported what sounded like a Jamaican accent. Dawn was blonde and tall and had an "Ivory girl" appearance. Andrea, the quiet one, was also tall and dark. You couldn't miss them; all three were strikingly beautiful, a year or two older than most of the kids, and kept pretty much to themselves. I also got the impression that they came from money, and a lot of the Newark kids who danced on the show seemed to be from low-income families. At any rate, the trio was not popular with the first-tier regulars.

Barry Landers as floor director.

CHRISTINE DOMANIECKI: Gale, Dawn and Andrea came on, I guess it was September of '65, and these were three attractive girls that came out of nowhere, they didn't go to any of our schools, so as far as I was concerned, I really didn't know them. They hung out with themselves and that was it. They appeared for a while on the show, but weren't really the regulars that stayed on for a year or two. From the get-go it was me, Pach, "Little" Sue Parinello, of course "Big" Sue Mercedante, Joette, and Diane "Top." They lived around the same area in north Newark and they all attended Barringer High School. I went to East Side High School which was Down Neck [Ironbound]. We were probably equidistant from the Mosque Theater. I was older than they were.

KEITH HAKALA: The only thing I remember was Dawn and Gale were sort of, you know, top bananas in the echelon, so they had more of a snooty attitude, but Dawn was so cute! And the name — "Dawn," was just very hippie-like.

CHRISTINE DOMANIECKI: I think it was October of 1965, we got a new cameraman (Joe LoRé), and he was a young guy about 19 or 20 years old. All of a sudden there was "fresh meat" at *Disc-O-Teen*, and the girls obviously all zeroed in on this guy. Joe was our age, so when he came on the show everybody was kind of flirting with him and just trying to be really cute because he was a cute guy. He was real sweet, and I remember Dawn, Andrea and Gale jumped on the camera and started flirting with Joe. Well, Joe didn't go for that and he asked them to please step off the camera immediately because he couldn't move, and he wouldn't stand for it. He said, "I don't give anyone rides." At that point he scored big in our hearts, because we really didn't like these girls, because they came on and they were snooty, they weren't really friendly with us. And I think we were all a little bit jealous, because they were so cute.

JOE LORE: When I started my job at Channel 47 I was assigned to video control, which was a position you couldn't get in too much trouble with. Watching *Disc-O-Teen* on the air and watching these cameras — that's what I wanted to do, I wanted to be a cameraman, I wanted to be down on the studio floor. And the fact that there was a load of young girls down there, made it even more attractive. Arnie Giordano was the cameraman, and I will never forget, he would wheel the camera around, and when he was setting up from one position to the other, two or three girls would hop onto his camera and he would roll them around the floor. And it was those girls [Gale, Dawn and Andrea]! I loved the girls, but I was dead serious about my camerawork. So they came over to me and wanted to jump onto my camera and I said no.

Gale, Dawn and Andrea, a couple of whom eventually became teachers, came in one day and announced that they had gotten bit parts in the about-to-be-filmed *Up the Down Staircase* (1967), which was to star Sandy Dennis.

RICH: It was tough getting the sound right, wasn't it? For the live bands, the teenage bands?

ZACH: Oh, yeah, that was very tough, it was only Joe LoRé who you could count on. Well, he really liked the music.

RICH: Well, he was younger, so he was probably more into the music. Did the high school bands ever get a chance to rehearse before they went on?

ZACH [*disappointedly*]: No. No, there was usually some live show on just before we went on the air, well, often there was, anyway, part of the time. Mrs. Meyner I think was on just ahead of us. [Helen Meyner, wife of then New Jersey Governor Robert B. Meyner.] Could have been her, I'm not sure. 'Cause we made Pete Seeger wait for an hour or so before our show went on. So, I don't know. But nobody ever got a chance to rehearse. You usually let them know how many microphones they needed for the group, but I guess it was pretty standard. You know, a drum and two other mikes, maybe.

RICH: I have a recording of one show when you implored the bands, you said, "Before you come on, practice, practice, practice!" [*Zach laughs*] I guess some of them didn't sound so good.

ZACH: Well, I don't know whether they had a chance in the control room, I don't think they did, to hear them ahead of time. That's why we were always glad that Joe Loré was in the studio on duty. We knew that he would make an attempt to make it sound good.

JOE LORE: Channel 47 was just the greatest learning experience because you really worked with the basics, and all we had was a basic straight board, it had absolutely no processing whatsoever. You'd plug the microphone into the wall, it went into the mixing console, and it went out over the air! Many times the band was setting up while the show was on the air. When the band would finally come on, you had to mix them on the air. I was very much into audio quality and making sure the music was right. And I knew the music, and when I was on the mixing board and doing audio for *Disc-O-Teen* I tried to put all of my talents to work to make sure that they got a good mix. The audio position, that took talent. It took somebody to know how the music should sound, I don't care how good you are at turning the knobs and looking at the levels, you need an ear to know how the music should be mixed, and then you need to know technically how to do that. A lot of the engineers that were there either didn't know that or they really didn't care!

Sometimes bands would go on and all you would hear was a bass drum or one singer...

I often wondered if any of the hundreds of high school bands that passed through Channel 47's Studio "A" may have later achieved some measure of success. While that question has remained largely unanswered, it has recently come to my attention that at least one band member went on to achieve just that. "Little Steven" Van Zandt, guitarist in Bruce Springsteen's E Street Band, also known as Silvio Dante in the hugely popular HBO series The Sopranos, was in one of the bands and remembers those days.

The Left Banke on Disc-O-Teen a *full year before their hit "Walk Away Renee."*

STEVE VAN ZANDT: Well, I'm a big Zacherley fan. It would have been, I'm guessing 1966, maybe? Our drummer, Bobby McEvily, his mother, who we called "Big Mama," was our manager, and his father had a "hookup" — either worked for the TV station or something like that. That's how we made the (Channel 47) connection, through his father. We made our TV debut! I grew up in Middletown, New Jersey, which is considered part of the Jersey shore, I guess. We had a bunch of bands in those days, but I think it was The Source; I think it was really my first real band. I was the lead singer and guitarist and arranger. I think we played the first original song I ever wrote, which I tried to find when I started my radio show. I was going to play it and nobody has it! The song was called "Traveling," and it was sort of a George Harrison-influenced song about taking a spiritual journey. Of course I had no idea, really, what I was singing about, but you do it with great enthusiasm when you're 16!

I reminded Steve that his band was most likely part of a contest on the show, and asked if they had won. He laughed, "I guess not! Actually, we usually did win whatever band battles we were in back then, and I'm wondering if because of the "fatherly" connection, you know, maybe the fix was in for us. I don't remember winning. If we did win it couldn't have been much."

The February 25, 1966, taping was the scene of an appearance by another soon-to-be-famous band, the Left Banke. It was also the first time since I had been attending the show that Donna did not show up. I was obviously disappointed, but I also felt a curious feeling of relief. It was kind of an emotional vacation not to have to wonder where she was, who she was dancing with and if she still liked me. Besides, this new band was pretty good. By this time, rock band hairstyles were becoming much longer, and bass player Tom Finn sported a look that John Lennon would make popular in late 1968 — down to the shoulders and parted in the middle. At that time, early 1966, when the most "outrageous" hairstyles belonged to the Beatles, the Byrds and the Stones, Finn's look seemed to really "push the envelope." The Left Banke's big first hit, "Walk Away Renee,"

Emperor Zachius using my artwork on a toga party show.

which would reach Number 5 on the charts, was about a year in the future, but they lip-synched to a couple of tunes that would appear on their first album — "I've Got Something on My Mind," and "I Haven't Got the Nerve," written by keyboard player Mike Brown. They only made one visit to *Disc-O-Teen*, but went on to have two hits — the second, "Pretty Ballerina," reached the Top 15 in the beginning months of 1967. Their sweet melodies, punctuated by a signature harpsichord and string quartet got them dubbed a "Baroque Rock" group, a designation I believe they didn't much care for.

March 1966's first costume show incorporated a Roman theme. The predominant color in the studio on Friday the 4th was white, as almost everyone wore togas fashioned from bed sheets. For some reason a huge, pale green curtain, always in place but rarely used by *Disc-O-Teen*, had been drawn around the studio and had the effect of making it look a bit roomier and more polished than usual. This was probably because the general cluttered look of the outermost edges of the room was cut off from view. Even though the set was comprised of homemade pillars strewn with "cobwebs," a makeshift stage and large gray boxes (painted to look like stones) for kids to dance on, whatever was stored in the back-rows of folding chairs, musical instruments, discarded props, flats, etc., could usually be clearly seen on TV. The word which best described *Disc-O-Teen* was "informal;" even the doors to the studio would occasionally be picked up by the cameras, sometimes catching people entering or leaving! An up-and-coming band called the Gingermen were the guests that week, looking very trendy, modishly dressed and long-haired, and as far as anyone knows, they're still up-and-coming. I took my usual position off to the side shooting pictures and occasionally helping Barry, when he suddenly handed me a peaked cap and told me to crash the show as a tour guide, the "tourists" being the kids who had shown up that week minus costumes. Zach looked very much the part in a flowing green robe and laurel wreath, and while he chatted with the Gingermen I improvised some hokum about "Emperor Zachus" holding court up on the stage, while some Christians were being thrown to the lions in the background. My friend Keith Hakala (alias Kharis the Mummy) was home on another leave from his Merchant Marine duties and immortalized the moment with my trusty 8mm camera.

Meanwhile, back on the home front, Herald Square was moving on to bigger things. In March they had been booked to play at a WMCA Good Guys all-star rock concert at Stevens Tech in Hoboken, New Jersey, hosted by the very congenial "Dandy" Dan Daniels. Their job was to play as a general dance band and provide backup for any act on the bill that needed it. Daniels promised the band that he would mention them the following day on the air, and he did, in this transcript taken directly from a tape of his show:

> So at anything like this there's no such thing as star billing, as a matter of fact we started off with a great start, Chuck

Jackson, and the place really swung for about three hours, I think it was the longest continuous show I've ever been a part of — Chuck Jackson. The fabulous Outsiders were there, my friends, and they are tremendous in person, the people who have the Number 5 record, "Time Won't Let Me," three guys from Cleveland, one guy from Pittsburgh and one guy from Denmark in the Outsiders. Johnny Thunder, Ronnie Milsap, a blind boy who sings with so much soul, the Critters, the boys who have the "Younger Girl." Best drummer I ever saw — Jack Decker with the Critters. Day Trippers, Runarounds, the Geminis, Janie Grand and a guy from Peter, Paul and Mary who is maybe the nicest human being I've ever met, forget how talented he is, Peter Yarrow of Peter, Paul and Mary, he came along and put on about a 40-minute show. I also want to mention the band that played for most of our acts and the band that played for dancing, they're something else! Some guys that call themselves the Herald Square. I hope to work again with them soon, they were fantastic.

Barry had been telling me from the day I first inquired about a job at WNJU that his intention was to "start me off the same way he had started" in television. My assignment was keeping the kids (and anyone else) away from the studio's main monitor so that he and Zach could see what the show looked like on the air. It wasn't hard at age 20 to feel like the biggest cheese in the fridge when you had some chickenshit authority to order people to "keep to one side, please, Zach has to see what's going out!" I was convinced that this was leading straight into a TV career and I tended to take it very seriously. In other words, I did anything Barry told me to do. It came to a nasty head one afternoon. A little man named Chet, one of the more strident members of the stagehands' union and probably a shop steward, read me the riot act after Barry told me to tell him that a couple of props were needed. Chet pulled me into his office and let me have it: "Listen, you're a nice kid and I don't want to get you in any trouble, but if you *ever* tell anybody on this floor again how to do their job, I'll have you outta here so fast it'll make your head spin!" It was my first experience with unions.

BARRY LANDERS: Chet would do that to anybody. You weren't the only one, I got my ass chewed out by him, you know. You finally learned how to handle Chet. Here's what you did: You said, "Chet, listen. In your opinion, do you think ..." and he would say, "Yeah, that's good," and he would do it. As long as it came from him, that was the key.

One day Zach took me aside and had a very quiet talk with me. It was about my "working" in the studio for Barry. He was, as always, courteous and low-key as he tried to make his point: "You know, it may not be a good idea for you to be trying to function as if you're working here. I know that Barry has you helping him out, but it can be a kind of testy place, what with all the union guys and people getting upset because you're not 'official.' It might be a good idea to be more in the background, you know what I mean?" I knew exactly what he meant, but the message went in one ear and out the other — I was hooked on *Disc-O-Teen*, the girl I was infatuated with, and the whole allure of the broadcasting world. I was pretty sure that Chet had complained directly to him, and he was doing what was right by taking me to the side. The great thing was the manner in which he admonished me, as gently as anyone possibly could, never once making me feel unwelcome there, just sort of asking me to take a couple steps back, to be more careful, to re-evaluate my actions at the station. I was not hurt or offended for one second, very unlike me at that time, which was attributable to Zach's diplomacy in handling the situation. I don't recall changing anything about my behavior, except I NEVER interfered with the union people again; I gave them a very wide berth. I seem to remember some minor

Zach wolf-howls in his Disc-O-Teen *office.*

flack from Chet later on about my taking pictures and movies in the studio, but I told Barry about it and he became very angry and promised to set the guy straight. It was a nice feeling to have one of the producers of the show on my side, despite union rules.

In the meantime, the costume shows continued.

JOETTE MARTIN: I remember an Indian outfit once, I don't know what the show was, but I remember being interviewed about it, and we were laughing before the show that I had made it from some curtain material like two hours before, as we were wont to do [*laughs*], and Zach came out and said ('cause I'm part-Indian, and he knew that at the time), "Oh, was this your grandmother's outfit?" or something, and I said, "No, I just made it," and he said, "Oops! Someone's in trouble for using the curtains!"

CHRISTINE DOMANIECKI: Spy shows were the rage. There was *Man from U.N.C.L.E, Get Smart* and a lot of other things on television, so you kind of made believe you were your favorite spy. I luckily had a trenchcoat and a big hat, dark glasses, a scarf and I was there. And Zach was getting posters from kids, sheets with the names of their favorite groups, and he would hang them.

One of my favorite costume shows was the "Spy" show. Taped on Friday evening, March 25, it was a hodgepodge of black suits, raincoats with slouch hats, plastic Tommy guns and dark glasses. The "party" in the office afterwards was memorable, because I had brought pictures of the Rolling Stones that members of Herald Square had taken backstage at the November concert and a half dozen girls were screaming for me to have copies made for them. If I remember correctly, this was also the time my Polaroid fixative made Zach think the office reeked with the smell of wine. I had brought along my tape recorder again (never afraid to push my luck) which captured a vivid audio portrait of what it was like to hang out in Zach's digs before and after Friday night tapings. They were like this:

4:00 p.m.: Just enough time after work to take a quick bath, slap some Old Spice on my face, jump into the Chevy and head south to Newark, trying like hell to make it to the Mosque Theater in time for the 6:00 live show. Usually it was impossible, since I was bucking rush hour traffic, but if I was lucky I'd arrive there for at least the last half of the show. I had another friend, my old *Shock Theater* buddy Steve Shaffer in tow, which was handy because of the amount of cargo I was carrying: my Polaroid, the movie camera, tripod and tape recorder. The radio blasted the latest Top 40 hits on the ride down: "Shapes of Things" by the Yardbirds, "A Groovy Kind of Love" by the Mindbenders, "When a Man Loves a Woman" by Percy Sledge, and the Righteous Brothers' "Soul and Inspiration," among others. This evening we entered the Mosque a bit later than usual, emerged from the elevator between shows, and the corridors were thick with teens dressed in black. The crowd was larger than normal, which generally made for a more exciting show. For some reason I decided to "play it cool" as far as Donna was concerned and virtually ignored her for the first two hours. You know, adolescent stuff. Steve must have found something to do somewhere, because I wound up hanging out at Barry's desk and started my tape recorder running while Zach laboriously typed out the script for the 8:45 p.m. taping of Saturday's show. The slow click of the antique black typewriter would be interrupted occasionally as Zach called out the name of a song, like "Surfin' Bird!," followed by more clicking.

Deejay Charlie Greer is Zach's prisoner on a Disc-O-Teen episode.

It was comical to observe him clacking away on what looked like one of the very first typewriters ever made! Barry's phone rang a very weak ring. I offered to answer it, but Zach ignored both me and it. A minute later, director Jack Wilson, a thin, no-nonsense man with a shock of wavy, graying hair, brought the typing to a halt. He had an idea for some mid-show lip-synching schtick and needed the participation of one of the regulars. The following is taken word for word from my recording:

WILSON: Hello, Big John! Now, is what's-her-name here? What's that tall girl's name with the long hair? Linda? She here? She's not gonna be here, huh?

ZACH: Well, somebody else will do it, that's all.

WILSON: How about, uh, I wonder if Gail knows it?

ZACH: Sue Mercedante'll probably be here.

WILSON: Are you sure?

ZACH: Well, what's-his-name, Dennis Ferrante is gonna be here, so she's gotta be here.

WILSON: Yeah, but they don't go out now, he just told me. He hasn't talked to her in quite a while.

[*Zach laughs a long, silent laugh at the tentative nature of teenage romances.*]

ZACH: We'll pick somebody, don't worry. You mean you want 'em to hear it first?

WILSON: Oh, yeah. I wanna tell 'em what they're gonna have to do.

ZACH: I tell you who could do it if she comes, that's Chris.

WILSON: Yeah, she'd be perfect for it.

Jack Wilson left and Zach continued work on the script. With that, I could hear Donna's voice outside the office. The door, never locked, swung open and in she bopped, in black from head to toe including knee-high boots, looking for some little doodad she had left in there. She then started questioning Zach, who was in no mood to be diverted from the completion of an outline for a show that was to begin within an hour! God she was cute, but right now I was tempted on Zach's behalf to ask her to leave. She then started pumping him on what songs were to be played on the show:

> DONNA: Do you have any of the Rolling Stones on here?
>
> ZACH: Yes, "Last Time." That's the dance contest, that's the dance contest [a polite laugh, never looking up from the typewriter]. Al-l-l right now, let's see —

A small example, but very telling. Even when he was under time constraints, I never saw John Zacherle be anything but charming and polite during the whole run of the show.

> RICH: In between the shows, the kids used to hang out in your office. Didn't that hinder sometimes your getting work done?
>
> ZACH: No, the only work we had to do was pick the music and not much else. And maybe some craziness I might be doing.
>
> RICH: Well, you basically wrote the show, didn't you? I remember you typing the scripts.
>
> ZACH: We had a script, did we? We had to give something to Wilson or somebody, I guess, I don't know. We pretty much winged the thing most of the time.
>
> RICH: Do you have any memories of Jack Wilson?
>
> ZACH: The director? Yeah, he was very cheerful and nice, but he felt that they were all on the lower end of the old totem pole by working there, this UHF station, you know, and working much harder than they would have had to work in other studios because it was just a very small staff, you know. I'm sure it was a union situation, but they didn't get a lot of help or relief, I guess that's the word. Somebody said he got sick and died, is that true? What was the other guy, the little short guy that lived in Manhattan?
>
> RICH: Another director?
>
> ZACH: Yeah. He was nasty.

Joe Lore reveals: "It was Ray Walker. This was back in the days when unions were very, very strong and very much a part of the business, a lot of the union rules were right to the letter, and those were the circumstances that Zach had to work under. Ray was the chief engineer. He was very active, so he was not only chief engineer, he was a Technical Director, he did everything."

> BARRY LANDERS: He was old-time Channel 13, you know. He didn't like the kids, he didn't like the show, he didn't like anything. He didn't like the music, and he was in charge of the engineers. I think he did things to sabotage it in my personal opinion. You know, where he'd keep the music low just to piss Zach off. One day Zach got so upset he ran up the back stairs, ran into the control room and he put Ray against the wall. And I don't think there was a problem after that.
>
> CHRISTINE DOMANIECKI: Jack Wilson used to walk around with a shoe with the toes cut off. The sole was on the bottom, but it was like an open-toed shoe that he made because he had the gout.
>
> JOE LORE: Jack was great. I started in broadcasting in 1964, and he is in the top ten directors that I worked with. I worked with some of the best directors in the business and not only was he a great director, he was just a great person. He was very, very, very sharp, and just got along together with the crew, and part of the success of *Disc-O-Teen* was because of him.

BARRY LANDERS: Jack was one person sober, then one person drunk. He'd go out in the afternoon, I'm just finding this out now, I didn't know it, he'd go out with Ray Walker and some of the other guys and they'd belt about three or four down before they came back, and if it was time for the show and Jack was gonna do it, he'd be half snockered. And he loved it that way — he was a drunk! He was very well-respected. He could be mean, though. Ray was a drunk too.

The taping commenced, and Chris did the bit with two other "spies" wearing ape masks and lip-synching to the Peels' novelty song "Juanita Banana." The show opened with a fake explosion and ended with the dance contest. Zach sported a light trenchcoat and dark glasses, had "disguised" himself by whiting out his usual facial shadows, and had noticeably longer hair, grown over the winter months. He always wore it short, but this was the beginning of the era when men were starting to wear Beatle-style coifs. Someone asked him if he was going to let it get any longer, but Zach said he was getting some flack from his mother, who had remarked that he was beginning to look like one of "the new people." I managed to shoot another cartridge of 8mm movie film and snap a roll or two of Polaroids between stints at the monitor, trying to do my unofficial "job" for Barry. A semi-pro band, the Henchmen, played live and later joined Zach in the office to chat and take some pictures. My tape recorder was still running:

ZACH: Well, now, you want to take a picture?

MANAGER [*with a heavy New Jersey accent*]: Henchmen Manager. Yeah, in or out?

ZACH: Well, let's do it in here, it's a crazy place.

MANAGER: Yeah, very wild.

ZACH: All right, now, are you all in? Can you see everybody? All right, smile, confound it! [*Looks around*] Well, I gotta get the duck. Duck?

MANAGER: Oh, the duck. Gimme a shot with your duck. Put that duck on your lap.

ZACH: He's liable to do things on me. [*Laughter from everybody*]

[Zach spots my tape recorder and jingles his keys into the microphone. Doing himself one better, he begins to pour his rice pudding onto it.]

RICH: Oh, no, no, no! Rice pudding on my microphone!

[Zach shoots a fake Tommy gun at it instead.]

ZACH: Well — we've gotta clean up and get outta here, that's a fact. How long does it take you to get home?

MANAGER: About an hour.

ZACH: Have you got any help there from the Harlow's? [Harlow's was a Long Island club where the group was performing.]

MANAGER: Yeah. We may do a return engagement very shortly — within another week or so. But right now we're, uh, hot and heavy on doin' some little small, you know, one-night shots out on Long Island.

ZACH: Any hope on a record or anything?

MANAGER: Well, uh, we got a couple guys writin' some music, but nothing definite yet.

ZACH: You gotta get a sound, and something original and all that stuff. Who would ever think those Knickerbockers would come up with a Beatles sound and sell records? [The Knickerbockers were a New Jersey group who had a big hit with "Lies," a Beatles sound-alike.]

MANAGER: Yeah, that's right.

ZACH: Now these Outsiders did the same thing, right?

RICH: What group did they imitate?

ZACH: What's the name of that song?

RICH: "Time Won't Let Me."

ZACH: "Time Won't Let Me." That sounds like the Rolling Stones, right?

RICH: I said Dave Clark Five. [*Zach puts the record on the record player.*]

HENCHMAN: Sounds like Paul Revere and the Raiders to me.

ZACH: A real imitation, isn't it? Well, people say that you have to come up with something new, but there they —

[*Zach puts on a record by the Vagrants, a short-lived but solid band featuring Leslie West, later to form the supergroup Mountain.*]

ZACH: Who does that sound like?

RICH: The Byrds?

ZACH: The Byrds! You're right, you're right. [*One of the group shows Zach a photo of his sister.*]

ZACH [*wide-eyed*]: That's your sister? Does she sing? Dance?

HENCHMAN: Yeah, she's a belly dancer.

ZACH: Is she really? Where does she work? Does she work down on 8th Avenue? That's what you call work! That's really hard work. No kiddin', it's like doing push-ups all day.

HENCHMAN: Can you make that out to Joyce? My sister Joyce.

ZACH: Sister Joyce? She's a nun?

HENCHMAN: No — she's my sister! [*Lots of laughter as Zach signs pictures*]

ZACH: All right, men. Out you go. [*shoots at them with toy Tommy gun*] Out, out, out, out!

After the Henchmen left, and it being obvious that Zach wanted to get home after a long day, I decided to do the only logical and considerate thing: hang out even longer, my tape recorder still recording. The Byrds were giving a show downstairs in the Mosque Symphony Hall the following day, which I was planning to attend. This would be only my second live rock'n'roll concert:

ZACH: I got two guns I didn't use here.

RICH: Zach? Will you be at the Byrds concert on Sunday?

ZACH: No, I'm dubious. ...To me, hearing them in concert is not that great a thrill because it isn't such great sound ... [*John the Cop walks in*]

ZACH [*brandishing the toy Tommy gun*]: John, do you wanna show up on Monday at the range with one of these? [*The toy burps out a loud "bullet" barrage.*]

JOHN THE COP [*indicating the duck*]: Don't scare our pal there.

ZACH: Well, I've gotta put him in the — take him home [*to his mother's house in Flourtown, Pennsylvania*] tonight.

JOHN THE COP: You're really gonna take him home, John?

ZACH: I don't know why, it's a problem, but I'll do it. I feel sorry for him in there. I don't know, if I take him out and let him run around in the garden, but he's not gonna like it coming back here.

JOHN THE COP: It's cold out, too.

RICH: But does that really affect ducks?

ZACH: No, but he's not used to it, he hasn't been out all winter, that's the thing I was concerned about.

JOHN THE COP: It was a good show, John.

ZACH: Well, it was a wild kinda show, we should've had you in there, never thought of that. Barry said he got in it by mistake!

JOHN THE COP: The little kid could dance though, right? The last song? The one who won the prize?

ZACH: Yes she could. The rest of 'em weren't that sensational, one problem was the first song I picked — it's funny, I thought "Last Time" was a good dance song, but they really didn't get moving with it. You can go very fast with "Last Time," but they didn't really warm up to it. In fact, I was a little bit afraid to play the other one, I thought that they'd be better with "Last Time," and I was tempted not to use the second one. [*Zach leaves the office for a minute and Barry comes in.*]

RICH: Good night, Barry. [*I hand him the microphone.*]

BARRY: It's been a pleasure.

RICH: Insulting me all the time.

BARRY: Insulting you all the time, but don't feel badly, Rich, because if I've said anything to offend you, believe me [*laughs*].

RICH: Do you really want to see those movies some time? I mean, should I bring 'em in some time?

BARRY: Uh-huh.

RICH: I don't know, how can you show 'em, where? [*Zach comes back in.*]

ZACH: Bum-bum-bum-bum-bum …

BARRY: Ah, we'll show 'em in the control room.

RICH: Good, I'll bring 'em in when I've got an hour — I've got over a half hour's worth of movies now.

BARRY [*sarcastically*]: That's good! Say good night to John Zacherle too.

RICH: I did already. [*Zach makes a duck noise.*] He's doing a duck imitation.

BARRY: That's the duck doing an imitation of John Zacherle.

ZACH: See you later on, have a happy. [*Shoots off again.*]

RICH: Zach, right after this I promise I'll leave. What about "Lemme outta here" [his intro from his WOR days], did you forget about that? From the old Channel 9?

ZACH: "Give me some light! Let me outta he-e-e-eere!" [*followed by a wolf howl and a final Tommy gun burst*]

RICH: Good night.

Chapter 9
Ducks and Daydreams

This little bird, she can fly away.
No salt on her tail, no cage to make her stay.
— "No Salt on Her Tail," The Mamas and the Papas

In one of my interviews with Zach, I asked him about the duck that regularly appeared on his show.

RICH: You did one commercial by having him eat the Fischer's Bread, and he didn't want to eat it, and you were going, "For God's sake, eat the bread, eat the bread!" [*Laughs*] And he eventually did. How did you get that duck? What was that all about?

ZACH: We bought some baby ducks once after I had the big duck. I don't know whether the duck was full-grown or where it came from. I have no idea. But he was there for quite awhile, and he stayed in the office over the weekend, we left him water and food.

RICH: You had a plastic pan with water in it.

ZACH: Yeah. And I eventually put him in a stream down in Philadelphia. I told you how he —

RICH: When you let him go. There was a story about that.

ZACH: I let him go, yeah. I let him go on one side of the stream and the other ducks were across on the other bank in the water. And I let him go — I was in costume too. I held him up in front of the camera and kissed him goodbye or something and put him with his friends.

RICH: Wasn't he "set upon" by another duck?

ZACH: He was, yeah, he literally went across the water, I said he went underwater, he actually [*makes swishing sound*], he must have swum, I don't think they go underwater to swim. But he went across, just thrashed his way like a bullet across the stream to join the other ducks, and he was immediately grabbed by a male duck and had sex there right in front of all the other ducks. Then he shook himself off and everything, actually it was a her, it was a her duck, obviously, a she-duck. It's the last

I ever saw of the old duck. I think I may have gone back and looked for her the next week, I used to go to Philadelphia there. My mother was probably still alive there.

RICH: It must have been sad to let the duck go. He was kind of — *she* was kind of a pet.

ZACH: Yeah, well, you know, I'd keep him in a big cardboard box and bring him down to the studio when it was time to have him seen, I'd open up the box and the first thing he'd do would be to stand up and stretch and flap his wings. Just like a trick, you know. But it wasn't a trick, he was just bored being inside the box.

Zach showed the duck's flight to freedom on 8mm color film on Friday, April 22's 6:00 show.

JOETTE MARTIN: Somebody reported him to the board of health. I remember that because in Newark I had had a chicken for awhile, I hatched a chicken as a sixth-grade project. I think they said, "You can't do that." The duck was living in a milk crate or something at the station, and they said, "No, no, you have to get rid of that. You can't keep poultry in a commercial building," or something. Zach was on one of the telethons, I think Channel 11, and brought the duck, and said he had a trick that the duck would do, and of course whenever you put a duck down when you've been holding it they flap their wings. And it did that and they said, "Oh, you've trained it!"

CHRISTINE DOMANIECKI: Zach had about 10,000 records that he would listen to once and they'd go into like the trash pile. And he had a lot of regular laundry rope, you know, that you'd hang your wash out on. He put all these records on this

Zach with an amoeba and Pach.

piece of rope. That was going to be the grand prize [in a dance contest]. There were these geeky guys that came in and all of a sudden Barry says, "Go ahead, dance with that guy." I was dancing and the guy was not hip looking, nothing going for him, and next thing I know he was awarded all these records, because we won as the best dancers. And it wasn't that we were best dancers, and I shouldn't say it was rigged, I think Zach just wanted to get rid of the records and he didn't want to hurt anyone's feelings, so he picked me because I was a regular.

LINDA PACE: I remember winning a modeling contest on the show. Somebody came in from a store in Manhattan. I think there were five of us and we modeled these outfits from the show and then I was voted the winner and I got to keep the dress. I remember that I had a fan club! I think it was maybe one or two girls that lived in Paterson, and she used to write into the show often about me, and about, you know, she loved watching me dance, this, that and the other ... and then she wound up getting some tickets to the show and coming in and I met her and she gave me this big plaque that said "Pach Forever on *Disc-O-Teen*." She'd take lots of pictures of me and send them to me and write to me. It was, you know, amazing, that I would have a fan club at my age! It was cute, she was a really nice girl.

BARRY LANDERS: They loved it! I mean Pach loved it. Sue loved it. The fact that they had this — and they were jealous, I mean, I used to go in the girls' room afterwards. You should have seen the writings on the walls! I'm serious, you know, it wasn't very nice. You never found that in the men's room! Worst I've ever seen, absolutely. And they guarded their realm jealously.

For some reason I could never fully understand, but was grateful for, Barry endorsed my hanging around and picture-taking, even though I was really doing a minimal amount of "helping out" in the studio. Some time around late March or early April, a new kid, Rich Fertell, assumed these duties, but he had one advantage over me: He was a paid employee of the station. I hated him immediately. I was enjoying my unique situation at Channel 47, especially the attention of scores of attractive teenage girls, and now here came an interloper to throw cold water on it. As it turned out, Rich didn't last too long, and I got the impression that he was staying after his normal hours to hang out at the show, pretty much the same as I was doing. I think what I didn't like about him was that he was a "take charge" type who made himself very visible in a way I would not. Truth be told, he was doing the job the way it should be done, but I've never been partial to "out there," look-at-me personalities. Even Zach, in his crazy persona, didn't exude that quality. Well, some time after the departure of "Fertell from Hell," Barry showed up with a beautiful woman on his arm. After the show, he asked me to come into Studio "B," a tiny room where they'd do the local news and the cartoon show *Junior Town*, with "Uncle" Fred Sayles. It was empty now, and Barry asked me to shoot a couple of Polaroids with him and this gorgeous blonde in an embrace. I did, and they came out beautifully. Later on, up in the office, I had them lying on Barry's desk drying out from the usual chemical swipe. Zach got a look at them, picked them up and said, "I think you'd better find a very deep, dark desk drawer, lock this up inside and throw away the key." My usual snail-paced savvy was operating a bit more efficiently that day and the picture was destroyed. Barry was obviously indulging in some extra-curricular activity.

The April 8 taping featured a special Zacherley event: the Dinosaur Egg Roll. It was basically a race, with four or five contestants rolling dinosaur eggs (played by melons) across the dance floor. The prize: the four baby ducks Zach had mentioned above. Zach had a thing for ducks. The "eggs" themselves, Zach explained, were millions of years old. How did he know exactly how old? He indicated that if you looked closely, there was a number written on each "egg" (most likely the price of the melon). For example, a "39" meant that the little rarity was 39 million years old, and so on. I always thought that the 39 stood for 39 cents — Zach was always one to educate. Also on the show was another low-level show biz personality, female singer Chi-Chi.

There was never a lack of young "talent" on hand as long as all the record labels were pushing artists they thought might benefit by some exposure on the show. A few of the bands, including the Critters, the Blues Project, Blues Magoos and the Left Banke, did go on to have some success, but the majority of the other hopefuls slipped silently into obscurity. Some of *Disc-O-Teen's* guests who hit the performers' graveyard included the Explorers, the Henchmen, the Deep End, the Primates, the Luvs, Vito and the Overtones, the Eight Feet (four girls), Johnny and the High Keys, the Artie Ehman Trio (featuring a blind drummer), the Corvairs, Donny Vann, Gayle Hanness, Scott Fagan and a band called the Ascots, who eventually changed their name to the Doughboys. More about them later.

JOETTE MARTIN: Donny Vann was a singer, he came down quite a few times. A good-looking young kid, wore the nice sharp suits then, the thin tie, gray collarless suits, and he was extraordinarily polite to us and held the door open for us. That's very heady stuff when you're 15 and people are pushing you aside.

Drummer Richard Heyman remembers the Ascots experiencing the technical problem that all live performers on *Disc-O-Teen* shared:

RICHARD HEYMAN: When you appeared on that show, as far as a live performance, you couldn't hear yourself sing. There was no P.A., so the bands were singing into mikes that went directly into the studio mixing board. The band couldn't hear the singing and the studio audience couldn't hear it, all you heard was the instruments. I used to feel so nervous and worried for Myke Scavone, our lead singer, because I didn't know how he did it. There was one time, I guess it was pre-taped because I got to actually watch it, when we did "Paint It Black," and I remember thinking, "Wow, Scavone's really singing on key!" I often wonder how many other TV shows were doing that because it was frightening.

The Lovin' Spoonful visit Disc-O-Teen *in May 1966. (Photo courtesy John Zacherle.)*

Some time in the late spring, *Disc-O-Teen* played host to a guest band on a day I couldn't attend. I hadn't quite gotten over the disappointment over missing the Rolling Stones event the previous November, and now I was going to be absent during a visit by one of my favorite bands, the Lovin' Spoonful. They were Kama Sutra recording artists, their appearance a result of Barry's close relationship with the record label. I did get to watch the show when it aired, and all I remember about it was the procession of girls shaking hands with John Sebastian, Zal Yanovsky, Joe Butler and Steve Boone during a playback of the Spoonful tune "Didn't Want to Have to Do It." Some of the girls even kissed some of the band members, and I started to get jealous as Donna approached, feeling certain she'd bestow a kiss on at least one of the guys. To my surprise and delight, she shook all of their hands, and at the last second jumped up to give Zach a peck on the cheek! Zach later described to me a

Myke Scavone, soon to be lead singer for the Doughboys.

party he attended in the rear courtyard of John Sebastian's Greenwich Village apartment building around this time, and how much he enjoyed it.

BARRY LANDERS: They were great. They were cordial, they were Zacherley fans, which helped a lot. They were extremely talented; John Sebastian was just a knockout. He was wearing a Jewish star with his name on it, with "John" carved into it, and I admired it, and I said, "That's really a beautiful piece." Well, he sent me one with my name carved in it that I have to this day.

CHRISTINE DOMANIECKI: Zal Yanovski, the one that just passed away, was my favorite and he signed my forehead. I think they had a dance contest and I didn't win.

JOETTE MARTIN: They judged a dance contest and they picked one of the little collegiate-looking high school girls, I think Zal said "because she wasn't dancing lasciviously."

On Monday, May 30, 1966, *Disc-O-Teen* taped a special Memorial Day show. A college buddy of mine, Keith Mirenberg (another Keith!), had agreed to come over to Bergenfield from the Bronx to take the pilgrimage to Newark with me and see what all the talk was about. He was also a Zach fan and was eager to meet him, but my stories of a bevy of teenage girls and a big dance party was, I'm sure, a larger draw. I also confided in him the sad story of my infatuation with the unreachable Donna, which bonded us in a way, since he was having girl troubles of his own. It was slowly dawning on me that Donna had nothing more than a slight adolescent crush on me. It didn't matter—I only had eyes for her, and I lived by the words to the Critters' "Younger Girl," another song I had come to identify with. In it, a guy meets a girl who is too young for him and finds his decision to wait for her too painful to bear. My situation was perfectly reflected in these lyrics:

Should I hang around acting like a brother?

In a few more years they'd call us right for each other, but why?

If I wait, I'll just die.

I gave Keith a tour of the studio, and he was instantly hooked by what it represented. He had just broken up with his girlfriend (whom he would marry two years later) and the prospect of meeting someone to take his mind off it seemed pretty good; in fact, the odds were in his favor that he would hit it off with someone in a studio populated largely by young females. Keith did manage to arrange a few dates with Patty, a new girl on the show. She was nice but, I felt, a bit troubled. As I had mentioned earlier, temperatures in the un-air-conditioned studio would skyrocket, particularly during a hot summer like the one of '66 when the thermometer hit 100 degrees on more than one occasion. On those sweltering days, we made our way down to Newark by the usual route I had been taking since the winter: Garden State Parkway South to Exit 143A, down Springfield Avenue to Market Street, then onto Broad Street, right onto Kinney Avenue, where we parked the car in the funky little parking lot.

The Mosque Theater was right across the street. Summertime inside the studio was almost unbearable. In between dancing to the recorded music, kids clustered around the one large stand-up fan, the only relief from the smothering heat. During this time, Patty danced furiously on one of the risers, a tortured expression distorting her face. She quickly earned the nickname "Patty Pain" from the regulars because she often looked like she was in agony, and after a while she started suffering from heat prostration and would pass out on occasion. I still don't understand why she wasn't barred from dancing on the show, at least until the problem could be resolved or the weather got cooler. I (and others) began to get suspicious that it was all an act, or at least exaggerated, to call attention to herself.

CHRISTINE DOMANIECKI: Patty had blonde hair, not the greatest face in the world, but she really, really wanted to become a star, she wanted to be a dancer, she wanted to be in show business, and she was on the show, but we thought she was a little too fast, too different from us, so she was probably on the periphery of the regulars.

Another old friend from the past was unpacked and trotted out on that Memorial Day show: Gasport, Zach's pal from the Channel 7 days, who lived in a burlap potato sack. Gasport resumed his duties on that day, which consisted of moaning, crying and literally just hanging around. Gradually all of the Cool Ghoul's original cast members were finding their way back to their master.

On Sunday, June 5, a Young Rascals concert sponsored by Foreign Languages Elementary Schools was held at Bergen Technical School, a Hackensack vocational school. Backing them up were two bands that had been featured prominently on *DiscO-Teen*, Chips & Co. and the Gingermen. I attended, eager to see the Rascals, a New Jersey band, and one of the hottest groups at the time; their string of hits included "Good Lovin'" and their then-current "You Better Run." Zach and Barry were there, and I believe the event was basically being run by them. Again Barry pressed me into service, acting as if he were doing me a favor by involving me, and placed me at one side of the stage with instructions to prevent any girls from rushing it. Bear in mind, I had bought a ticket like everyone else and was prepared to enjoy the show from my seat. I just didn't know how to say no to Barry; he was a very forceful personality and I was basically shy. My one memory of "guarding" the stage was physically grappling with a young girl who seemed determined to make it up there. Thinking back on it, it took a lot of chutzpah on Barry's part to shanghai me to do a job meant for security people when I had paid to see the show. But that was Barry, and at that time I was in awe of anybody working in the television business. I still have the ticket to that show, and I'm astounded to see the admission price was a whopping $3.50, designated as a "donation"!

Later that week at the Channel 47 studios, I paid my usual visit to Zach's office, and he had a poignant story to tell. He said that it had been extremely hot the day of the concert and that he and someone else temporarily escaped the heat by going across the street into the thickly shaded Hackensack Cemetery. Wandering around and reading some of the stones, he said he came upon one "about so high and so wide" (he indicat-

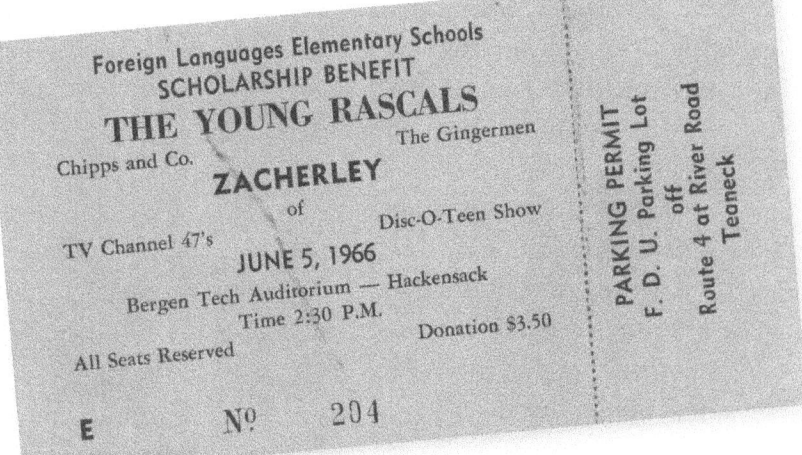

ed with his hands) with the name **SCRIVANI** inscribed on it. I told him that he had stumbled upon the gravestone of my father, who passed away when I was 16. The look on his face was one of shock. "That was your *dad*?" he intoned with genuine surprise. I guess he felt I was too young to have lost my father.

BARRY LANDERS: We were doing a show and I think Zach was hosting it in either Asbury Park or Atlantic City, I'm not sure, but we had the Rascals. They would come out all the time with us. And Felix Cavaliere. I was at the back pier with my son Richard, who was maybe about 12 years old at the time, we were sitting in the back talking — I remember the ocean right behind us, and Felix wanted me to manage them! "Take us over, please do it," and I said, "I can't do it, I can't do it," and I could see my son going, "Please, Dad, please!" They were the Young Rascals then.

I once asked Zach about a live *Disc-O-Teen* event in Central Park.

ZACH: We have still pictures of that, what do you call 'em? Kodachrome slides. I don't think any of those concerts were ever filmed, that I recall, I never did see them. That was a great place to have concerts, it really was.

RICH: Who did you have there, do you remember? Were there live bands?

ZACH: Yes, I remember one with Tina Turner and her husband Ike. Ike and Tina, that was a great show. But I'm not sure which show it was where the girls were dancing, I don't know who that was. And the Beach Boys, I remember introducing them and throwing Frisbees with them.

RICH: Was it at the Wollman Rink?

ZACH: Yes, the Wollman Rink, the ice rink. It was a really great spot, everybody had a good time there. If you didn't get a ticket you could sit around outside and hear the music anyway, it was easy listening, as we say. Did they charge to get in there or just give out free tickets?

RICH: I wasn't there, but I did see a Procol Harum concert and I think — was it surrounded by rocks, and you could sit up on the rocks and look over?

ZACH: Yep.

RICH: Okay, I saw Procol Harum there but I wasn't involved in any way with the *Disc-O-Teen* show.

ZACH: Well, 'cause I say I don't know if they charged or if it was just first-come first-served tickets, I don't know.

RICH: And some of the dancers, some of the "regulars" from *Disc-O-Teen* danced there?

ZACH: They danced on one of the shows, and I don't know who the band was, who the main attraction was. Seems to me it was during the week — I don't know. I can't really remember.

Zach throws Frisbees at the Wollman Rink concert.

According to Joette Martin, The group that played when we did the Central Park concert was the Fragments of Love. We hated them. It was in '66, it was the Lunchtime Music Series, and it was at the ice rink. There was an article in the *Daily News*, center page, five of us out there, we danced and we gave out autographs. The Fragments of Love didn't want us on stage because we were distracting people from them, which was probably a very good thing. We had bright colored miniskirts, bright colored tights, and black and white and very mod-looking outfits. We had a great time.

LINDA PACE: I remember doing some Central Park shows with Zach where we were actually dancing on the stage, and walking over to the park from his apartment and him taking his bike and hanging out there. We were walking over and he was doing his thing over there, greeting and meeting people and I have a really neat picture of us standing there with his bike, and my little white short dress and my go-go boots. He just exposed us to so much at that time, you know? Here we were, 14- or 15-year-old kids, and it was just great, just great. Not a lot of people get to do that. I remember when I moved during the *Disc-O-Teen* time, some of us went into Manhattan and walked around and he was helping us select some little things for my new room and everything. You know, again — just always so caring and concerned and considerate of us. A wonderful guy.

Chapter 10
Summer of '66

But at night it's a different world,
Go out and find a girl.
Come on, come on and dance all night,
Despite the heat it'll be all right.
— *"Summer in the City," The Lovin' Spoonful*

The Critters returned to the show for an advance taping on Monday, June 20, to debut their brand-new hit, "Mr. Dieingly Sad," but were minus lead singer Don Ciccone, who had just started a four-year tour in the U.S. Air Force. Don had sung lead on "Younger Girl" also, but on most future releases the voice of lead guitarist Jimmy Ryan would dominate, as on their first album, soon to be released. The band actually played a live set on the air, quite unusual on *Disc-O-Teen* for a pro group with an album due out, and included their versions of "My Little Red Book," the Lovin' Spoonful's then-current hit "Did You Ever Have to Make Up Your Mind" and the Rascals' "You Better Run." Their career was starting to take off, and they had been invited to tour with Dick Clark's Caravan tour during the month of July. Zach asked Jimmy if he'd get to meet Clark, to which he replied: "I don't think so — I don't think he goes on the tour, I think he just sits in his office and makes money." Zach recalled, "He's a grand old boy, I've known him for many years, you know, from the old *Bandstand* there, I used to go down there on Halloween and raise cain." He then made reference to the Lovin' Spoonful Show as he told the Critters: "I'm sorry we didn't have any experiments here. When the Spoons were here, we had a great amoeba operation, but they were so violent, their techniques on the operating table, that the S.P.C.A. got after me and I had to cut out the amoeba experiments." I took a generous amount of pictures there that day, and by this time had, along with my friend Keith, started to dance regularly on the show, sometimes making the pilgrimage to Newark as many as three times a week. The Critters show aired on Saturday, June 25, 1966.

RICH: I went up in the control room a few times, I was "allowed." And I remember being shocked. I was 20 and I was very sheltered in a way, and I didn't know — didn't hear too many people using curse words and stuff.

ZACH: Oh, all that, huh?

RICH: Not in the "professions," you know? And I went upstairs in the control room and I swear, I don't know whether it was Jack Wilson or [Zach already laughing in the background] whoever was calling the shots was going, "That one with the big tits! Come in on the one with the big tits! Yeah,

Zach displays a clay Frankenstein bust I made. Note the dreaded Kama Sutra logo on the wall.

now oh-h-h, that one over there!" [*Zach is in hysterics.*]

ZACH: Well, there you are! You've answered the question, that I didn't — I never heard any of that. That's funny [*more laughing*]. I believe it, though!

According to Christine Domaniecki,

I used to go up to the control booth. I was one of the few people who was invited, I don't know why, but I would hear different conversations, and the guys would zoom in on different female body parts. Most of the girls, if they were not voluptuous, were left alone, but if they really had a figure these guys were zooming in on them. There used to be a program there called Senorita TV right after *Disc-O-Teen*, and one of the girls from that show would appear a lot on *Disc-O-Teen*. She would wear extremely provocative clothing, like white cotton pants without any underwear, and believe me, she was not a natural blonde!

Leaving the show on those warm, magical evenings always left me in a pensive frame of mind. As music of the era buzzed through my head, the tunes created an otherworldly, hypnotic effect. It was as if I knew that this was a special place and time. The Beach Boys' recent album Pet Sounds became my personal soundtrack, an anthem for that summer, and I, through my dreamy fixation with Donna, related to Brian Wilson's melancholy melodies and lyrics; his were songs of lost love, alienation, poignant and heartrending songs, even, as one writer said, sad songs about happiness. Donna had disappeared from the show for over a month, probably on vacation with her family, and I sometimes took to driving through the Ironbound section of Newark before turning onto Route 21 toward home, hoping I'd catch a glimpse of her walking the steamy, shadow-filled streets. I never did, and on my way back to Bergenfield I'd console myself with the thought that tomorrow was another day, and my next visit to the show would probably be more lucky; she had to be back some time. It's amazing how such gloomy recollections can be recalled many years later and mentally reworked into some of the best memories of one's life. I guess when human beings in self-defense remove the hurt from such bittersweet moments, what's left is the elation of our senses, fine-tuned and working at peak efficiency, reminding us that, even with the pain, we are truly alive. I also had my friend Keith, living his own pain, to share it with, and that was great solace.

There they were again, sitting patiently in the bleachers, waiting for a ride home from Zach. The 16-year-old was a quiet, pretty Italian girl who had just danced on the show, the older woman was her mother, a gray-haired, thin woman, with an air of polite gregariousness about her. They sat silently and waited for all the hoopla to die down, for Zach's office to empty. It was nearing the end of June, and later that evening at Bergenfield High the Class of '66 senior party was to take place. Thanks to the chutzpah of one of the

A gift from Herald Square: a new record player for Zach's office.

Herald Square band members, Zach had agreed to make an appearance. That afternoon I was to hang out at the station and Zach would eventually follow my car north to Bergenfield, get into makeup at my house, go over to the school and do the party. Things settled down in the office, and Zach walked out to the bleachers and up to the waiflike duo waiting for their ride home. "I'm really sorry," whispered Zach, "but I have an affair to host tonight and I won't be able to take you home."

Overhearing this, I obnoxiously chimed in: "Oh, that's all right, Zach, the party isn't until later tonight, so you'll have plenty of time!"

A glare from Zach, then back to the mom and daughter: "So," he continued, "I'll see you next time. When's your next bus?" "Really, Zach," I interjected loudly, "there's no problem! You can take them home and make it to the party in plenty of time!" Zach, without missing a beat: "Well, well, I'll see you next week, get home safely now." They got the message and began to leave. Then: "Rich, could you come into the office a minute?" "Sure, Zach!" Zach went in and closed the door. I said good night to the mother and daughter, walked down the short hallway and opened the door to the office. Zach was behind his big black desk, laughing until I thought he'd cry. "Oh—I can't believe you! I just can't!" More laughing, and now I'm starting to see what I'd done. "I was trying to get out of it graciously tonight and then you — oh! I can't believe it!" More laughing.

I wanted to slink out through a crack in the wall. How could I have been so thick? "Oh, well, forget it," he finished, "what's done is done." I think Zach actually got more of a kick out of my naive blundering than the annoyance he obviously felt.

I got home first. Zach was originally planning on following me, but felt his mind might wander and he'd lose me, so I gave him directions to my house. My mother, nervous at the prospect of meeting the famous ghoul, expecting a lunatic or, at best, someone quirky, had made coffee and laid little pastries out that Zach would, as it turned out, never see. After a while he called on the phone. "I got all screwed up with the directions, sorry — I felt I'd better ask someone how to get directly to the school, so I'm here — come on over!" Disappointed that my mom wouldn't get to meet him and sorry for the trouble to which she had gone, I ran over to the high school in time to see Zach in full makeup signing autographs and holding forth for the students completely in character. He stayed for the entire party, I'm sure helping the band's stock to rise dramatically with their classmates that summer. Since he wouldn't take any money for it, later on, on the air, band members Dave and Frank presented Zach with a new record player for his office.

On Monday, July 11, Herald Square returned to *Disc-O-Teen*. Since winning the show's first contest and playing on the same stage with the Rolling Stones the previous fall, the band had played the Cheetah, a fashionable Manhattan discotheque, found itself a manager and were preparing to record a single, "I Do Love You Baby," written by a professional songwriter. They were also about to begin a summer tour to promote the song, and in a concession to commercialism their name was

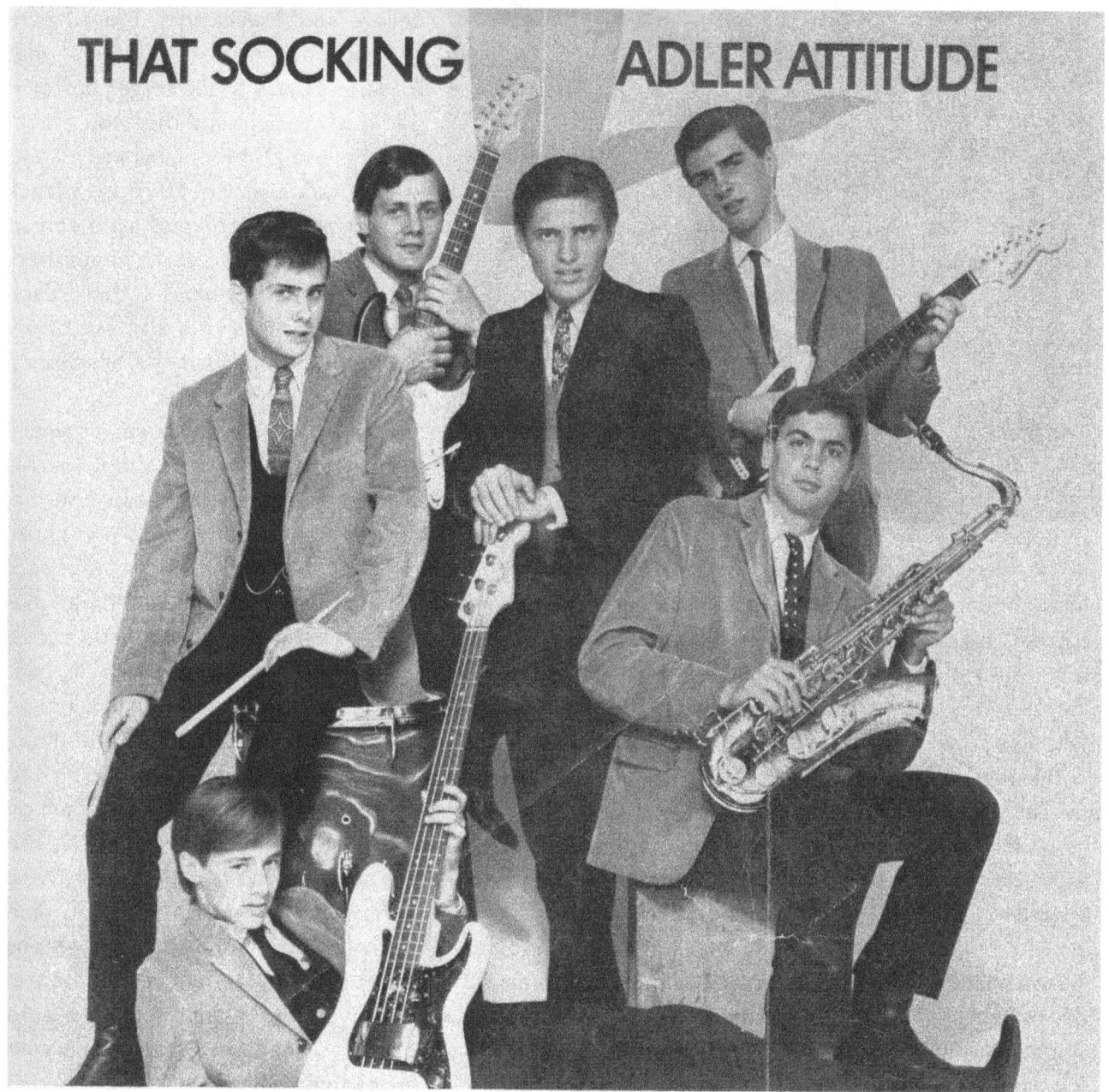

This great photo of the Cat's Meow was included in an Adler Socks flier: Standing, drummer Kurt Meyers, rhythm guitar Dave Meyers, lead singer Frank Youngblood and lead guitar Doug Scrivani; sitting, saxophonist Bob Ariosto; on floor, bass Doug Schaffer.

changed to The Cat's Meow at the behest of the Adler Sock Company which was funding the tour. Hundreds of semi-phony publicity fliers about the band members were dispensed in the form of a glossy handout with the band's picture on it surrounded by plenty of advertising for Adler socks ("THAT SOCKING ADLER ATTITUDE"). It looked like the band was actually going somewhere.

Also scheduled to appear on the Saturday hour-long show was another band who had, by July '66, a song in the Top 40 in the New York area. The Fugitives were another mod, long-haired group typical of that era and the record was called "Your Girl Is a Woman." Remember it? I thought not. They had introduced the song on the June 3 "Senior Day" show, during which they had also judged the customary dance contest. It was a bit amusing for me to hear Herald Square-Cat's Meow lead singer Frank express his dismay at the fact that the group had to share air time

Herald Square, now The Cat's Meow, on their Adler Socks tour. (Photo courtesy Doug Scrivani.)

with the Fugitives; with a surprisingly headstrong attitude, he seemed to have quite an inflated opinion about the status of Herald Square. To me it seemed a fabulous opportunity to be given so much air time even on a small UHF station like Channel 47, but thinking big was probably a better formula for success, and it sure seemed that may have been in the cards for them at that time — some measure of it, anyway. Conveniently for the band, at the last minute the show was notified that the Fugitives could not appear, and Frank got his wish: "The Cats" had the show all to themselves. The taping was held on Monday, July 11, to be aired on July 16, and Zach decided that if he only had the one group he'd play them up real big, as stars in the making, sort of "They started out on *Disc-O-Teen*, and who knows where they'll end up?" He had them autographing girls' hands and lip-synching the Rascals' "Good Lovin'." As Zach said on the show: "One thing you have to learn when you're a star, of course, is to sign autographs and things like that, but you also have to know how to lip-synch, and we're going to give you a little lip-synch lesson right now. Who's the soloist? Who sings 'Good Lovin'' in your outfit?" The newest member of the group, Bob Ariosto, was the one who got the honor.

Zach introduced the band as "The Cat's Meow — future stars!" and they played their first set: the

Herald Square (aka The Cat's Meow) returned to Disc-O-Teen in July 1966.

original "I Do Love You Baby," Dionne Warwick's "Walk On By" and the Turtles' "You Baby."

This was followed by a live commercial (which Zach always did so hilariously) for Moonshine, a cheap ($1) cologne aimed at teenagers. It came in the form of an atomizer the size and shape of a disposable cigarette lighter. The scent was supposed to be so irresistible that it came with a license to use it. The following is an excerpt from this particular day's commercial, demonstrating how inadvertently funny Zach could be while trying to sell his sponsor's product:

> You can't get this anywhere but through Channel 47. This little spray dispenser here, little aerosol job, you know, like everything is in this world. Everything's either plastic or aerosol spray, or — you know how it is in this world. It's terrible, terrible! But it's true. It's true, and we're all used to it and it's lovely.

The Zacherley humor almost always offset the boredom of the commercial, and in this case left Moonshine's atomizer with a mixed review. But whatever the sponsor, they always received at least three times the minute they probably paid for thanks to Zach's ad libs. The Moonshine wind-up gimmick was to find a male volunteer who, upon being sprayed with the stuff, would immediately be set upon by as many screaming girls as Zach and Barry could line up. The boy would have to run around the studio to avoid being torn apart by these girls, who supposedly couldn't resist the scent. Classy stuff, and pure *Disc-O-Teen*. In case anyone's interested, included in the show's roster of sponsors were Buitoni, Bic Pens, Fischer's Bread, Angelo's TV Repair, Robert's Technical School, and the Cheetah, the brand-new booze-free discotheque.

RICH: I remember you always fooling around with the Fischer's Bread.

ZACH: There was the greatest thing we ever did, I remember dropping a loaf of bread from the top of a stepladder to a table below. I said to the cameraman, "just follow it down." And I pushed it off and it landed, bump! "Fischer's Bread" [*laughs*]!

RICH: It landed just the right way? In front of the camera?

ZACH: Right!

According to Joette Martin,

We actually had sponsors! In fact one time, I don't even know if it was a real commercial or just a schtick, where we did the Bic ballpoint pens, and dropped it down and we all danced all over it. We jumped on it and danced on it and Zach wrote something with it and actually I think it almost didn't write! We had Fischer's Bread, with the logo of the little girl on it. We had the same loaf in there until it got green.

BARRY LANDERS: The Bic pens? Remember that? He'd throw it into the floor, and into the ceiling, and he'd step on them, oh, it was unbelievable! Then he'd write with it.

The Cat's Meow next judged a dance contest, and then was ready for their second set which was to close the show, "My Little Red Book" and a super-long version of "Dancing in the Streets," during which lead singer Frank's microphone pulled out of its socket when he decided to take it off the stand and walk around the stage with it — a technical no-no. The mikes were never intended to be removed and there was insufficient wire on them to move more than few feet. As a result, Frank couldn't be heard until Zach ran to the rescue and, after it was reconnected, he held the mike aloft until the set was finished, probably sending the volatile Ray Walker into a hysterical frenzy. At about the same time, rhythm guitarist Dave Meyers broke two strings on his guitar. Embarrassing, but minor mishaps.

I don't know if it was common practice at Channel 47, but sometimes (probably for bands that might be "going somewhere") in the control room, a 7 1/2 IPS reel-to-reel recording would be made of the performance directly from the sound board, and one was done on this occasion for Herald Square–The Cat's Meow. I'm not sure if the tape was meant for the engineers or if Zach needed it for some reason, but it was given to the band to keep and I still have it to this day. I remember the quality was top-notch back in 1966, much better than the recording I made off the air on the 16th. That afternoon the band left before I did, and because Zach knew how I sometimes tended to walk off and forget things, he refused to let me take the tape home with me, wagging his finger and warning, "You'll only lose it!" I knew even back then that he was beginning to get to know me. He held onto the tape to make sure it got into the right hands. Ironically, when I listened to the tape recently, the sound had degraded so that it had an overabundance of bass and a somewhat "dull" sound, whereas my recording off the air still sounded acceptable!

The summer of '66 continued to simmer, and Keith and I were almost daily visitors. The temperatures soared and my Chevy Bel Air, hot as blazes inside would, at this point, first make a side trip to Hasbrouck Heights to pick up Patty, then continue south, eventually to the scorching streets of Newark. Late one July afternoon, Keith and I were about to leave Zach's office, when he raised his finger in an "I just remembered something" gesture, and reached deep into the pocket of his undertaker's jacket which was hanging on a hook on the wall. He came up with four yellow tickets and handed them to me, instructing us to have a good time. On it was written "Sound Blast '66," and the list of artists on the bill that night at Yankee Stadium was astounding: Stevie Wonder, Ray Charles, the McCoys, the Byrds, the Beach Boys and more would all be performing.

Well, we had four complimentary tickets, so we now needed two dates. Keith immediately asked Patty, and I scoured the halls of Channel 47 to see who was still there and might be interested. One of the regulars, Ilene Baranik, seemed excited at the prospect. She looked quite young; thinking that she might be too young, as in Donna's case, I asked her to get her mother's permission. (I asked Ilene at the 1991 *Disc-O-Teen* reunion if she remembered that, and she said she remembered the concert, but not calling her mother.) The concert was one of the high points of the summer, as Keith and I sat high in the stands of Yankee Stadium with two cute dates, the warm breeze rustling through everyone's hair, rock music wafting through the sultry air — and all for free, thanks to Zach.

One of the exciting perks that came with hanging around the office after the show was rooting through the stacks of promotional 45 RPM records that constantly poured in to the show, similar to the volume that would, I imagine, be delivered regularly to AM radio stations playing the Top 40 hits. More often than not, Zach would let me go home with a handful of them, especially if they were doubles of ones they used on the show. I used to look for tunes by artists I recognized, even if they weren't hits, or, more commonly, never got any airplay at all. I still have a handful of these by artists like Bob Lind, Sandy Posey, the Hondells and many others. More often than not we could "preview" these on Zach's little record player that he used to select the song roster for each evening's show. Being a Beach Boys fan ever since the release of their classic Pet Sounds album the previous May, I was particularly taken with one tune by a group called the GTOs, a driving "car and girlfriend" song called "She Rides with Me." It sounded like a Beach Boys hit, and I noticed that it had been written by Brian Wilson and Roger Christian, who had collaborated on a number of Beach Boys recordings. Zach had used it on the show and it had special summer feelings attached to it for me. There was only one problem: the record I held in my hand was the only copy. By this time I would feel totally at home in the office, as Zach accepted my presence there and even shared his dinner with me at times! I picked up the record, turned to Zach and asked, with my usual casual resolution, if I could take it home. "There's only one thing," I added. "There's only one copy. What does that mean?" Zach, without missing a beat, and probably a tad annoyed, shot back, "It means there's only one copy!" Somehow, likely due to his extreme good nature and the chance that the song had outlived its usefulness on the show, I walked out that night with the record, which I still have, and I have never seen the song released anywhere since, not even in collections of rare '60s recordings. I did manage to find it by accident on YouTube years later—the same recording, only the group was called Joey and the Continentals.

During an uncommonly quiet period following one of the Friday night tapings, I questioned Zach about the old *Shock Theater* shows. I was particularly interested in how he reacted to technical mishaps, such as when he set up one of his little "break-ins" during a movie and the engineers failed to make the camera switches correctly and the joke failed to come off. He has since told me (on an episode of my cable TV show *Front Row*) that he just accepted it because either they didn't have enough setup time or "we made it too difficult for whoever was doing the switching." But that night in 1966 I remember him telling me that he'd get so frustrated with it that he "could hardly sleep that night." He also added that by the time they were ready to go on the air live at 11:15 p.m., he always felt like he'd rather to go to bed. I probably asked him about those technical errors because I was witness during one *Disc-O-Teen* taping to my only experience seeing Zach angry (although his handling of it was typically tactful) with the engineers. They had tried some technical trick, I can't remember what, but it took so long that it held the taping up for about 20 minutes. I can still see him looking into the camera during down time and saying quietly to the guys in the control booth, "And you call yourselves engineers …"

At the show, there were moments I just wanted to laminate and take home with me. One day Zach started talking about the old Universal horror movies, which had been running practically nonstop (except for a brief period in 1961) on local stations. "You know, they should take all those films and lock them up in a vault for about ten years," he lamented. "They're shown way too much." I seized the opportunity to ask him the famous question that I'm sure he has heard at least a thousand times since, "Which one is your favorite?" thinking then that he actually enjoyed horror movies the way I did. The answer was then, as it is now, *Son of Frankenstein*. He loved the sets, the craftsmanship, and Bela Lugosi as Ygor, who he didn't recognize until halfway through his first screening. During another conversation (this is the moment I'd like to laminate), he asked a few of us in which vampire movie it was stated that the image of a vampire would not show up in a photograph when it was developed. Of course, Know-It-All Scrivani had the answer — there was no such movie. Zach insisted there was (I have since been informed that there indeed was — 1958's *The Return of Dracula*). We went back and forth until, bolstered by my perceived expertise in the field I found the temerity to shout, "Listen, you don't know who you're arguing with!" If you can visualize Zach in fun "losing it," jumping up on his desk, shaking his fist in full character and screaming, "I don't know who I'm arguing with?! *You* don't know who *you're* arguing with!," you can get some idea of the moment, as the absurdity of arguing about vampire lore with the king of horror hosts became clear.

About midsummer another novelty song, "They're Coming to Take Me Away, Ha-Haaa!" by Napoleon XIV, hit the charts and zoomed up to Number 3. It had gotten a lot of airplay on the local radio stations, and Zach and Barry felt the song, a kind of insane rhythmic rant by a soon-to-be asylum inmate, fit the quirky nature of *Disc-O-Teen* and played it throughout the summer months. Eventually, when the kids heard the march-like drumbeat that began the song, they would grasp each others' shoulders, form a line, and stomp around the studio in circles as if being led off to the funny farm en masse. I was in earshot of Barry and Zach during one such episode and heard Barry complain to Zach that he didn't like it, they weren't dancing, and it just looked weird. "Oh, let them do it," Zach countered. "I think it looks great, and they're having fun." Barry was overruled.

One Friday late in July, Zach took me aside and pointed out a visitor to the set, a teenager standing off to the side, wearing a Don Post Phantom of the Opera mask (see photo on right). "This kid's mother has been calling the station and asking me to talk to him," Zach whispered. "He's been a fan since my Channel 11 days, and his mother says he's so obsessed with me and the show that he neglects his homework. Nothing she does seems to help. What am I supposed to say to him?" He wanted to do the right thing, and clearly felt pressed by the concern of the kid's mother. I had no solution. Zach decided to feature the kid as the next "victim" in a Moonshine commercial. I guess the kid left happy, because I heard no more about it, and if I read Zach correctly, I'll bet he gave the boy a bit of advice about the importance of doing his homework.

August was a busy month at the show, with an appearance by the Tradewinds, who'd had a hit with the East Coast surfing song "New York's a

Zach with "the problem student."

Lonely Town," and were about to have another with a bit of pre-psychedelia called "Mind Excursion." This was quickly followed by another Critters visit, fresh from their Dick Clark tour and anxious to promote their first album, "Younger Girl." A slight change in personnel resulted in a new drummer, Jeff Pelosi, taking over for Jack Decker.

Chapter 11
Clouds, Shadows and Guest Stars

Go to a show, you hope she goes.
I've got nothing to say but "It's okay."
— "Good Morning, Good Morning," The Beatles

Not everything that happened at the show was memorable in a positive way. As the summer rolled on, more young people from the Newark area got wind of the fact that there was a dancing show being broadcast in their backyard, and since the city had a sizable minority population, the show began reflecting a distinct ethnic diversity. Soon black and Hispanic kids began to outnumber the Caucasian population in the studio (Newark was also comprised of a generous helping of Polish and Italian families), temperaments clashed and tension began to grow. I remember a distinct effort being made to keep the show "balanced," by including a proportionate number of different races, but trouble was looming in spite of it. Fights would sometimes break out outside the Mosque Theater, and there were more than a few times when Keith and I would make tracks across the street to the car to avoid impending trouble. Racial tensions in that city finally reached a peak during the summer of 1967, culminating in the infamous Newark riots.

RICH: How about the time of the Newark riots and you only had three kids show up?

ZACH: Of course nobody was there, three kids came and their father brought them. Father of one of the girls or whatever, but three girls showed up and the Sweet Inspirations also showed up, they lived in Newark. So we had to do the whole show with them singing, and I don't know whether they sang a lot or what happened, it was all lip-synching.

RICH: The group featured Whitney Houston's mother [Sissy Houston], right?

ZACH: Yeah. And the three girls, so now we had a show [*laughs*]. Seems pretty absurd, but we did. Then the next day, I guess slowly *people* came back, and I'm sure the parents didn't like the idea of being in Newark in such a situation. It was a terrible time.

I guess there has to be a "most humiliating" story to sandwich in here somewhere, so this would have to be it. The day finally came, delivered on a silver platter by co-executive producer Barry Landers. I can't for the life of me remember what I had done; most likely I was poking my Polaroid around too many corners or just being in spots I shouldn't have, the wrong place at the wrong time kind of thing, when all of a sudden I was ordered out of the studio by Barry. I immediately retreated to the second floor above the studio, behind the glass partition, and watched the rest of the show from there. I felt like a third grader sitting in the corner, wearing a dunce cap. My truer nature would have driven me, having been thoroughly mortified, to pack up and leave without speaking to anyone, drive back home and never show up there again. That didn't happen. For some reason where *Disc-O-Teen* was concerned, somewhere deep down in my psyche I felt I really had some kind of crazy right to be there! Barry didn't blink an eye when he later found me sitting there. He simply explained (and this is chiseled in my brain) that I had "spooked" Zach! I'll never know if that was the truth or if it was just that I had annoyed Barry, but at the time I was embarrassed that I could possibly have caused Zach to banish me from the studio. Except for the injury to my pride, no permanent damage was done, the curfew was soon lifted and things went on as if nothing had ever happened.

September passed, Zach's birthday (his 375th) was celebrated on the air, and October was upon us. Patty, the girl Keith had been interested in and who had had the heat prostration problems during the summer, was now working as a dancer at the Metropole on 48th Street in New York City, a job her older sister had arranged for her. At the time I remember thinking that she was making an inroad into show business — ah, sweet naivety. This was in the days before the Metropole became topless, and she danced, as a photo showed, in a black leotard with fishnet stockings. I asked her what it was like dancing in a place like that, and she said that the only thing that bothered her were what she referred to as the "crotch-watchers."

On Monday, October 24, 1966, taping for the second annual Halloween Ball took place. I had decided to dance on the show dressed once again in my Frankenstein Monster outfit. The drive down to Newark was special that night; the Beach Boys' "Good Vibrations" had recently been released and was playing on the radio. Also memorable from that night was hearing the Supremes' "You Can't Hurry Love" for the first time, taking comfort from lyrics which urged patience when experiencing an unrequited love affair.

Barry Landers, shortly before he banished me from the studio.

As I entered the vestibule of the Mosque, weighed down by cameras and my costume, I couldn't help noticing someone camped at the side under the poster-filled glass display cases. His was a new face, and he was hard at work making up another person as a werewolf. I must have talked to him for a minute, but felt sorry that he had to do his makeup job out in the cold hallway. He was obviously there for *Disc-O-Teen*, but John the Cop, in typical form, wouldn't allow him up to the studio. My compassionate reaction to the young man's plight was to snap a Polaroid of the half-completed make-up and continue on upstairs. Such was my first glimpse of Michael R. Thomas, future professional makeup artist. Later on I was lumbering around in my Frankenstein costume when I saw the werewolf guy (now completely and impressively made up) and a second Frankenstein Monster with a different look than mine (his outfit incorporated a version of the Monster's woolly vest from Son of Frankenstein, mine was the straightforward black-suited version) about to dance on the show.

MIKE THOMAS: Rich Scrivani also came dressed up as Frankenstein's Monster, and when the two of us looked at each other it was like two girls being at the prom, both wearing the identical gown, like, "Who do *you* think you are?"

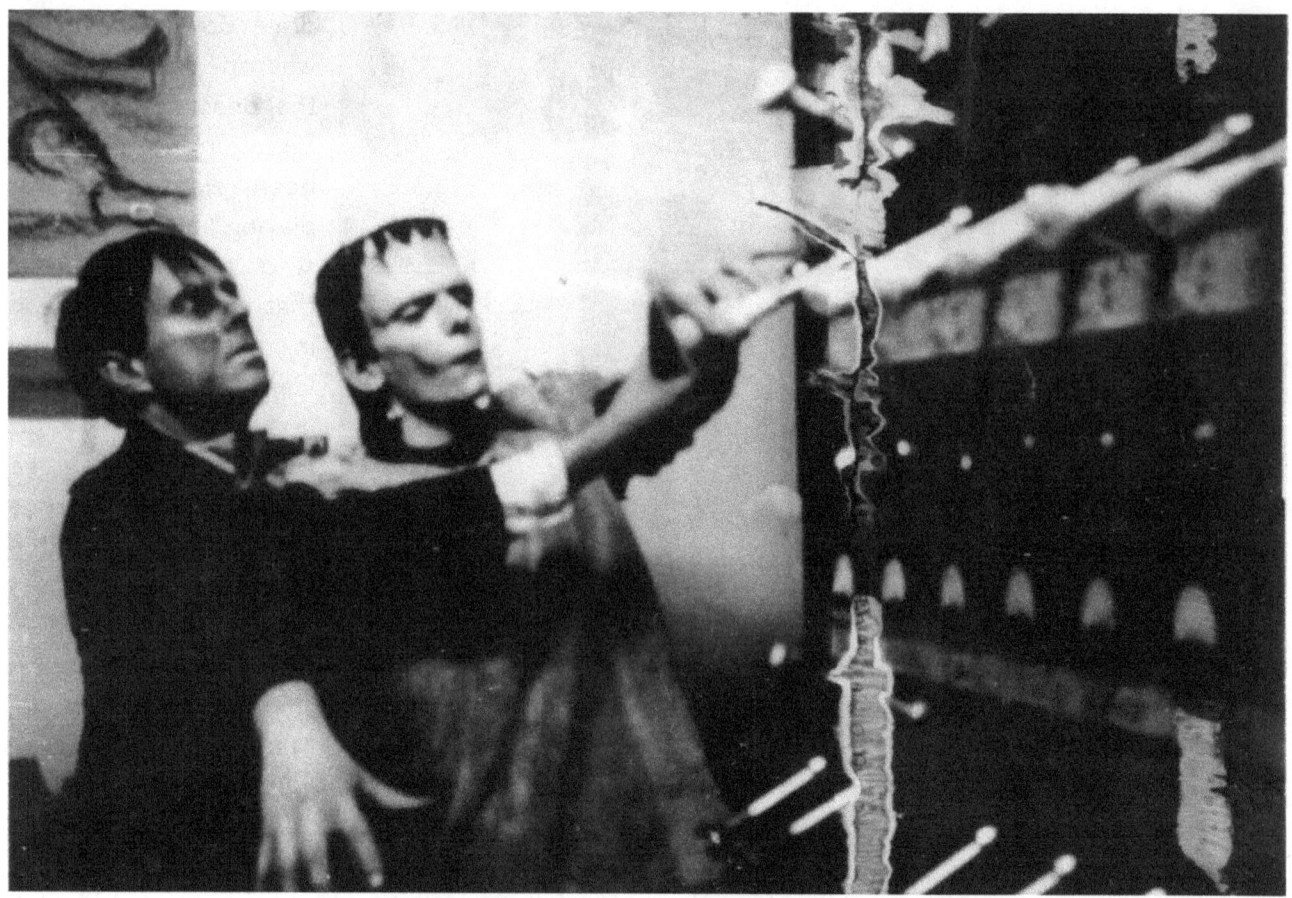

Zach and Mike Thomas revisit Bride of Frankenstein.

What really struck me, though, was the undeniably professional look to both of Mike's makeups. This was someone with real talent, and would, I felt, make something of himself as a professional. I was right, and ten years down the road his career as a makeup artist would include a regular stint on a groundbreaking new NBC comedy show by the name of *Saturday Night Live*. But all I could think of then was how annoyed I was that there was a more slick version of the Frankenstein Monster on the show. When I grumbled about it to my dance partner, 17-year-old Sharon Kiselyk, she very kindly consoled me, "Oh, you make a better monster — you're taller."

MIKE THOMAS: I gathered together all this pitiful makeup kit that I had which I kept in a corrugated cardboard box. By then I had already gotten Dick Smith's *Do-It-Yourself Monster Makeup Handbook*. In it were instructions on how to put crepe hair on a face and do a Wolf Man makeup. I had spent the previous summer working on a Frankenstein Monster outfit. My dad helped me with the costume. When we got to the Mosque Theater, John the guard wouldn't let us up. I sat my friend Greg Rondinoni down and began making him up as the Wolf Man. The kids then started coming in and Barry Landers came in. He took a look at Greg, half made-up, and he looked around and said, "Who's doing the makeup?" I pointed to myself and he said, "Well, what are you out here for? Come on in!" He brought us up and let us use the boys' room to finish the makeup.

Zach of course seized on this newcomer with enthusiasm and featured him in the type of little bits he had once done with me. I have to admit I was feeling left out; a new kid was on the block! Well, the truth is that I had had my 15 minutes, and here was someone who could really do it, who obviously had a career ahead of him in the business. I had brought along another friend, Joe Hannemann, to handle the chores of taking pictures (I think at one time or another, every friend I had had been to *Disc-O-Teen!*), and after the taping was over, Zach grabbed Mike and Joe, headed over to a side room which housed all the huge levers for the studio lights, and had Joe take a Polaroid of Mike as the Monster reaching for one of the levers, with Zach trying to hold him back. I thought trying to recreate a scene from *Bride of Frankenstein* was a neat idea, and Mike was thrilled.

> MIKE THOMAS: Zach wanted to recreate the moment in *Bride of Frankenstein* where the Monster has his hand poised above the lever. Even though I was a little bit taller than Zach, wearing those ridiculous eight-inch platforms, he kind of stooped down a little bit to make me look even bigger, and held his hand out and put it on my arm. I can remember Zach saying very quietly, "No, no. Don't do it. Don't pull the lever!" to get the right expression on his face, I guess. Man, how I longed to have that photo. For years and years and years, every time I thought about *Disc-O-Teen* I would think, "I wonder what the hell ever became of that photo?"

I would see Mike at least a half-dozen more times at the show and whenever I'd get the chance, I'd engage him in monster trivia quizzes. His knowledge of the classic Universal horror films was up there with mine (not an easy thing to match, even back then). After a few more encounters at *Disc-O-Teen*, in flawless makeups as different creatures that included Count Dracula and a perfect death's head Grim Reaper (accomplished with nothing more than shadows and highlights), he would disappear from my life until a chance event reunited us 25 years later at NBC Studios in New York, where we had both been working under each other's noses for 15 years!

Mike Thomas in his own Grim Reaper makeup.

> MIKE THOMAS: During the Halloween '66 show, Barry approached us and said, "Listen, what are you guys doing on Halloween?" If it wasn't Halloween proper, it was the Saturday of Halloween weekend. We said, "Nothing. Why?" He said, "Well, I would like you guys to show up at a dance at the South Plainfield High School, because Zach is going to be hosting and we would like to have you there to kind of 'beef up' the occasion." Of course Barry said, "I can't pay you!" But we were just happy to get dressed up and show off. And so we showed up and I think we walked around among the kids that were dancing on the floor, and I can remember that Zach was auctioning off his original three-quarter length double-breasted coat that he wore on *Shock Theater*.

(I guess the auction didn't happen or someone had a change of heart, because as of the summer of 2004, Zach was still in possession of his original

"V" did not stand for Victory on the Disc-O-Teen set.

coat, took it out of his legendary closet in my presence and tried it on. It was a tad tight and a bit threadbare, but he could still button it!)

It's at this point I should mention what may very well have been a significant symbol of the '60s that I believe originated among the mini-skirted and bell-bottomed teenyboppers who populated this out-of-the-way, one-of-a-kind dance show. Somewhere along midsummer of 1966, a group of the girls began making a unique gesture at the camera. It consisted simply of the first two digits of the right hand held in the air in a sort of V-for-Victory wave, swinging the arm back and forth while dancing. The kids made a point of doing it while the cameras were in a close-up, and anyone who saw it knew it had to have another meaning all its own. This was about a year before the same gesture was used to signify "peace," by the way. Being supremely unworldly, I finally asked my friend Sharon what the hell it meant. She told me it was a symbol for the word *crunch*, which even I knew had to have a deep, dark implication.

I pressed Sharon further, until between loud, obnoxious giggles I finally figured out that it must be a symbol for the king of all obscenities, the "F" word. More accurately it was a way to communicate between a certain group of adolescent girls which guys they thought were hot and who they would "do it with." Well, "Crunch!" became a byword around *Disc-O-Teen*, and Zach even had a bunch of official T-shirts made up with "ZAC 47" on the front and **CRUNCH!** emblazoned on the back, above an enormous hand in the "V" sign position. Zach never knew it, but he had commissioned a run of what had to be the most obscene T-shirt ever designed! I have one in mint condition, in case anyone's interested.

CHRISTINE DOMANIECKI: I'd like to believe that one of the "regular" regulars started it, but there were a whole bunch of girls who would come to the show, Leslie and Sharon, Stacy and Ilene and others, and we were sitting around in the place across the street, the soda shop — Nick's. We were sitting in a booth, and one of the girls pulled out a copy of *Rave* magazine, which was from England, and I remember someone pointing to an English guy's picture. He had these really nice jeans that were incredibly tight, and worn very, very thin and faded around his privates. And she said, "Ah! *Crunch!*"

On Friday, January 6, 1967, I wandered in off cold, windy Broad Street, strolled up the 30-degree rise that was the marble foyer of Symphony Hall, said my "hello" to John the Cop and took the familiar small, clanking elevator up one floor to the offices of Channel 47. Upon entering Zach's office, I beheld a startling sight: There he was, glumly looking up at me with a huge bandage covering his right eye. At first I thought mild-mannered John Zacherle had been in a fistfight.

RICH: Can you tell me the famous eye story?

ZACH: Was it *Famous Monsters* where I cut my eye? Russ Jones came to visit me. He painted my portrait for the cover of *Famous Monsters*. He still calls once in

The famous "dirty" T-shirt.

awhile from California. And I had picked up some magazines and brought them with me in my car, and when I went to unload them, it was late and dark and I stacked them up in my arms, and new magazines are very slippery. You can't do that, you can't carry them around because some of 'em will slide right off your arm. And in this case they slid and I went over and hunched up to grab 'em, save them, and when I got upstairs a guy says, "Hey, your eye's bleedin'!" I said, "What're you talkin' about?" He says, "Your eye's bleedin', you cut the white of your eye!" I got a paper cut right up on the eye, it just missed the pupil. It was dripping blood.

RICH: On your eyeball?

ZACH: Cut me right on the eyeball, yeah. There's a skin like on your eyeball, the white of your eye. Anyway, Barry or somebody, it was late in the day, found a doctor, I don't know if he was an eye doctor or who he was, in Newark, and we went down on, I think he was right down on Main Street. You came out of the Mosque Theater and turned left on the way to the Weequahic Diner, remember the Weequahic Diner? [Weequahic is pronounced *Week*-wake.] Famous old diner. Anyway, this old guy stitched up my eye. He put a big patch over it. You must not have been there, so I did the whole show —

RICH: I was! I have a picture of it. Did you ever see the Polaroid I have of you with that big bandage on your eye?

ZACH: Yeah, I've got a picture of it. Somebody, I guess *you*, must have taken it.

RICH: I was there that night.

ZACH: It was really annoying, and slightly painful because when you put a stitch in your eye, you know, they have to tie a knot or something and… They left part of it hanging out so that you'd close your eye and it wouldn't snag. The next day I had to get the scissors out and cut it off, it was so annoying. And it only lasted a couple of days, and it healed up nicely.

RICH: Do you remember how you went on the show that night? Because I do. I also have a photo of that, how you covered it over.

ZACH: No idea.

RICH: You wrapped your head up like the Invisible Man.

ZACH: Oh, yeah?

RICH: Yeah. And put dark glasses over it, you know, just to cover up the eye patch.

ZACH: Really?! Oh!

Because of Zach's eye injury, he hosted one Disc-O-Teen episode dressed as the Invisible Man.

RICH: I don't know how you explained it to the audience, but you went on the show with your head wrapped in bandages.

ZACH: That was pretty clever! [*Big laugh*]

The show had its share of guests who would just show up and hang around, but one day apparently two soon-to-be superstars showed up:

CHRISTINE DOMANIECKI: About the time that *Star Trek* was really hot, Leonard Nimoy and William Shatner came to the show. I had watched a couple of episodes, but we were following some English group or whatever group was in town, so we really didn't have that much time to watch *Star Trek*. All of a sudden these two guys appear on the show. And I just remember Zach bringing both of them over to Pach and me and introducing Pach to Leonard Nimoy, and he said something Italian to her and kissed her hand. I said hello to William Shatner, and I thought he was gonna eat me with his eyes! I said hi and goodbye because I really wasn't interested because they weren't English and they weren't in a rock group. They came in in their space-suits and everything!

LINDA PACE: I also remember meeting Leonard Nimoy on the show. Shatner was there too. I don't remember too much talking to him, but I remember talking to Leonard Nimoy and Zach introducing me and saying, "This is Pach." And he said, "Oh, Pach! What a *bella fache* [pronounced 'fach']!" which means "beautiful face," because Leonard Nimoy, I guess, spoke Italian.

Chapter 12
The End of an Era

The song is over, the song is over,
Searchin' for a note, pure and easy
Playing so free like a breath rippling by.
  — "The Song Is Over," The Who

"I wish I had the records we threw away," said Barry Landers. "The 45s we used to sail across the office and try to catch on our fingers."

In the fall of 1966, rumors started circulating that *Disc-O-Teen* was going to be dropped. Station manager Ed Cooperstein (or "Big Ed" as Zach called him,) apparently had been thinking seriously about discontinuing the show. Almost immediately the kids launched an "anti–Big Ed" campaign, not only protesting the show's possible demise, but canvassing, painted signs and all, for the extension of the show from 30 minutes to an hour!

Zach and Barry allowed the protest signs to be seen on the air, and Zach seized the opportunity to place some angry "phone calls" to Cooperstein during a few of the shows. At one point Mike Thomas, again in Frankenstein Monster makeup, bellowed, "BIG ED – NO G-O-O-D!" into the microphone. The point was well made, and as implausible as it may seem, the show not only avoided the graveyard, but on November 2 it became official: *Disc-O-Teen* would soon be expanded into an hour-long show. No one knew it then, but the campaign helped buy exactly one more year for the program.

CHRISTINE DOMANIECKI: Zach was having some kind of a contest, I can't remember what it was for, but there were tons of postcards and letters, and he would keep those boxes in the office. I remember Diane and I and a couple of the other regulars walked into the office and we made believe we were drawing a winner, I picked out a card, and the guy's name was Bob Schwab. We just laughed for days, we couldn't stop laughing because it was such a weird name.

During this final year of the show, the guests included some

Marsha, Sharon and Joette protest

Zach welcomes the Blues Project.

light and some heavy hitters: the Blues Project, a once-again reinvented Critters on December 30's Reptile Ball costume show, the Doors, featuring a hyper-stoned looking Jim Morrison, who spent the bulk of his time staring blankly into the camera, a band probably no one remembers: Lothar and the Hand People (so named for their featured instrument, a theremin), pop singer Keith ("98.6"), Rick Derringer and another member of the McCoys, the Blues Magoos from Greenwich Village, and a much-anticipated appearance by the Rascals, which never happened. No one could say that *Disc-O-Teen* didn't deliver some pretty impressive talent for a low-budgeted show.

RICH: Did you ever get pressured to have to play certain songs?

ZACH: Some 45s came by mail, from the distributors, but I never remember ever having a call from anyone asking us to play anything like that. I never did.

RICH: Were they sent along as freebies to promote them a little bit?

ZACH: I don't think so. Danny Fields, who was the promotion man at Channel 7 when I got to New York, eventually became a promotion man for Electra Records, and he sent us the Doors and I forget who else. The Lovin' Spoonful came through Kama Sutra, right? Yeah. I don't know what the connection was there. Well, it was the only dance show in New York, you know? So they said "Well, what the hell?"

RICH: The McCoys were on.

ZACH: Wow! Gee, that's interesting, I forgot about that. But like I said, the only reason that they would ever do it was the fact that it was the only dance show. Clay Cole hadn't started and all that stuff. At least I don't think. When did he start?

RICH: I think Clay Cole was around on Channel 11.

ZACH: He wasn't doing a daily dance show though.

Zach welcomes "98.6" singer Keith.

RICH: Then he opened a discotheque down the street from *Disc-O-Teen*, remember?

ZACH: Did he? Really! I didn't know that. [Author's note: *The Clay Cole Show*, an *American Bandstand* clone, ran on WPIX Channel 11 in New York from December 1963 until December 1967.]

RICH: Clay Cole wasn't there, they just used his name, you know. Kids would go over there and dance. I remember watching The Doors' visit on the show. I couldn't make it that day.

ZACH: They walked around, you know, and they were lookin' over the girls, and the girls weren't all totally attractive or knockouts, but there were a few. And they located them, I guess. Jim Morrison did anyway, just wandered around. At one point Morrison walked past me and was wandering, as I used to walk through the crowd as they were dancing, and I don't know if the kids were excited about them or not, they obviously had a first big hit they were playing, which was "Light My Fire," yeah, okay. And we must have played that before they got there because it was a big hit. And, ah, danceable. He walked past me and says, "This is the god-damnedest television show I ever saw!" You know, sort of under his breath as he passed me. Because they were so loose and I guess everybody seemed to be having a good time. And the whole set was probably so freaky-looking, because beyond camera range was a wrestling ring and other sets they had set up for interviews. It was a whole big dance floor, it was — used to be the, whatever you call it, the ballroom for the Mosque Theater.

According to Joette Martin,

I was with Joanne Onischuk then, she was the blonde Jane Asher–looking type, and Jim Morrison was talking to her, of course they gravitated to her, she was very cute, and he said, "We're going to be at the Steve Paul Scene on Tuesday, why don't you come and we could have a drink" or something, and she goes, "Oh! Maybe." And afterwards she's jumping up and down saying, "I gotta go see them!" But her mother wouldn't let her go into New York alone on a Tuesday night.

RICHARD HEYMAN: For some reason the Doughboys happened to be there, maybe we were just hanging out. I just remember being upstairs, because you could sort of look down onto the studio from upstairs. I remember the interview where Jim Morrison just became totally mute, he wouldn't say a word. Zacherley kept trying to be funny and humor him and Morrison would just stare into the camera and give this kind of zombie look, and he'd walk right up and put his face right up to the lens of the camera. I don't think he ever said anything on the air during the whole interview. It was very bizarre.

LINDA PACE: I remember meeting the Doors on the show. I remember them coming on, and I used to love that song "Light My Fire," I was so excited. But what I remember about that day was that Jim Morrison seemed to be so out of it, and when I got close to him, he was such a really, really phenomenally good-looking man, but he [had] all this stuff like caked in his hair. I don't know what it was, but it was amazing. I thought he was really out of it. You know, I was naive in those days too, but he had all kinds of stuff caked in his hair. It almost looked like something he had been eating or something, or he had slept on it.

Barry's memories of Jim Morrison were a bit more effusive:

He was a total asshole. He wouldn't take direction, number one. I told him what we wanted them to do because of the parameters of the cave. I mean it was a small area and we needed two cameras in there, one for wide shots and one for tight shots, and he proceeded to just prance around like the asshole that he is, or was, I should say. I have no regard for the man, even as a talent or as a singer or as a supposed human being. He mouthed some obscenities to the camera, he flicked his tongue at the lens, very close, in a very obscene gesture, and all in all it was a very unpleasant experience. He was also an alcoholic. He was an unpleasant personality who we had to deal with, that's all. They were big stars as you know, and let me put it this way to you: He was underwhelming. And I'm being kind!

By the latter months of 1966, Barry had taken a shine to a band that had appeared on the show under the name The Ascots. They were a good-looking bunch, and their lead singer, Myke Scavone, sported a thick mane of shoulder-length hair and a voice resembling Mick Jagger's. They had won the 1966 Battle of the Bands contest (Herald Square had won the previous year) and were given a recording contract with Bell Records. Soon Barry, now their manager, came up with a gimmick: He dressed them up in World War I infantry outfits and changed their name to The Doughboys. A record was cut, "Rhoda Mendelbaum," which supposedly received some airplay on WMCA, one of the two hot AM radio stations at the time. However, drummer Richard Heyman, in his book *Boom Harangue (Life in Mid-Century Through the Eyes of a Rock'n'Roll Survivor)*, claims none of the band ever heard the strains of "Rhoda Mendelbaum" emerge from any radio.

Christine Domaniecki with the Ascots, soon to become the Doughboys. Myke Scavone is on the right.

BARRY LANDERS: They were called the Ascots, and I saw them at the Rheingold Festival in Central Park. I was working on the show, and I said, "These guys are gonna be big." I got the idea for the World War I costumes and I went out and bought them. They could have been big, they could have been huge. But there were a lot of problems with dope — Willy Kerchover and Myke Scavone.

Author's note: Scavone read the preceding quote in the first edition of this book and told me he never had a problem with dope.

RICHARD HEYMAN: First prize was a recording contract with Bell Records, which at the time was a big deal because that later turned into Arista Records, but at the time it was considered a major label even though it was independent. Barry liked the band from our appearances, he was from South Plainfield and we were from Plainfield, so he was close by, he knew of us. I think in the Plainfield area we were considered the top band around. It was probably more through the show

Herald Square being presented with a recording contract by Steve Jerome.

at first that he found out about us. When he became our manager, we used to have band meetings over at his house in South Plainfield, and he thought we needed to change the name. I don't know if it was him or someone else who actually came up with Doughboys, but it certainly wasn't me. It was determined that we should wear World War I uniforms and we went into the East Village and bought authentic uniforms with spats, the hats, etc.

Barry thought we should do some novelty songs. He kept telling us we should sing old standards with a rock beat — that was his approach to it. When we got signed to Bell Records, we were assigned a producing team known as the Jerome Brothers. They had just produced the Left Banke's first two singles, "Walk Away Renee" and "Pretty Ballerina." We were excited about that and they came up with the material for us; nobody in the band was writing any songs yet. They came up with this song "Rhoda Mendelbaum." I was just flabbergasted by the ridiculousness of it all: "What are they trying to do to us?" We were trying to be like a real cool kind of garage, "Stonesy" band and we're given this song called "Rhoda Mendelbaum." I thought, "That's the end of us!" But we did the best we could with it, and they subsequently put on a string section after we left the studio, which was surprising. I'm sure it was written as a novelty song, and we tried to make it a little more like garage rock. It was totally our arrangement. They just gave us a demo and we went back to Plainfield.

The Doughboys' second offering, "Everybody Knows My Name," a pleasant tune and distinct improvement, was also their last:

RICHARD HEYMAN: We were assigned that song as our second single. It was written by Bob Gaudio of the Four Seasons. I remember Gregory's Music in Plainfield was selling it and the salesman there said he didn't think the last one was going to do anything, but "This one has a chance, it's gonna be a hit." So we were so excited. We used to do the WMCA Good Guys shows promoting it, and they promised us up and down if we did their shows, that they were going to play it. They did play it a bit. It never charted or anything, but they played it.

Before the Doughboys faded into obscurity, Barry managed to get them a gig opening for the Beach Boys at the Mosque on Saturday, April 29, 1967, a show he emceed. I was there with two friends, and we will never forget our first experience with actual physical, ear- and skull-splitting pain as the Doughboys played the opening chords of "Rhoda Mendelbaum" onstage. Their standup organ was amplified so loud that all we could do was stare at each other in abject pain and disbelief. Mercifully, the unbearable decibel level lasted all of 20 seconds, and the remainder of the concert was rendered at a far more comfortable volume level.

The rest of the concert was fabulous. A group called the Buckinghams ("Kind of a Drag," "Susan") shared the bill and the Beach Boys capped the show with their latest #1 hit "Good Vibrations," complete with cello section and an electro-theremin played by Mike Love. It was a thrill seeing those five guys, familiar from album covers and TV appearances, up there in three dimensions wearing those famous blue-striped shirts and white chinos, and I was impressed at how full-bodied their vocals sounded live. The only thing missing was the presence of Brian Wilson, who had stopped touring two years previous so that he could stay at home to write and produce.

One ugly incident marred the afternoon. Carl Wilson, Brian's younger brother, had declared himself a conscientious objector (the Vietnam War was growing in intensity) and was awaiting an arrest and the possibility of jail time. I assume that due to this, and because anti-war sentiments wouldn't be popular for another year or so, some boneheads in the audience started balling up paper and aluminum foil and began lobbing them at the band. It got so bad that at one point Al Jardine almost got hit in the head and muttered, "Hey, that was close!" in one of the most embarrassing moments I have ever spent in a concert hall. Mike Love stopped the show, walked to the edge of the stage and, in a very surly tone, warned: "You will cease with the throwing of missiles, or we'll come down there and knock some heads together!" The missiles stopped and the show continued.

RICHARD HEYMAN: It was very exciting, I remember it was still sort of in the era of the screaming girls, like that real kind of mid–60s concert feeling. We thought we were on our way to being rock stars, though it didn't really happen. The big letdown was when Dennis Wilson started a fight on stage with our lead singer in front of the crowd. We were mortified. They were a little uptight because Carl had just gotten arrested the day before or that very day for draft evasion, so there was kind of a tense vibe in there.

It was some time in the early months of 1967 that my relationship with Donna began to warm up a bit. By this time, we were speaking on the phone quite frequently, and I had even been over to her house, an old two-story affair in the Ironbound section, not far from the Mosque. I had met her parents; her father, I believe, didn't trust me (there was a significant age difference). But her mother liked me and could see that my intentions were as good as they could be. During one winter evening's phone call, Donna asked me if I passed close enough to her house on my way to *Disc-O-Teen* that

I could pick her up. This was the closest thing yet to a "date" for me, and I was ecstatic. So for a time, every trip I made to Newark involved a loop around into the Ironbound to take Donna to the show. It wasn't much, but in light of the circumstances and my frame of mind, it was enough for the moment. What she didn't know was that if she had lived in Sri Lanka, I would have made that side trip gleefully!

One winter evening, I came home from work and it was one of those nights where it just felt good to change into pajamas and settle in. I grabbed some dinner and switched on the TV to watch *Disc-O-Teen*, feeling totally relaxed. Donna had not been going to the show much lately and I never expected to see what I was now watching: a gorgeous close-up of her dancing on one of the risers. Between chewing and swallowing, I had changed back into my clothes, jumped into my car and was pulling out of the driveway before the storm door slammed. I don't know how I possibly avoided being pulled over by the police, because I was averaging at least 70 flying down the highways toward Newark. Since the show had been lengthened to an hour after the November protest campaign, I knew, barring any traffic jams and a few red lights, that I could *just* make it before it ended. My tires screamed as I pulled into the Kinney lot. I ran across Broad Street, paused for a second to get my breath, and "casually" walked into the Mosque. As soon as I entered the studio, one of the girls said, "Hey, Donna's looking for you!" and I knew I hadn't jeopardized my life in vain. Out she walked as if on cue. After explaining to her that I had gotten stuck in rush hour traffic, I asked ever so casually, "Oh — would you like a lift home?"

That night I got to spend a quality 20 minutes with Donna, and it was worth it; that's the kind of crazy thing you do at that age.

College studies, new jobs and a changing life kept me away from *Disc-O-Teen* during the last few months of its run. By then, the usual familiar faces of the "regulars" were for the most part gone; everyone was getting older, priorities were being shuffled and younger kids started to filter in. In many cases, the kids were so young that *Disc-O-Teen* was in danger of resembling a children's show. Even the dancing had changed: The classic '60s dances the original kids had done (the "Frug," the "Swim," the "Pony," the "Jerk," etc.), was now replaced by a single gyration which consisted of nothing more than standing in place, knees bending slightly, while moving the arms up and down in time with the music. It wasn't so much dancing as swaying to the beat, and it took so little effort that it just looked silly. Even Zach seemed less interested in the show, his between-the-songs business having lost some of its pizzazz, his talks with the new kids more perfunctory than inspired. The end was near, you could feel it in the air.

The third and final Halloween costume special (October 28, 1967) seemed comprised of these young teens and even preteens. There were a few familiar faces, but not one of the first tier of regulars could be seen. The costumes, somewhat inventive and a bit artistically complex in the early days, were now largely rubber gorilla masks and blackened faces. The popular rock group, the Box Tops ("The Letter," "Cry Like a Baby"), hung out, interacted with the kids and at one point got a little physically rambunctious with Zach, as lead singer Alex Chilton jumped on his back during the horseplay. The Box Tops didn't play live, but two of their hits blared from the overhead speakers for the kids to dance to. "Neon Rainbow," their latest single, was one of them.

> RICH: You had a group of regulars who were very nice. They were on all the time. Christine was one of them.
>
> ZACH: Yes yes yes, that's right, and they all came back for the last show, too, which was nice. It lasted two and a half years, didn't it? Something like that?
>
> RICH: Yes, only two and a half years.

According to Barry Landers, "They had trouble selling it because it was UHF. If that show had been anywhere else, it would have been number one in the country. Zach would have been a super, superstar, because everybody loved it. The bands came from all over."

> WENDE SASSE: Cooperstein fired my dad. I'm not sure what went on, but Cooperstein, I guess, was trying to sell the station off or whatever, to make some money, so that's why I think they were deciding to make it all Spanish. I do remember my father was very upset about that, that they were trying to shut it down, and my father and Cooperstein got into a huge, huge fight, and I think Cooperstein fired my father and my father went in front of the board, and there was some dirt he had on Cooperstein — Cooperstein was not exactly the straightest guy. It got a little ugly.

> JOETTE MARTIN: They just announced before it that this was going to be the last show. We thought there'd be more of a prelude to that, or a workup to a last show or something, but that was it. It was already getting a little sporadic, and falling apart. We called everyone and we all ran down.

> JOE LORE: It was billed as the "two-and-a-half-year anniversary" show. It was never alluded to on the air that that was going to be the last show, but we knew it was the last show. As a matter of fact, for the very last shot I pulled my camera all the way back to the back wall of the studio with a big wide shot of the whole studio, and then at the very end of the show they fed in applause.

The last show, broadcast November 4, 1967, was treated with no more ceremony than any of the others. The only indication of anything special was Zach's announcement that it was *Disc-O-Teen*'s "two-and-a-half-year anniversary," hardly an occasion for celebration. One thing did look different, and welcome: half the original regulars, so long absent from the dance floor, were back. Visible once again were Christine Domaniecki, Joette Wrubel, Linda Pace, Wende Sasse and Sue Mercedante. In his Dracula getup was Mike Thomas, visibly subdued for a reason I learned only a few years ago:

> MIKE THOMAS: On October 30, 1967, I called the studio and Barry Landers picked up the phone and I said, "Hey, I haven't been on the show in a while, and because tomorrow is Halloween I was thinking of showing up in costume." And Barry said, "Oh, no, babe. I'm sorry, but we taped the Halloween show on Saturday. I tell you what: Go ahead, show up in costume, that's a good idea. It'll be a good sendoff for the show." I said, "What are you talking about?" He said, "Well, the show's over." I said, "You mean for the season?" and he went, "No, babe, we've been cancelled. Tomorrow is the last show ever." My heart sank.

The final guest band was the one-hit wonder group Every Mother's Son ("Come on Down to My Boat"), who, like most other pro ensembles before them, simply walked around the studio when they weren't cavorting with Zach in the "cave." A second guest was there, a Columbia Records recording artist with the moniker Brute Force. I couldn't for the life of me figure out his act; he behaved like an improvisational comic, spoke in a quasi-poetic style with a confusing staccato delivery and lip-synched to his recent release entitled, incredibly, "To Sit on a Sandwich."

Christine, caught candidly in a close-up dancing on a box during the song, exhibited a distinctly "thumbs down" expression, appropriate for the nonsensical novelty number which was obviously foisted upon the show in an attempt to give Mr. Force some much-needed exposure. As soon as she realized she was on camera, her face transformed into a radiant smile.

Zach couldn't resist the temptation to recreate a bit he had done on the show previously: a pantomime of Sonny and Cher in which he enlisted Pach to be Cher to his Sonny. Zach wore a "wig" that looked suspiciously like a mop and did his best to lip-synch to "I Got You, Babe," with middling results:

> LINDA PACE: I think Barry approached me one day about doing it because people used to say that I resembled Cher so much. And we talked about doing it, and what we were going to do and everything, and then we did it that one time, and it was just so funny, and it was great! Zach never knew any of the words, and I knew every one, you know? I took it so seriously, and he was just so funny.

The show ended with Zach climbing onto the bandstand, gently shooing off the array of newcomers dancing there, replacing them with the small group of original regulars, all dancing to the Dave Clark Five's version of "You Got What it Takes." Joe's camera dollied back, far into the nether regions of the vast studio, the tiny figures swaying to the music seeming to wave "goodbye" for the last time, John Zacherle doing his famous "underarm" dance on center stage. Fadeout. No one watching the show outside of the inner circle had a clue that it would not be on the next day or any other day. *Disc-O-Teen* was gone with a whimper.

> MIKE THOMAS: It was very ironic that on the last show, of the two only existing tapes, one of them being the last show, I got a speaking part. Zach interviewed me and my friend Nicky Taber [who wore werewolf makeup in the episode]. I was very lucky. I can remember being extremely depressed that the show was over, but kind of trying to still impersonate Count Dracula, and if you see the tape you can tell that I'm pretty sad. One of the things that really sticks in my memory: when the show was finally over and the music faded out and all the kids stopped dancing and were just milling around and everyone's saying "so long" to each other, and some of the kids were crying. I was kind of choking some tears back until I saw one of the prop men wheeling Isobel's hamper across the floor, and he kind of lifted his head and signaled to one of the other prop men and pointed to the hamper and said, "The end of an era." I went, "Uh-oh, here it comes," and it was everything I could do to keep from crying. I can also remember somebody asked me for my autograph, and I said, "You've gotta be kidding!" But I kinda figured that if they were getting Brute Force's autograph, they might as well have mine!

> RICHARD HEYMAN: Zach was so down-to-earth and so nice to everybody. There was none of that kind of "I'm a celebrity and you're just a kid," he was very respectful of everybody he talked to and it was so nice to find out that somebody you watched on TV was genuinely a great guy.

> BARRY LANDERS: When Eddie Cooperstein and Herb Greene decided that they were going to kill the show, I mean, that was like death. It was like somebody died. It was like a stake literally through our hearts, honest to goodness. Zach wanted to make sure it was low-key. A very quiet day, very somber day. The girls were crying, we all were. It was like a big dark cloud descended upon the entire place, and we didn't want to talk about it. We didn't discuss it in the control room, we didn't discuss it in the office. Zach was trying to be as stiff-upper-lipped as he possibly could, but I know he was heartbroken. Everybody was. Except Ray Walker, maybe…

Postscript

Shortly after the end of the show, on December 29, 1967, a group of the girls paid Zach a visit at his New York City apartment:

> JOETTE MARTIN: It was after the show was over, we all went out to visit him one

day on invitation, I think it was Chris and me and Pach and "Big" Sue and "Little" Sue, and he took us to Earl Doud's house — he did the First Family albums and he also wrote for Mad Magazine. He introduced us to our first huge stereo set with earphones, it took up the whole place. I think he played Pink Floyd, and he had a kinkajou in the closet! And while we were walking over, Zach pulled out a bottle of Anbesol, spilled it on the sidewalk, and we said, "What's that for?" and he said, "It must hurt, all those people walking on it all the time."

And Donna? I kept in touch with her for four years after the show's demise. I was dating a lot of other girls (a few of them from *Disc-O-Teen*), but for a while I saw quite a bit of her, and took her roller skating, horseback riding (actually she took me on these outings) and to two rock concerts: the Monkees at Forest Hills tennis stadium in the spring of 1967, and Procol Harum at the Fillmore East in the summer of 1970. I even helped teach her to drive. It was fun while it lasted, but the age difference, rather than becoming meaningless as in the John Sebastian song, prevented any substantial relationship. Also, the dreaded "friendship" syndrome had formed, in which she had become so accustomed to our platonic association that my eventual romantic overtures were spurned.

My contact with her ended, unpleasantly, in 1972. I hadn't had contact with her for over a year, and one night the phone rang. Donna was calling to ask me for a favor: Her new boyfriend was starting up a rock band and needed about $500 to buy some equipment. Could I help them out? Still being a bit love-struck but fortified emotionally by the amount of time that had passed since we had last seen each other, I told her I couldn't help her. I bristled at the thought of her nerve, asking for a handout for her new squeeze! I told her that if *she* were in need, it might be a different matter. Some months passed. Very late at night, the phone rang again. It was Donna announcing that she had a personal problem and needed money — $500. My heart was ripped out, but at the same time I was furious at this utterly transparent attempt at deception. Luckily I had the presence of mind to offer to help her solve her "personal problem" discreetly, in a manner that would also require less money. I reasoned that anyone in the predicament she described would have kissed my feet for an offer like that! I had called her bluff; she hesitated, then told me in a disappointed tone that she would prefer to handle it herself, she'd rather just have the money. I told her I wasn't a fool, that I knew exactly what she was trying to pull.

I also told her to go to Hell.

In 1991, when a group of us were putting together a *Disc-O-Teen* reunion, I offered to try to contact her. I figured that what had happened years before when she was just a teenager could be glossed over, but I had no way of knowing how she would have felt about the incident 19 years later. I got as far as a phone call to her mother, who told me that Donna had been married and divorced, then engaged again. It was a shame that she didn't get to attend the one and only *Disc-O-Teen* reunion, but that's another story for later.

Chapter 13
Radio Days

It's very strange trying to describe the end of an era, which the conclusion of *Disc-O-Teen* certainly was. More to the point, it was the end of John Zacherle's television career. No one knew it was coming, no announcements had been made, there was no ballyhoo. It was simply there one day early in November, and then it wasn't.

Since September 1967, I had moved on to a new job, one that made the regular trip to Newark less feasible, and more importantly, we were all older and a lot of us had gone on to other things. But there was something about knowing that Zach and crew were no longer there that left that familiar void — once again, what was he doing, and when, if ever, would he turn up with a new show? The dance show had left, I would learn, a mark on many of the kids who "lived" there, had impacted their lives and in many cases, as in mine, shaped the course of their personal and professional lives. One sunny but cold day in January 1968, on an impulse, I packed up my 8mm camera and tripod, took one last ride down Route 21 to the Ironbound section of Newark, made the familiar right onto Broad Street and parked in my old parking lot. No one was around; the city seemed eerily quiet. There was no excitement under the big glass dome fronting the Mosque Theater, no teenage girls in dotted and striped bell-bottoms waiting to get in. I had never seen it so deserted. Then, to purge the empty feeling and officially say "goodbye," I photographed the lonely-looking Symphony Hall and its surroundings, eerily devoid of any sign of activity, no kids waiting at the doors, no rock'n'roll about to happen in the evening and no Zach. He had found a home at WNEW-FM radio in New York City and was about to embark on the most satisfying phase of his career: that of FM disc jockey, a job that would take him into the late 1970s.

Zach recalled making the transition after the show ended, and getting into radio:

ZACH: Sometimes after the show, I would visit with my friend Earl Doud, who lived near me on the Upper West Side of Manhattan. I'd become friendly with him when he came to me one time when I was doing the horror movies and he was a fan and was writing for Jack Paar. And so he arranged for me to be on Jack Paar's show one night and do a takeoff on *Dragnet*. I had "lost" one of my monsters and Jack Paar and — what's the other guy's name?

RICH: Charlie Weaver [Cliff Arquette].

ZACH: Charlie Weaver! They were the detectives and they were trying to find my missing person. A ghoul of some kind. I've still got the audio of that.

RICH: I've got a copy of it.

ZACH: So I'd stop at Earl's house after *Disc-O-Teen* and he'd be watching, he watched in the daytime, and he was all excited about the little girls and so on, and his wife was cooking dinner. He was the first one that I ever knew that had earphones, you know, headphones, and he had a lot of great equipment 'cause he made a lot of money on that First Family album that he produced. And when *Disc-O-Teen* ended, he said, "Why don't you go

Zach the deejay at Central Park in 1970.

down to WNEW-FM? They're changing their format."

I went there and talked to the guy and that's all I did, I didn't try to sell myself I said, "Well, I know a lot of this music." And he also was already collecting albums, he was a big fan of WOR-FM, with Murray the K and Scott Muni. They were the first ones to play albums on FM in stereo. And just at that time they were giving up that format and going be the first station in New York on FM and in stereo that would play Top 40 songs. Only the hits. And WOR dropped the album format. WNEW-FM had an all-girl format, all the announcers were ladies. And they were playing sort of big band music, mixtures and stuff, the same stuff they were playing on WNEW-AM. But the government had made a rule that you couldn't play the same material on both AM and FM, and they decided to go with rock album cuts on FM. So I went down to see the guy and he confessed to me later that he went home and asked his son if he thought I would be a good deejay! The kid was a fan and he said, "Sure!" [*Laughs*] So I got weekend work and then very shortly after that, I remember they had a concert in Central Park with Jefferson Airplane. They introduced all of us and I got a big cheer because all the kids remembered me from television, I guess. So that next week I got a full-time job. That was 1967. I wore my undertaker's jacket with Mod flared striped pants. I guess I was insecure at that point [*large laugh*] for whatever reason. Got a huge cheer and, I guess I'd been on just weekends at that point.

I don't know if it was simply coincidence, but just over a month after the last *Disc-O-Teen* show, I landed a job at NBC television's New Jersey Film Exchange, a job that would take me into New York City about 18 months later. This turned into a career of 33 years: first as a film editor, later a videotape engineer, and eventually a technical director. The first year of the job, with my exposure to hundreds of 16mm syndicated and network TV shows, jump-started a lifelong hobby of film collecting. It was a very strange feeling — leaving Newark, where I was accustomed to going at least once a week for over two years, was like leaving behind a lifestyle. All the kids I knew and had gotten friendly with were now only memories, preserved in a collection of hundreds of Polaroid snapshots.

Almost immediately after I had started working at the Film Exchange, having regaled my new friends there with stories of the show, rumors surfaced that a "new" *Disc-O-Teen* was in the planning stages, this time to originate from New York. But it turned out to be just that — rumor. No sooner had I heard about all this, than a plain, white postcard arrived. It was from Zach. It read:

> Hey, Rich — (using up my post cards before the rates go up) Many, many thanks for all you did to make old *Disco* a great show. No kidding — your taking pictures was a big thing and kept a lot of kids with smiles on their faces while our cameras were on them!! Hope to be on radio show soon — and eventually a TV spot. Good luck to you old boy. — Zac.

I once asked Zach if doing *Disc-O-Teen* helped him feel prepared to do FM radio:

ZACH: Oh, I never even considered radio. *Disc-O-Teen* I just enjoyed doing, I didn't think of what the future would be. And of course I must have realized that music was changing, but it hadn't changed to the extent where rock'n'roll ended up in the late '60s. It was getting there, you know, but we did play the Doors and things like that; that was a lot different than an old Bobby Darin record or something like that.

RICH: I guess what I'm asking is, was it a good training ground for FM radio?

ZACH: I don't know if it was a training ground as much as it was a chance to get another job. I never thought of being on the radio. I mean, I didn't know what it was like to be on the radio, I had no idea. I never sat down in a studio where a guy was playing the hits of the day. Ah, that's not quite true, wait a minute. Occasionally I would be on the Murray the K. show. Was I still on the air when I did that?

RICH: I don't know, I never heard you on Murray the K. You'd have to say what year it was.

ZACH: Well, certainly, certainly, wait a minute. What's the guy's name on ABC? He got in trouble with the payola.

RICH: Alan Freed?

ZACH: Alan Freed. Now that would have been the very first person I ever sat in with while he was doing his show. I visited him because he came down and visited me. The announcer for my show also would be announcing his station breaks on radio — he was upstairs. So he came down and visited me while I was on the air. I remember going upstairs once or twice and being in the studio where he was — I think, I'm not sure, he may have had an engineer or maybe he was handling the records too, but he certainly had a mike in front of his face, whether or not he was actually putting records on the turntables I don't really know. Can't remember. But it wasn't anything that excited me or got me thinking about, "Gee, I could do that." I never thought of it, I was just a guest on the show.

A radio show — really! I wondered what kind of show it would be. Not long after that, a co-worker told me that he had heard Zacherley spinning records on WNEW-FM; Zach was now a full-fledged disc jockey, playing rock'n'roll in stereo. I didn't quite know how I felt about that. I was hoping that "TV spot" he had mentioned in his card would materialize quickly, and that he would be back where he belonged, but that was never to be. Aside from guest appearances and a couple of instances hosting movies over 15 years later, Zacherley would never again have his own television show. In the early '80s, WOR rehired him for a one-time presentation of the 3D movie *Gorilla at Large* (1954). I recently viewed a tape of his antics on that show and was struck by how young and energetic he still appeared (he was around 64) and how funny his schtick still was. Frolicking with an actor in an ape suit, Zach demonstrated how to make a Zacherley Daiquiri by squeez-

ing bananas out of their skins into a punch bowl filled with various repellent ingredients. He then attempted to build a mate for "Joe," the ape, using some arm bones, a bit of fur and the Zap Machine. The latter imparted a couple of nasty shocks to Zach, one of them appearing unsettlingly but hilariously real! The funniest moment came when "Joe" discovered the camera and began some uproarious posing and mugging. In 1990, Zach returned to WCAU in Philadelphia for a show they called "The Return of Roland." The movie he hosted was the 1972 stinker *Moon of the Wolf*.

Things were changing. The vibrant creativity, the freedom of expression that was the center of gravity of the 1960s, was in full bloom. Psychedelic rock gave way to a re-appreciation of the blues; country and western–flavored rock albums; new groups and supergroups sprang up everywhere. The Jimi Hendrix Experience exploded onto the scene. Traffic and Cream gave way to Blind Faith; the Who created the first rock opera "Tommy," which was to become legend, eventually spawning a movie; the Moody Blues changed their original personnel and re-invented themselves, giving way to symphonic rock; the Beatles led the way through all of it, and in their efforts to top Brian Wilson and the Beach Boys' "Pet Sounds," they produced the milestone "Sgt. Pepper's Lonely

According to Steve Van Zandt, "I loved it when Zach came onto WNEW. That was our FM station when AM turned to FM around '67 or '68, somewhere in there. For me, it was just great because he just continued to be Zach, who was a huge, huge part of my childhood. People wonder why I'm a misfit, outcast and freak; Zacherley, Soupy Sales ... things like that."

RICH: What was your best working experience in FM radio?

ZACH: By far, it would be WNEW-FM because the music was all so new. I hate to use an expression like being "blown away," but it was such a big change, even from the music we played on *Disc-O-Teen*. *Disc-O-Teen* music was all mono mostly, and by that time everybody was running out and buying stereo sets, and high fidelity was in the air. It was astonishing, the records coming from England were amazing. They were so wonderfully recorded, and we were doing the same thing here in many ways. But I think they were a little ahead of us somehow. To be sitting there handling these records, and 45s, I'd been pretty good at throwing records, 45s, across the air and having Barry Landers catch them with his finger, you know, through the hole? And back and forth, we had games going and we were very good at it — record toss. But suddenly we've got these beautiful LPs to handle and we had total freedom to create an evening or an afternoon or a morning of music, I mean it was just amazing. We actually handled the

Zach emceeing at the Fillmore East, circa 1970.

Hearts Club Band." The Rolling Stones followed up with their own Xeroxed version, "Their Satanic Majesties' Request." The world of soul gave us Sam and Dave and Joe Tex. Out of the Yardbirds would emerge Led Zeppelin and Jeff Beck. The universe of rock music was expanding fast. In the middle of all this change and enjoying every minute of it was John Zacherle, fast becoming one of New York's most popular disc jockeys.

records and cued them up, you know, and threw the switch to turn them in motion.

RICH: No engineer?

ZACH: The engineer handled the volume. And it was really neat, you could really turn your record back and forth and get it right to the spot where you wanted it to segue and bang, bang, you know, it felt good when you did that. No breaks between the songs, from one artist to another.

And then getting to hear them live down at the Fillmore, which was the best of all possible worlds because it was never the same when they ended up in the big arenas. It was terrific and it was exciting, but it was three times as loud [*laughs*]. To hear them in a place at least that small and maybe smaller, occasionally. There was a theater across from the Fillmore which seemed maybe half the size, I'm not sure, called the Anderson. To hear people and maybe be a little bit closer to them, you know. And then eventually the Bottom Line — they're thinking of closing the Bottom Line, have you been reading about that? The building is owned by New York University, and Stanley, I can't think of Stanley's last name, there were two guys that ran it. [Author's note: Allan Pepper and Stanley Snadowsky.] In the years of the Vietnam War, they both were teaching to avoid being drafted, and after the war ended they opened up the Bottom Line. Anyway, that was a great place too, because they had often fairly big time people playing in there. I guess my first experience was the Bitter End, which is a tiny little place in comparison. Did you ever go there?

RICH: No, I never did go to the Bitter End. I used to go to the Fillmore a lot.

ZACH: The Bitter End is a very small place, and it started out as a folk place, very small stage, and when you go in there they have all these posters of Bob Dylan and everybody who used to be there. I think I first went there when I was at WNEW and occasionally introduced groups. I remember introducing Joni Mitchell. They had a buffet, and then she got up and did her songs. First time she'd been in New York. And some other people that I can't remember, the same thing. We were there for WNEW because the record companies knew we were possibly a sure thing to play something if it was good from a new artist. That was great to get invited to these grand openings, so to speak, of somebody's career.

RICH: And WNEW-FM was at the center of it all?

ZACH: All those good things happened at WNEW because they had competition, WCBS-FM was trying the same thing, WPLJ was also free-form, and some college stations too. WNEW-FM really was a pioneer in getting music out and having a good team, you know, with the music and we had the deejay thing and the uniqueness of handling our own records. That goes back to the days when WNEW-AM was a powerhouse playing big band music — Frank Sinatra and so on. When WNEW-FM was founded, the manager of the station made the decision that the studios would be built so that the announcers still had that hands-on experience. And there were still union rules that required an engineer, but they felt that the disc jockey should have some physical contact with the records, so to keep the turntables in the studio next to the announcer and not in the control room next to the engineer. And it really made a difference, it really did. You would clean your records, you know, and make sure there was no dust on them and put them down and be careful where you set the needle, and had your earphones on and you could cue it up just right, you know? It was kind of exciting.

RICH: Tell me about meeting Ringo Starr.

ZACH: Oh yeah, that was at WPLJ, and it was an odd thing, they had a studio that didn't have a wall, a glass window, between the announcer and the engineer. So I would pick a record and hand it over to him across the console and he would stick it on the table and fire it up. And then to the left was another window into a larger studio. At the far end it had its own control room too. But it was a larger room than ours and I remember it hardly ever being used, but one day suddenly there's Ringo Starr lookin' in. He had been around the corner on the same floor. The WABC guys had had him on as a guest, so somebody brought him around so he could be on FM, you know? So I got excited and we both made motions like "come around," and that's when I found out that he knew all the words to "Dinner with Drac" [*laughs*].

RICH: Did the rest of the Beatles know the song?

ZACH: I don't know, but he said, "Oh, we'd hear all the records from America." Well, that's true, they did that, that's all they did was listen to American music. I don't remember if he said "we" listened or anything, but he said, "I remember that one, sure."

RICH: You know where they probably heard it? Pirate radio stations.

(Photo courtesy John Zacherle.)

ZACH: Ah, yeah, because it was banned in England and I don't know if they heard it or just got a copy of the record or how they operated there. What information they had about what the hit records were — maybe it was magazines in England to let them know what the hit records were in the United States. And maybe the guys who ran the record stores, maybe they were shipping stuff over. In those days I guess they were, because there was a market for music from America.

RICH: They were probably as hungry for American music as the Russians were for the Beatles. Do you remember anything else you spoke with Ringo about?

ZACH: No, I don't remember any more, just small talk, he was on some kind of a tour. He was visiting ABC, which was in its final days of glory as a big-time, number one station. It was just a few years after that that they turned it upside down, you know.

RICH: How about meeting Frank Zappa?

ZACH: Yes, he was really a friendly cat. Zappa's music was very hard to "choreograph" sort of into the rock'n'roll that I felt we were featuring on FM, at WNEW-FM, anyway. It was a little far out there.

RICH: But you met him at a party, didn't you?

ZACH: Yes, sure, I did. And also I introduced him at the Capitol Theatre in Passaic. We had more of a big long talk there, and I was surprised, I think I expressed my surprise to see that he used — his musicians used written scores. I've always admired rock'n'rollers that they can do a concert and have no music in front of them. It's all from memory. But he put up music stands and he had scores for each instrument. Whether it's because at that time he didn't have a band that he held together or he changed musicians or whatever. But I thought, "Jeez, all these guys have to know how to read music [*laughs*]." You sometimes think that maybe there may be a few guitar players who don't know how to read music today, they do it all by ear. He was great, and ... we spent some time, that's the most time I ever spent with him, actually, in his dressing room. They were practicing and coming over to each guy and pointing to the music, some spot in the music where he didn't think the guy got the right idea, you know?

RICH: Did you get to know any other rock stars?

ZACH: I never really hung out with any of them. And I'm not sure that any other people did either. Pete Fornatale may have done more than anybody because I think he had more guests on the air. I never had many guests late at night on the show at WNEW, and I just don't remember, there may have been some when I was at WPLJ. But it wasn't a regular thing. It was all a deal with the record promoters. They would have to get permission from the program manager at the station. I don't really think they pursued that very well, 'cause I never really had people dropping in at all. Or one a week even, which I think probably was a mistake, they should have done more of that. At WPLJ at least.

RICH: Did you say you knew May Pang?

ZACH: I met her through a girl who worked at the Record Plant, and somehow I found myself up in Allen Klein's office and May Pang was working there. And I think that's how I first met her, I maybe met her in a recording studio, I forget which. Always nice, she was really a very pleasant person. But everybody accuses her of screwing everybody and things like that. Well, she became friendly with John, right?

RICH: Lennon?

ZACH: Yeah.

RICH: She wound up going out to L.A. with him in 1973 on that famous "lost weekend."

ZACH: You know, I think she stayed with him a long time, I'm not sure.

RICH: Oh, but you didn't know her back in the '60s? Because I found a letter from her that she had sent to you, I think in 1969.

ZACH: Well, maybe, maybe, I don't know that she met me when I was doing the horror stuff. *Disc-O-Teen* was my first experience working with music.

Zach stayed at WNEW-FM until February 1971. From there he found a home at WPLJ, the FM side of WABC Radio. He was never as happy there as at his former radio station due to the more stringent policies. The freedom, similar to college radio stations, to create his own playlists at WNEW was a hard act to follow.

Deejaying – the work Zach enjoyed the most!

I decided to call Zach toward the end of his stay at WNEW, and found, to my delight, that he remembered me. After he asked if I still lived in New Jersey, I told him of my luck in finding a job in television, how I'd always hoped to find one at Channel 47, and, ironically, how fortunate it was that I hadn't. He told me that he had been offered a job on WNEW's TV station, Channel 5, hosting *Creature Features*, which at that time was showing the classic Universal horrors that had launched Zach's TV career. He said that he would do it on one condition: if he could also keep his radio job. The station said, "No way," and so did Zach. He had found his new love, radio, and the music that he played was something he just couldn't give up. We spoke for a few more minutes and said our goodbyes, and I wouldn't see or speak to him again until an evening in 1982.

RICH: There's a CD that exists where you introduce the Grateful Dead at the Fillmore East. I understand that Bill Graham, the owner, was there.

ZACH: I was going to come down the aisle in a casket carried by the ushers. They had firemen and policemen in the auditorium so no one would smoke any dope and cause any problems. But either the firemen or policemen decided that if a casket was carried down the aisle, that the people would get so excited that they might start a [*laughs*], an uproar or something. So they said, "You can't come down the aisle with a casket." So they carried me out quietly in the box and set me down in the semi-darkness next to the center stage. But on the CD you can hear Phil Lesh, I think it is, you can hear him talkin', "Well, it looks like we got Halloween here." He could see who it was in the casket. Some of the band members could have been from New York and might have seen me on television as they grew up, but the Grateful Dead people, most of them were from out west, raised out there. So it ended up that I was not carried down, but I was in the casket. It was kind of exciting, I was up there on the stage and they're all there tuning their instruments a little bit. I don't think it was totally dark, it may have been as dark as it can be and not fall over the stage. I think I must have been standing up next to the microphone when somebody said, "Let's have a light on the announcer, please!" And I made a comment, "I was supposed to come down here blah, blah, but the policemen thought there'd be a riot, so here I am, here." Then I started scratching myself, and I said, "I got this itch over at Channel 47. Crabs, got the crabs," or something, I made some comment about crabs, I was scratching myself. I didn't make too many comments, I always regret — there's another case where I really don't like to listen to it because I forgot something really important. It was an amazing evening, it was the "Love" group and the Allman Brothers, and then the Grateful Dead in one evening. Holy Moses, I mean, really. And they were waiting all night, you know, to hear the Dead, but they'd already heard so much wonderful stuff from two great groups. I wish I had made mention of that. Maybe Bill Graham or somebody in between when they introduced the groups, said something about what a wonderful night it had been — I wish I had said it. I do remember saying "It's Sunday morning, and on this glorious Sunday morning — The Grateful Goddamn Dead!" That's when the lights went on. But I really wish I'd have made some comment about how many great evenings we'd had there at the Fillmore. It was not the end of the Fillmore, it wasn't that. It's just that it was such a great place.

RICH: So Bill Graham was there that night?

ZACH: He was always there, yeah.

RICH: I thought he stayed at the Fillmore West.

ZACH: He split his time between them, yeah. He was a tough guy. I heard him a couple of times, I can't remember the guy who was in charge there. Very nice guy, very quiet. I was sitting talking to him one time one night in the office about something that was happening or was going to happen in the future, and all of a sudden I heard Bill Graham on the phone to somebody, and he just — oh, boy. He was a tough bargainer, and he was mad, he came out and he says, "God damn guys! I put 'em on here first!" What he would do, he says, "Okay, I'll give you a shot, but you've gotta come back one more time at the same price." Something like that. And they would try to break out of that. "No, God damn it, I gave you your shot and you've done good now, and you owe me one!"

Graham knew what he was doing, you know. He not only made money but he made a wonderful place for everybody.

RICH: He's dead, isn't he?

ZACH: Yeah. Helicopter ran into a high-tension wire in California.

Throughout the 1970s and early '80s, I would hear John Zacherle's voice on FM radio from time to time. In my opinion, the '70s was a strange decade. The creative forces that were inherent to the '60s seemed to have stalled; the people and the styles looked somewhat like the previous decade's, but something was missing. It was as if this era didn't know where to go. Hair was longer, worn that way by almost everybody, including me. The nonconformist behavior which sprang forth naturally, if a bit naively, during 1967's "Summer of Love," was now embraced by middle-aged corporation executives and hippie wannabes. Recreational drugs, once looked upon by the straight populace as the beginning of the end of civilization, were everywhere. If you were around people who earned above-average salaries, there was a good chance there would be some cocaine nearby. Coke and pot were no longer limited to the back rooms of recording studios and the parties of rock stars; it had become part of Corporate America.

My job had moved me into New York City in November 1969. Having worked contentedly at the Jersey Film Exchange for less than two years, I was reluctant to have to commute to the city with its subways and noise, but I realized that to turn down a position in the Big Apple, where the real action was, would be professional suicide. A union member and making good money, I became a second assistant film editor in NBC's network film center, and worked my way up to first assistant, a title I held until April 1980. At that point, the use of film had gone the way of the dodo as far as broadcasting shows and commercials, and many of my fellow film editors had gone over the wall to the videotape department. But I stayed to the bitter end, and one day I found myself staring at the proverbial pink slip. Being inherently lucky all my life, it wasn't long before I landed a vacation relief job followed by a permanent one in the videotape department. I was not heartbroken to leave my film "career" behind; it wasn't too exciting. Aside from being lent out to the local department to assist on a few 16mm documentaries, it had consisted mainly of splicing commercials into network protection prints for air.

Working in the edit room of the NBC Film Center one day, I was listening to WABC-AM's talk station when host Malachy McCourt announced Zach as his guest for the afternoon. John Zacherle was working at WPLJ-FM at the time, and took questions from callers. For the first time in my life, I got up my nerve and called in, lucky enough to talk to Zach for a few minutes. I asked him if there was any truth to the rumor that disc jockey Pete Fornatale had visited *Disc-O-Teen* once upon a time. The answer was yes and he had even danced on the show!

By the summer of 1982, I had been working full time for over a year in the videotape department. WNBC-TV had just purchased the rights to air the old Gothic soap opera *Dark Shadows*, which they planned to run weekday mornings at 3:30 a.m. To kick off the series, a big launch party was given on June 10 at the Magique Disco on Manhattan's East Side, home of innumerable late-night glitter clubs. I had heard that, in addition to an appearance by Jonathan Frid, who had played the part of vampire Barnabas Collins on the show, there would also be present another celebrity: Zacherley. I was going with a bunch of friends anyway, but I was anxious to meet up with Zach again.

The atmosphere at Magique was cordial and fun, the drinks flowed freely, and those who were into it danced to recorded disco music. The

57-year-old Frid made the rounds with a cane, due to a possible health issue; no one ever found out for sure. Not long after meeting Frid, I spotted the welcome and familiar form of Zach, in full makeup, making his way toward us. I held out my hand, introduced myself, and immediately tried to jump-start his memory by telling him I had been a regular visitor at *Disc-O-Teen* 16 years before. Disappointment set in almost immediately: He had no memory of me. He chatted amiably with our group and started to move on, obviously wanting to make the rounds of the entire room, when he stopped and turned back toward me. "Were you the one with the camera who was always taking pictures?" he asked. "Yes!" I shot back, so pleased that he had remembered. We spoke a bit about Jonathan Frid, and I said something dumb like, "I think more people here are interested in seeing you," at which point he cut me off, not wanting to garner more of the attention than Frid. (I would find out years later that this was very typical of him; I've never met anyone more humble about his own career.)

Seconds later, someone in charge of the entertainment interrupted and led Zach away to have pictures taken with Frid. That was the extent of my meeting with John Zacherle that evening, and would be the last time I would speak to him until the waning months of 1990. I wondered how he had been getting along, knowing he had been absent from WPLJ for a couple of years. But what bothered me more was the scant mention he had gotten later in the WNBC leaflet "News from Channel 4," which had made the rounds at work. Instead of preceding his name with something like "legendary TV horror host," it simply read "another famous ghostly guest named Zacherly [sic]." Were we really that far removed from Zach's glory days? "Famous ghostly guest," indeed. It was depressing.

Chapter 14
Timelines Cross: *The Disc-O-Teen Reunion*

RICH: When Kevin Clement started up his Chiller Theatre expo, a lot of the *Disc-O-Teen* people converged at the first one to see you again and talk about the reunion. Did you enjoy the reunion?

ZACH: Oh, it really was great, that was amazing. I just really had not been in touch with anybody and now they were all there! Twenty-five years after *Disc-O-Teen*!

Horror and sci-fi conventions were nothing new in the fall of 1990, but Kevin Clement, a burly, friendly-faced man with a passing resemblance to the Grateful Dead's Jerry Garcia, had attended several of them and decided that he could do it better. He did. Opening his first convention in the Halloween season of 1990 at Fairleigh Dickinson's Rothman Center in Rutherford, New Jersey, he packed the house by having Zacherley as his first special guest, along with Jonathan Harris of the '60s TV show *Lost in Space* and actress Dyanne (*Ilsa: She Wolf of the SS*) Thorne. But there was a special dimension added to this affair: a group of former dancers and attendees from the old days at *Disc-O-Teen* were converging on the Horrorthon for a sort of "pre-reunion" gathering. Among the alumni were Christine Domaniecki,

Zach and Pach at the first Chiller convention – an emotional reunion.

Joelle (Wrubel) Martin, Linda "Pach" Pace, Mike Thomas and myself. To "prime the pump," I had already sent Zach a video of the 8mm movies I shot in the Newark studios of Channel 47 some 24 years previous, and he called me back ecstatic about them. "I'm going to watch them again and again," he sang into my phone machine after he had seen it for the first time, and I could tell he was genuinely excited about seeing all the old faces in the films and about the reunion to come. It was my first contact with him since that evening at the disco Magique back in 1982.

John Zacherle, slightly grayer, but looking much younger than his 73 years, was in costume and makeup and ensconced at a table in a corner of a hallway of the Rothman Center busily and happily meeting his old fans, who made up a line that showed no sign of ending. Suddenly he found himself surrounded by a small group of "Transylvanian Teenagers," as we called ourselves, none of whom he had seen since the end of *Disc-O-Teen*. Zach hastily called a break for himself, closed the table, and hustled us all into a nearby elevator and into a small private room. There we all officially "re-met" and discussed the upcoming "official" reunion which was scheduled to take place in four months.

To begin at the beginning: Through the years, my older brother Steve had mentioned on several occasions what a good idea it would be to have a *Disc-O-Teen* reunion. I had never gotten the show completely out of my head and often the mood would hit me to take my dusty photo albums out of the closet, thumb through the drying-out pages and remember. I had inherited from my father the habit of "archiving," and had, in six albums, every shot I had taken on the floor of the show, complete with names, dates and what was going on during those moments in the show. I also had thought of a reunion but never had the organizational skills, or, truth be told, the drive to try and organize one myself. Then one day in the summer of 1990 I got a phone call from my old dance partner from the 1966 Halloween show: Sharon Lawson (formerly Kiselyk), one of the few people from *Disc-O-Teen* with whom I had kept in touch, and she told me that Christine Domaniecki and Joette Martin were working on precisely that. Sharon had Christine's phone number and I called her immediately. She called me back a couple days later and set up a meeting at Joette's apartment in Nutley, New Jersey.

My emotions during the drive to Joette's apartment were, to say the least, vibrant. I had always had an appreciation of the past, but *Disc-O-Teen* held an importance for me unmatched by almost anything else. It had been my first exposure to a television studio, my first experience being smitten by a girl, and the show had provided a turning point in my life. And in the middle of it all, in effect helping to orchestrate it, was my hero — Zacherley.

The meeting at Joette's was charged with nostalgia. Upon seeing these two women for the first time in over 20 years, I couldn't believe how little they had changed. Pleasantries were exchanged, and Christine, Joette and her husband Tony, sat me down to watch, to my amazement, a video of the last episode from November 1967. I had no idea that there was anything left of *Disc-O-Teen*, being that the usual practice at Channel 47 was to immediately erase the two-inch tapes following the Saturday afternoon broadcast. It turned out that two episodes had survived, thanks to the foresight of Joe LoRé, who "liberated" them when the show ended and kept them at his video facility in Peachtree County, Georgia, through the years. Suddenly there on the screen was the familiar and beloved studio — the cheesecloth "spider webs," the riser boxes painted to look like stone pedestals, Zach's home-base "cave" set in the corner, and the kids — those young faces. Years melted away as we watched the old dance steps and listened to the familiar music. I was awash with nostalgia; I had not attended this final show, but recognized about a dozen faces, among them Christine, Joette, Linda Pace, Sue Mercedante and Michael Thomas in Dracula makeup. Coincidentally, I had audiotaped the show in 1967 as a memento, knowing that it was the last, but I never dreamed I'd see the show again on video.

CHRISTINE DOMANIECKI: We were talking about having a reunion and Tony's the one that got on the phone and called Zach. If Zach didn't give us Joe LoRé's number, he found Joe somehow, and up until, I don't know how many months before the reunion, everybody was calling and we were going down Memory Lane. Everybody had their thoughts and memories about *Disc-O-Teen*.

At first Christine, who was to play the role of detective in locating many of the people involved in the show — either staff, dancers or members of bands — felt that Zach should be offered whatever pay rate he charged to perform, but it turned out that the man wouldn't hear of it; he was as much a part of this affair as anyone else, and didn't want to feel like he was anything special. As he later said on the reunion video, "You couldn't keep me away from this!" So Zach was set, and the major task was to locate everyone else and decide on a place. That place became "The Hop" in Totowa, New Jersey, a dance club with a '50s deco and theme — actually a decade early in spirit for Disc-O-Teen, but a serviceable place with plenty of room. My contribution was to compile a list of most of the hit tunes played on the show, a job I could have done in my sleep. I also made a few phone calls, one of them to the long-lost Donna, whom I thought would enjoy attending and would have, as I had, forgotten the negative spirit of our last correspondence. Either I was mistaken about her or she simply had no interest, because after locating her mother, and emphasizing that this would be a once-in-a-lifetime affair that Donna would enjoy, we never heard back from her. It's possible that she was embarrassed about the off-putting circumstances behind our last contact. Maybe it should have fallen on someone else to track her down.

I can't remember the precise date, but it was sometime shortly after my reacquaintance with Christine and Joette that the former called me up all excited that she had tracked down another former "Transylvanian Teenager" — an important one. There was double reason for excitement: (1) Mike Thomas, the kid who had performed those extraordinary makeups on the show, had been located, and (2) he was currently working as a makeup artist for Saturday Night Live at NBC Studios in New York. He had been there in a freelance position since practically the inception of the show, working in the same building with me for 14 years, and never had our paths crossed! What made it more incredible was that since videotape had taken a major bite out of the film department's workload, I had had so much spare time that I was often hanging around Studio 8H watching Chevy Chase, John Belushi, Garrett Morris, Dan Aykroyd, Gilda Radner, Bill Murray and others rehearse. Had I run into Mike, I probably wouldn't have recognized him anyway.

I approached the door to SNL's makeup room on that October day with nervous excitement as I prepared for another journey into my past, about to meet another member of the long-lost Disc-O-Teen family. Would he remember me? Would I be shocked at how he looked? I knocked on the door. An attractive young lady opened it, and immediately I spotted a guy with a graying beard joking around in the back of the room, whom I was pretty sure was the man. Upon looking closer, all doubt was removed. Glued firmly on both sides of his neck were perfect reproductions of the Frankenstein Monster's electrodes, a nod to the Halloween show that was to be aired that week. Twenty-five years melted away on the spot. I walked over, introduced myself, and instantly produced one of my photo albums. I opened it to a Polaroid shot of a 17-year-old Michael made up as Bela Lugosi's Dracula with the incomplete caption, "Mike ___, monster authority and modern-day Lon Chaney, in another of his makeups for the 'Reptile Ball.'" I shook his hand and said, "Finally! What the hell is your last name?" He told me "Thomas," and I was finally able to fill in the blank. As if the coincidence of working so near each other wasn't enough, I also found out that he had been living in an apartment in Bergenfield for the previous 17 years! It seemed we were destined to meet again.

JOETTE MARTIN: Oh, dear, tons of work. I think we found "Big" Sue, "Little" Sue and Pach through Paul Russak. He posted some of the fliers, we made fliers, we put something in the paper, and WCBS-FM very nicely announced it. They mentioned it twice, and we got a lot of people through that. While we were digging people up,

Paul posted fliers down the shore somewhere and one of the Sues saw it. And Chris got in touch with Joe LoRé and he contacted all the technical people that showed up. It was a huge amount of work; it was like a wedding.

Preparations for the big night were proceeding smoothly, although it was relentless labor for Christine, Joette and Tony, tracking down name after name, crossing off the ones who were beyond locating, and tending to the publicity surrounding the event. At the top of the list was Barry Landers, whom we had given up trying to find for a very good reason: We had been told he was dead! The story went around that he had been working for the New York Yankees under George Steinbrenner, suffered a heart attack or series of heart attacks, and passed away some years ago. In a phone conversation, Zach himself explained what he thought had occurred:

> Well, he worked for Steinbrenner for awhile. He was happy as could be, because his father was a semi-pro pitcher or something. He got a job with Steinbrenner, and he was the guy that started Bat Day and Hat Day and all that stuff. He had me up there one time and took me up to meet Phil Rizzuto, and Phil was funny, he says, "Oh, me and my boys used to watch you all the time." Anyway, there was obviously a lot of pressure there, and I said, "Do you have to stay for the—" "Oh, yeah!" Barry says, "the night game, you're expected to be here at nine o'clock in the morning, and if there's a night game you stay until the last inning, and you're here the next day and nobody in the office goes home." He didn't say much about Steinbrenner, but he said there was a lot of pressure, you know, and later on, I don't know how many months later or how long he was there, he mentioned that two guys had had a heart attack and he had had one, and he left there and he was up in Middletown on the radio, and his doctor said he had to get away from that pressure in that office. So he was up there for a while and he died, he had a heart attack and died, as far as I know.

CHRISTINE DOMANIECKI: Finally one of the Doughboys, Myke Scavone, called and said that Barry Landers was not dead! He gave me Barry's number out in Scottsdale, Arizona. We got in touch with him and the rest is history.

The months following had the makings of some kind of bizarre soap opera. I was at work one afternoon when I got an urgent call from Christine, who gave me the most amazing news: the reports of Barry's death had been greatly exaggerated. She had spoken to him on the phone and gotten his address, which I copied down. I was eager to speak to him again. He might not be able to attend the reunion, but at least he knew it was happening and would eventually receive a videotaped record of the event.

On Wednesday, January 16, 1991, Zach and Christine appeared on a popular kids' show out of Newark, *The Uncle Floyd Show*, to promote the reunion. They were on for the entire half hour, exchanged playful banter with host Floyd Vivino, and even showed some clips from my 8mm movies taken in the *Disc-O-Teen* studio. How many people the show reached with the news we never knew, but we hoped that there would be *some* folks from the old days watching. Two days later, I found myself on the phone with Barry Landers, indeed alive and well — and he even remembered me! He recalled the Halloween show of 1965 and my Frankenstein costume, regretted that he couldn't make it east for the party, but offered to send a video of himself to play on the big night. He also said that he had a radio show out there and asked if I'd be interested in being interviewed over the phone for it. (Neither the interview nor the videotape materialized.)

In 2004, I discovered on the Internet a website run by Joe LoRé dedicated to WNJU, Channel

47. Down in the lower left-hand corner of the home page was a small list titled "In Memory Of," and at the bottom was the name Barry Landers. It looked as though this time it was for real. Not too many people get to die twice!

MIKE THOMAS: One time in 1966 or '67, Greg Rondinoni and I had gone to Newark and it was a four-day weekend and we both begged for as much money from our respective mothers as we could possibly get, which was like just a couple of bucks. We wound up paying for a room at one of the hotels in Newark, very inexpensive, but there went our food budget. So the following day we were in a Woolworth's real near to the Mosque Theater, and all of a sudden Zach comes walking in. We asked what he was doing and he said, "Well, I'm buying some candy for the guys in the control room. The candy machine doesn't have the kind of stuff that they like." He was always doing stuff like that for everybody. And he walked over to Greg and I don't know how he knew that we were starving to death, but he looked at Greg and said, "You look a little skinny, there!" and like, real quick, tucked like three dollars into Greg's shirt pocket. Then when we turned to protest, he was gone, he like disappeared! Years later, when we were doing the publicity for the *Disc-O-Teen* reunion and Christine and Zach had appeared on *The Uncle Floyd Show*, we went downstairs to the diner, and I finally had enough money to be able to reach across the table and tuck three bucks into his shirt pocket.

Here I am, greeting the guest of honor at the reunion.

The big day finally arrived, the culmination of Christine and Joette's hard work. Everyone felt the electricity and excitement as almost 100 partiers converged on Totowa's "The Hop" on Sunday, February 3, 1991. I arrived early, wearing a 1966-type outfit which included a black shirt with huge white spots (prompting Zach to dub me "Dr. Spot"), black corduroy pants and black walking shoes which Christine had helped me pick out. We had been lucky enough to have been offered the talents of two NBC engineers, Robert "Ratso" Rizzo and Bill Kanakaris, fans of Zach from the old days, who brought along state-of-the-art camera equipment and documented the evening for free. All they required were passes, their dinner, drinks and the chance to see Zach in person and they were thrilled to do the job. Being sort of "in charge" of the videotaping, I was supposed to meet them in front of the building at 4:30 p.m., but after waiting 15 minutes, they were nowhere to be seen. "Damn, they're lost!" I muttered to myself. I quickly forgot about them for the moment as I saw the familiar figure of Zach standing in the parking lot wearing a blue sports jacket, blue shirt and psychedelic tie which he later told us he bought at the Cheetah in the '60s. We spoke for a few minutes and he told me how much he was enjoying the tape of my movies from the show — he had just watched it again to jog his memory. All was well; my camera crew might be lost, but the guest of honor had arrived.

I next spotted a woman with red hair busily unloading what looked like huge paintings from the trunk of her car and went over to see if I could help. As the "paintings" were revealed, I recognized them immediately. One or two of them had hung in Zach's Channel 47 office, but there were a few that I had never seen before — all colorful renderings of the Cool Ghoul and imagined wife and offspring in various settings, and a beautiful wreathed portrait of the "family," obviously created for the Christmas holidays many years ago. In a moment I found myself looking once more into the radiant face of Rosemary Schroeder, aka Tafaro, aka DiPietra, *Disc-O-Teen*'s official house artist, whose creations went back to Zacherley's first *Shock Theater* days. It took me a moment to recognize her (she had long black hair in the '60s, and a face reminiscent of Los Angeles TV personality Vampira) but as soon as she spoke, I remembered her voice and warm, gracious manner that made me feel so comfortable at the show during my initial days there. Her paintings were to be added to a huge display inside the hall that included a collage of the best of my Polaroids, an old Doughboys poster, photos from various Disc-O-Teeners and a Peter Max–style mini-mural rendered in the finest psychedelic tradition. While looking new, it was obviously a genuine artifact of the past.

I decided I'd better head inside and check the scene out. There, all calm and unruffled, were camera crew Bob and Bill, all set up and ready to go. I told them I was afraid they had gone astray and were still searching for the place. They laughed and told me that they weren't about to take any chances and had come out an hour before I did.

I should have known better; these two guys were reliable and consummate professionals. "We really should have someone at the door interviewing the people as they come in," whispered Bob, and thinking that was a great idea, I volunteered for the job. In they came, one after another, and I stopped each one of them and asked them to tell their stories about how they discovered the show, how often they danced there and what the show meant to them. It helped flesh out what could have been a largely muddled and confused record of the evening's festivities. The only problem was, I had to miss a lot of conversation, a portion of the party and even my dinner to man the door.

The arrivals gradually thinned out, and it was time to enjoy what we had all looked forward to since the previous summer. After about an hour spent in his civvies, Zach changed into uniform, combed his hair down the middle and, *sans* makeup, strolled the ballroom looking once again like *Disc-O-Teen*'s maestro. The deejay, who called himself Sal Boy, had been instructed to play tunes from a list that we had compiled; he turned out to be next to useless, as he all but ignored the list and used music that he thought was appropriate. The problem was that most of his selections were released years after the demise of the show. While they might have been good to dance to, they added nothing to the evocative mood we were after.

Joe LoRé helped to remedy that by showing a special 20-minute video that he had put together especially for Zach using portions of the last two shows and a bunch of my Polaroids that I had still-framed onto tape for him. As Zach watched in a clear wash of emotion, everybody once more saw themselves in black-and-white dancing on the floor of Channel 47's Studio "A." Joe had done what Sal Boy was unwilling to do, added the appropriate music to the audio track: "Let's Spend the Night Together" by the Rolling Stones, "Gimme Some Lovin'" by the Spencer Davis Group and "You Got What it Takes" by the Dave Clark Five were three very representative songs heard countless times during *Disc-O-Teen*'s halcyon days.

(Photo courtesy John Zacherle.)

The remainder of the evening was pretty much filled up with dancing, eating, drinking and, of course, reminiscing. A fleeting feeling of disappointment pecked at the back of my brain when I thought of what Donna was missing, but I realized that the regret was more than likely for myself, and it soon passed. I danced with Christine and former regular Diane Topolewski, Sharon Lawson, Ilene Baranik (my date for the "Sound Blast '66" concert that Zach had given us passes to) and anyone else who would share the space. Then it was time for the Big Moment. As you remember, on the last show, Zach had performed a duet with Linda Pace by lip-synching to Sonny and Cher's 1965 mega-hit "I Got You, Babe." At the midpoint of the party, Linda was called upon to present Zach with a gift from all of his TV family, and without warning the strains of "I Got You, Babe"' burst forth from the speakers. I handed Zach a cheap wig I had brought, he put it on and they performed the bit one last time. Not only did this moment bring down the house and move some people to tears, but weeks later as I was assembling the best of the video taken by my NBC colleagues Bob Rizzo and Paul Scrabo, I realized that I had available to me, compliments of Joe Loré, the actual footage of the Sonny and Cher bit from the last *Disc-O-Teen* show! Not only was the footage usable, but luck had it that Zach and Linda from 25 years ago were standing in the same positions as they were at the reunion, making it possible for me to dissolve from 1991 to 1967 during their performance. To this day, it's impossible for me to watch it without a tug of emotion.

Even after the reunion, the past refused to remain in the past. On March 18, Christine called to tell me that she had gotten a call from a fellow named Steve Friedland, better known as Brute Force, the quirky singer who had been a part of the last *Disc-O-Teen* show. The next night I got a call from Mr. Force, who announced that he was coming into New York and would be stopping by the NBC studios. His reason for coming was to get a copy of the last show, which he was amazed still existed. I told him I was working on the midnight shift and that his visit would have to be in the middle of the night, which didn't deter him. In the wee hours of March 20, 1991, I was face to face with a very recognizable Brute Force, now obviously in his mid- to late forties. He seemed like a nice guy, and I ran for him the segments of the show in which he had appeared and made him a dub which he greatly appreciated. He then proudly announced that his 1967 single, the notorious and wonderfully forgettable "To Sit on a Sandwich," was about to be included on a CD compilation of various novelty tunes entitled "Crazy Rock." It was amusing to hear him say that he was very pleased the song would end up on any album which would feature the word "rock" in the title. He left shortly after I made him the dub, and I never recall seeing "Crazy Rock" in any record store's "rock collections" bin. But there's a good reason for that: I never looked.

It wasn't until Thursday, April 25, that I was able to present Zach with a final edited copy of the reunion. Christine, Mike Thomas, Joette, Tony and I met him for dinner at the Mt. Fuji Restaurant, high in the Ramapo Mountains in Hillburn, New York, for the official presentation of the tape. The next day I got a call with Zach's rave review and a request for a dozen copies for him to disperse among his friends. I couldn't have been happier to have pleased him so much. The 12 copies were hand-delivered to him by me on Sunday, May 12, at Kevin Clement's second Horrorthon (not yet known by the more familiar name of Chiller Theatre), still at the Rothman Center in Rutherford. Mike Thomas went with me and we attended Zach's first of many "lectures," during which he unspooled a 16mm kinescope of the intermissions from an old WABC *Zacherley at Large* show. I had no idea he had anything on film from that far back, but my memory of the show was still clear, having seen it in my darkened living room in the spring of 1959. In it, he performed, with the aid of cohort Gasport, a dig to reach the center of the earth. It would not be the last time I'd see this particular kinescope, and in a way it and two others in his collection would pave the way for something I never foresaw in my life, but I would certainly welcome and cherish: my friendship with John Zacherle.

In addition to the 8mm films, I had transferred to video 100 or so of the best Polaroid shots I had taken at Channel 47. They were originally meant for Joe LoRé, for use in the special presentation he had given at the reunion. I had already made a better copy of the 8mm stuff to send to Zach, and for good measure threw on the Polaroids at the end of the tape. Zach had never seen them before, and was deeply moved by it all.

I'd always hoped my hanging around the Channel 47 studios and snapping pictures (basically done to make me feel I was doing something, *anything* there, to justify my presence) would serve some purpose. After all these years, I knew it had.

As the months wore on, I began to receive phone calls from Zach semi-regularly. This surprised me, but I realized that I was no longer a teenaged fan (although I often still felt that way). I was in my mid-forties and Zach, now in his early seventies, had probably lost some friends to old age. He was retired, living in an apartment in New York City, and probably had ample time on his hands. I made a point of keeping in touch, but was careful not to overdo my phone calls to him, afraid I'd quickly wear out my welcome. What happened through the years was precisely the opposite, and I began to hear from Zach on a regular basis. He also, I should add, kept in touch with Mike and Christine, now officially a couple, Joette and Tony, and others from the *Disc-O-Teen* family. In one of our conversations, we spoke about the kinescopes he had from Channel 7 in New York and I asked, "When am I ever going to see the rest of them?," thinking of a screening at one of the Chiller conventions, nothing more. After a beat, he asked what I was doing the following week. "My God," I thought. "He's inviting me to come over!"

West 96th Street in Manhattan is easy to get to from Bergenfield, New Jersey. Over the George Washington Bridge, a quick run down the West Side Highway to the 96th Street exit and you're practically there. Zach's street is a wide, two-way affair, the only problem being, as in most of New York, finding a parking space. The apartment building was easy to spot, the carved wooden front door ironically appropriate-looking for a celebrated ghoul. I rang the bell. A few seconds later, that familiar voice, filtered through the electronics of the P.A. system, announced, "I-I-T's SHOWTIME!" The door buzzed open and I walked through a small entry hall, through a second massive door, and found myself in a dimly lit, echo-filled hallway with a single elevator, the type you see in almost all older New York City buildings. I entered and pushed 4. On the 4th floor the door slid open with a metallic "clang," I found the apartment and knocked.

The door opened and Zach, dressed in faded blue jeans and blue shirt, smiled that famous smile and invited me in. My first impulse as I entered the foyer above his sunken living room, was to look around for memorabilia he might have displayed to celebrate his career. Surprisingly, there was not much. One Zacherley photo taken during his year at Channel 11 was framed and hanging in a corner, but more prominent were the large oil portraits of various Zacherle ancestors adorning the far wall of the living room. Propped in a corner of the foyer to the left of the door was an artifact I recognized immediately, part of his set from Channel 11 and *Disc-O-Teen*. There it was, looking none the worse for wear, the old Gothic chair we all knew and loved. Zach told me he wasn't sure, but he thought it had come from the Shriners' Hall at the Mosque Theater, and that the only way he could imagine he had gotten it was by stealing it. Over the years he seemed to have developed a slight case of guilt at the thought that he might have actually pinched the chair from the Shriners!

I was then led down the two steps into the living room, and invited to sit in an easy chair to the right. The TV set was at the south side of the room, at its base a pile of videotapes and a VCR. Zach eased into another chair to the left of the set, picked up the remote and started the show. I savored the miracle of it; here I was, the consummate Zacherley fan, who as a kid had spent countless hours watching this man on my parents' black-and-white television, about to enjoy a private viewing of four rare kinescopes in his presence and in his home!

The tape rolled. Through the haze of time I first saw Zach as Roland, introducing 1931's *Dracula* and attempting to create a "Dracula Fizz" between acts; in the second segment, a voice screamed, "Give me some light!," bold, craggy letters spelled out SHOCK THEATER, and Zacherley performed his opera *Il Draculare*; after that, a new show title appears: *Zacherley at Large*, with Zach's famous center of the Earth "dig"; and finally, the last WABC New York show in which a white-coated man leads Zach away, out of the crypt, to join the other patients at Bellevue Hospital. Once in a while I'd sneak a peek over my shoulder at Zach, watching himself in amusement and cracking up at the pseudo-Italian titles producer Ellis Sard devised for *Il Draculare*'s songs. If he caught me looking at him, he'd screw up his face into an expression that seemed to say, "Do you believe all this?" When I would ask him what some ragged prop he was using was, he'd say, "I don't know — but something cheap!" His only other comment was, "God! Look at that makeup!" It seemed he had forgotten how much shadow and highlight he had used in the old days.

The show ended all too soon, and after a bit of conversation I felt I should head out before I ran the risk of making the visit too lengthy. I thanked him and said that it had been a great privilege, turned toward the door and noticed — ah, there were mementos of the old days on display. On a shelf behind the door stood various gifts sent in by fans of long ago, and one in particular caught my eye — a liquid metal rendering of Dracula, the Wolf Man (a pentagram emblazoned on his chest), and the Frankenstein Monster, all with accurate faces and done in painstaking detail. Attached to the base of the statuette was a plaque which read: "Tran-sylvania [sic] Horror Film Award to Zacherley for the Most Horrible Films on TV." Zach told me it was sent in during the Channel 7 days. On my way out the door, one of the last things I noticed were film cans standing up against the wall, and on one of them was a yellow label which read *Zacherley at Large*. Being a 16mm film collector, I thought to myself, "If God loves me, those will end up in my collection some day." And they did.

Chapter 15
The Chair

With Zach, I have discovered through the years, expect the unexpected. One winter day in 1997, the phone rang and it was the man with a question for me: Would I like to have the old Gothic chair he had used on his show? Would I *what*? Would I — could I — was I actually being offered that historic piece of furniture for my very own? I had, in the course of past conversations, described to him the basement of my house, which I had over the years transformed into a comfortable screening room–theater for the enjoyment of 16mm movies. He seemed to feel that the chair would make a nice addition to the setup, and since he needed room in his apartment for some filing cabinets, it was time to find a new home for his television throne. I think my response to his offer was something as original as "Is the Pope Catholic?," and I still couldn't believe that I was the one to be the recipient of one of Zach's most identifiable props. The chair went back at least as far as 1964's *Chiller Theatre* on WPIX, and I remember seeing it prominently displayed in the "cave" corner at *Disc-O-Teen*. After I told him I'd of course love to have it, he added, "Well, okay, then I'll go

Zach in "The Chair" at the author's home in 1997.

ahead and reupholster it." It turned out that the seat of the chair was in a somewhat sunken state, and not only was I getting it, it would be hand-repaired by Zach.

I secured a "Rent-a-Wreck" and we met at the apartment. The chair, having undergone Zach's surgery, was now no longer its original velvet-red color, but a tasteful shade of orange, both the back cushion and the seat. The chair's transport was a rather simple affair. After walking it down the four flights of stairs and wedging it into the truck, it was ready for the journey to its new home. I waved goodbye to Zach and sped off through the snowy streets back to New Jersey. The famous prop now resides in Bergenfield, waiting for the day someone incorporates the Cool Ghoul's legacy into a television museum of some kind, at which time I plan to donate it.

Probably the funniest phone message I ever received from Zach was the one that follows. Remember I had mentioned his feelings of guilt at the thought that he might have "stolen" the chair from the Shriners in Newark? The relief in his voice was palpable as he spoke:

Chiller head man Kevin Clement presents Zach with an award at a show.

> ZACH [*singing*]: R-Rich Scrivani! More history on the chair! I thought I stole it from Channel 47, but not true! I just found a picture of myself on Channel 11, and it's a big story about — "There's No Ghoul Like an Old Ghoul," or something like that, a picture of me standing up holding an amoeba in my arms, and right behind me is the chair. So I did buy it myself, and it probably was [*laughs*] a Baptist church chair. It didn't come from the old Mosque Theater, from *Disc-O-Teen*, because here it is, big as life! My God, that's amazing. I must have bought it in that same place that I bought the chairs for my house here. Kitchen chairs that turned out to be from an old farmer's house that they sold, I think there were 12 chairs at one time, I only bought six of them. They're still here. Dining room chairs they are, actually, but there's the chair! And this precedes *Disc-O-Teen*, it's Channel 11, there it is, I didn't steal it, I feel so much better! [*Long Zach laugh*] I think that's great! But to see it in this picture, oh, I feel like I'm no longer a crook!"

It wasn't long after this that I became the recipient of a few more Zacherley items: During a phone call in which Zach asked me to come over because he had "a gift" for me, I wondered what it could possibly be. Once more I made the trip into New York. Now we all have experienced what we call "mixed emotions" from time to time, but this occasion really redefined the expression for me. I called up on the intercom, and a few minutes later the maple-colored wooden door squeaked open to reveal Zach pushing a hand truck, maneuvering a small but weighty piece of equipment through the door. This I had never expected. Before me on the sidewalk lay one of his most celebrated laboratory devices, the purveyor of countless laughs during my years in front of the tube and hanging out at *Disc-O-Teen*: the Zap Machine. How many windup toy monsters had walked between the arcing Tesla coils of this contraption? Zach had used it countless times to amuse us — it was as essential to his act as — well — Gasport! And now he was giving it away? It was probably the first time in my life I ever felt equally happy (happy that I was to be entrusted with it) and sad (we would never see him use it on TV again!).

I looked up at him to thank him, and the words came to me automatically: "This means that you're never going to do the act again!" Zach's attitude was his customary matter-of-fact and more practical: "No, no, you have the perfect setup for all this stuff." It didn't help to quell the melancholy I felt; Zach was dispensing with the tools of his trade, preparing for the inevitable day when he would be completely done with the character that had made him famous. I assuaged my slight feelings of guilt at relieving him of so indispensable a part of his past by saying that I would be acting as an archivist, only "storing" it for him and keeping it safe, until the day that he would need these props again. It may have been a dream, but it made me feel better.

In the years following the reunion, regular visits to Kevin Clement's Chiller Theatre expos became a pleasant routine, not only to walk through the dealers' rooms and gawk at the amazing array of resin monster models, toys, posters, photos, videotapes and countless other items for sale, but to pay a visit to Zach's table, where, assisted by best friend Jeff Samuels, he was always busy, greeting a long line of fans eager to reminisce about the old TV shows. Chiller was also fast turning into a social event for me, because it was a place I'd always get to spend some time with friends I'd met through our common love of horror and Zach. Mike and Christine would turn up fairly regularly, Mike more often than not in an incredible makeup either as Ygor from *Son of Frankenstein*, Lugosi's Dracula or Karloff's Monster. Christine would alternate in exceptionally sexy makeups and outfits as the popular Elvira or legendary Vampira. For one Chiller, Mike had even convinced me to sit in his makeup chair so he could transform me into Lon Chaney, Jr.'s Dan McCormick, the "electrical man" from the 1941 Universal film *Man Made Monster*. It was all part of the allure of Chiller.

Another friendship had developed, one with Michael and Ruth Gilks. In 1992, Mike and his brother Rich had produced a CD with Zach entitled "Dead Man's Ball," featuring mostly original songs and new versions of a few selections from the "Spook Along with Zacherley" album. The entire project had been produced at Rich's home studio in East Quogue, Long Island; it was quite a creative journey from the night in 1988 when Mike had nervously introduced himself to Zach at the Dowling College show. Following the CD's release, Mike, Ruth and children Rachel and Evan would regularly turn up at Chiller; Mike would bring along his guitar and amp, providing musical backup for Zach as he performed songs from the CD to delighted fans. Mike would also play onstage with Kevin's group the Dead Elvi, a band created to back up Zach when he sang at Chiller's Saturday night parties: Zach would launch into "Monster Mash" and "Dinner with Drac."

Mike and I had started intermittently connecting by phone, and at one point he confided to me that Zach had gotten the feeling that I'd like to invite him to my house, but had never followed through. I took the cue to do just that, inviting Mike Thomas and Christine to make all of us a little more comfortable, and also so that Zach wouldn't have to be staring at just *my* face all evening. I had an ulterior motive too: I wanted to get a picture of Zach sitting in the famous chair, now proudly displayed in my screening room. I wanted proof for any Doubting Thomas that this was indeed the official Zacherley throne.

(Photo courtesy John Zacherle.)

The night came in March 1997. Mike Thomas, a master of the culinary arts, prepared Couquilles St. Jacques (seafood in puffed pastry), and for the first time John Zacherle set foot in the "Scrivani Mansion" (as he would later call it). The "Mansion" was, and still is, the Cape Cod house in Bergenfield where I grew up. After dinner we all sat by the fireplace in the very living room in which I had first set eyes on my celebrity guest on TV in 1958. I was impressed at how little Zach wanted to talk about his career, how much more he enjoyed asking questions about my house, its history, what it was like when coal was used for heat, and even expressing interest in helping me locate an overgrown access cap for the abandoned oil tank buried under the front lawn.

The rest of the evening was passed by a tour of my basement movie theater ("Wow, Rich, you've got a balcony!" "It's just a platform, Zach." "The heck, you say! To me, it's a balcony!") and film vault and a short screening of classic Warner Brothers bloopers with stars Cagney, Bogart, Edward G. Robinson, Bette Davis, etc. Zach really enjoyed it, and during the screening he turned to Christine and said, "Now, aren't you glad you came?" There was also a quick photo session with Zach sitting in The Chair, playing with a Groucho Marx ventriloquist dummy I had bought. Zach admired Groucho, and I once saw him express his delight at seeing his photograph sharing a page with Groucho's in a book about the history of TV.

A great evening indeed.

Chapter 16
The Saga of *The Zacherley Archives*

Some time during the spring of 1998, Zach got serious about releasing his old kinescopes on videotape. Portions of them had been a staple of his "Chiller" convention appearances, alternating with various TV appearances on Mike Douglas, Tom Snyder and Dick Clark shows. Almost every time Zach hit the podium, some fan would ask, "Are you ever going to put your old shows out so we can buy them?" Indeed, I would have been one of those people had I not many times heard of those intentions from the man himself. "Gotta do it, gotta do it," Zach would always murmur, and he really did mean it, because if you know him, unless it's something he absolutely plans on doing, you know it takes a fairly serious regimen of gentle but consistent prodding to get him to put his shoulder to the wheel. In this case, Zach grabbed *my* shoulder.

I had sent him an 8x10 blowup of the both of us, taken the night he posed in the chair, and the first mention of any serious intentions to put together the infamous four kines came via a casual mention in a phone message:

> Got your picture — what a picture! Or as Mr. Rogers would say, "Picture, picture!" Really great, came out great. And I don't know whose camera that was shot with, yours maybe, but it's amazing how well it was done, with available light and a flash, I guess. And we look great there! And the old [*laughs*] chair looks great against the wooden wall. I may have to borrow you someday and sit there and do my introductions to this tape if I ever get it together. Anyway, that was just a thought. And I should do an act with that little Groucho dummy you had there, that's great! Where'd you get that? I forget. Anyway, I'm out and I've gotta go to Philadelphia for a wedding and sing the 'Monster Mash' at my grandniece's wedding!

Well, with that I knew that Zach was working up to asking my help in getting the kine project together, and not only was I surprised, but extremely pleased and, above all, excited. My first instinct was to call my friend Paul Scrabo, whom I knew would jump at the chance to tape Zach's "wraparounds" to introduce each segment. Paul also had recently purchased a Beta video camera, which was at that time state-of-the-art in the video business, and had formed a company, PS Productions. He and his wife George Ann had been shooting interviews to be used in DVD releases of some of the James Bond films, in addition to other DVD projects. This setup was too good to be true. Zach wanted help, and we were equipped to give his venture first-class production values, plus both Paul and I were big Zach fans from way back.

The next message from Zach seemed to seal it all up:

> I'm pursuing again now this situation of coming over and using the chair and all that, and do a little shooting. It really wouldn't amount to a lot, because I'm just going to introduce, I'm gonna say, you know, what the history of the kinescope is, and you're gonna see one from Philadelphia, and three from New York, and

the date and so on, and I hope you enjoy it, and that stuff. And I don't even know as I run 'em along whether to introduce each one as it happens, they run about 20 minutes, each one. And then a closing thing too. We'll see what we can do. It shouldn't take long, I mean, I'm just gonna write it all down and practically read it, so I don't need retakes and all that kind of nonsense. And make it look kind of cheap like the films themselves were cheap, make a joke about the fact that I had no budget at all, we used to spend about 20 bucks on bananas and Jell-O and cauliflower for brains, you know. And anyway, not to make it a huge big production, but well done, you know. I've kind of looked over everything and made a little script and so we can do it, if you know somebody that has a camera we can certainly pay them to do that. It involves about five or six tapes that I can cue up and then we'll just run 'em just as they are. Okay, give me a call when you're free this week, next week, whenever, and we'll just have to do it, that's all. It's gotta be done, gotta be done.

The wraparounds were shot in March 1988. With the help of mutual NBC friend John Kourkoutis, we set up a makeshift set which consisted of nothing more than a dark blue background curtain (which wouldn't even be seen with the low-key lighting we'd be using), the Gothic chair and a life-sized wax figure of Henry Hull as the

Zach in position for the Zacherley Archives *taping with his old pal the WereWolf of London.*

WereWolf of London, an impulse buy I had made at Chiller a year or two before, and a prop with which Zach loved to play. ("Back in Philadelphia where all this started, was where I first ran into my friend here, Mr. Hull. He was a great old partner of mine when we used to hang out in London. Take it easy, old boy!") The WereWolf would be sharing the screen for Zach's intros to what would become *The Zacherley Archives*. The three of us were a bit nervous preparing to shoot these intros, never having worked with someone of Zach's reputation. I was hoping that we'd all come off professional enough to please him. Eventually I would learn that if you are competent, these type of concerns are meaningless when it comes to dealing with Zach.

Paul was (and still is) a master of many technical trades at NBC, his strongest suit being video and editing. His wife George Ann was a lighting director there and had worked on *Nightly News, The Today Show, Dateline* and many other live shows. In fact, all of us including our friend John, were NBC engineers in one capacity or another.

John was an equipment maintenance engineer and I was working in videotape with Paul. What we were missing that day was the presence of George Ann, who had given verbal instructions to Paul about lighting Zach. She was unable to be at the taping because she was visiting her ailing father in Key West, Florida.

The setup looked fine through the camera, the wax WereWolf was moved into place, Zach went into the bathroom and dabbed on some makeup (an extremely light version, almost a "suggestion" of the original), sat in the chair and was ready to go. Holding up a reproduction of his face on the cover of *Famous Monsters of Filmland*, Zach murmured, "It's me! I — used to look like this, now I look like this! [*laughs*] Time has a way of messing things up. This is the great old days here, back in the days of *Famous Monsters of Filmland*, you know, and Forry Ackerman and all those people." We were off to a rousing start, and all Zach had to do was introduce and provide some background on the kinescopes to follow. He followed his opening comments by comparing the discovery of the kines to that of the Jackie Gleason "Lost *Honeymooners*" kinescopes, adding, "Well, these weren't discovered, they were just stuffed in the back of my closet!"

The introductions finished, Zach read a laundry list of television guest appearances he had made through the years to include on possible future video releases. When he got to *The Pat Boone Show*, he just couldn't resist ribbing his old friend from the WABC days: "Pat Boone! Did you see Pat Boone running around in leather stuff lately? Ha, ha! A whole leather outfit, trying to change his image. Can't fool me, Pat! A 'born-again biker' is what he's trying to be, I think, I don't know."

The whole session ran only a couple of hours; what we got on tape was funny, pure Zacherley, and the picture came out sharp and clear. Zach took off for Manhattan, John for Queens and Paul for New Milford, about three minutes away by car. We were now all set to book an edit room and shuffle Zach's intros together with the old kinescopes. Or so we thought. The phone message below came the following day:

> I really felt I had let you people down in a way, because I didn't notice until too late that we really had the lighting set up for an interview rather like for your show (*Front Row*), but I realized afterwards we really probably should have gone for moody lighting. It could've looked very mysterious, you know, a little more dramatic and spooky. You let me know when you see it, and if you think we could do better with like an overhead light and all that stuff, making my eyes look dark and shadows and all, why we could do it sometime when you're shooting the other show and you've got everything set up.

This was not good news, especially for Paul, who is not fond of going back and redoing something when the results he has are fine. None of us thought the footage looked bad, but we all knew that Zach had a point. He eventually received a copy of the footage, and a few days later had another idea: "Maybe we should make the whole thing in black and white. That might not be a bad idea. Anyway, with black and white kinescopes it might be a neat idea. It'd give the whole thing a consistent look. That's my latest miraculous thought."

We hit on Palm Sunday as the next, and hopefully final, shooting day. Before this, Paul had come up with the idea of taking full advantage of Zach's presence that day by asking him if he would consider being a guest on our cable talk show, *Front Row*. Zach himself had planted the seed by suggesting that we do the Archives taping on the same day we would be doing an episode of our show. Well, we had nothing planned, but the opportunity to have a real name on the show seemed to have dropped in our laps. Zach, of course, agreed, and the next shoot went from being a quiet affair with only a few people present to a genuine genre event.

Present for this double feature of a day were Paul, George Ann, John Kourkoutis, Michael Brunas (co-author of the book *Universal Horrors*), Christine Domaniecki, Mike Thomas (who had gotten the green light from Zach to be his makeup man for the day) and myself. I, as host of *Front Row*, had done some homework and come up with enough questions for a two-hour interview, deliberately including questions I had never heard anyone ask before, knowing I'd have to edit myself as we went along. When we taped *Front Row*, the rule was to complete the entire half-hour without stopping, if possible. The look of the show was kept simple due to budget and space restrictions, and our set that day consisted of the usual dark blue velvet background curtain, two camp chairs, a table between them for notes and props, and two Zacherley posters hanging prominently overhead.

Zach arrived at about 9:30 a.m. He walked into the house sporting a Grateful Dead cap and announced, "This hat is in honor of Palm Sunday!" The ice was officially broken, and we headed down to the screening room to begin the *Front Row* shoot. Mike applied some basic makeup to us, and Zach sat across from me in the guest chair wearing a pale blue shirt, dark blue pants and matching sports jacket. I nervously studied my notes one last time and we were off. I knew that this installment would wind up as a two-parter, as had our premiere episode with *Universal Horrors* authors Tom Weaver and John and Mike Brunas — there was too much to talk about in a half-hour. In addition to the usual topics, we discussed Zach's Army days, his earliest acting experiences, and *La Belle*,

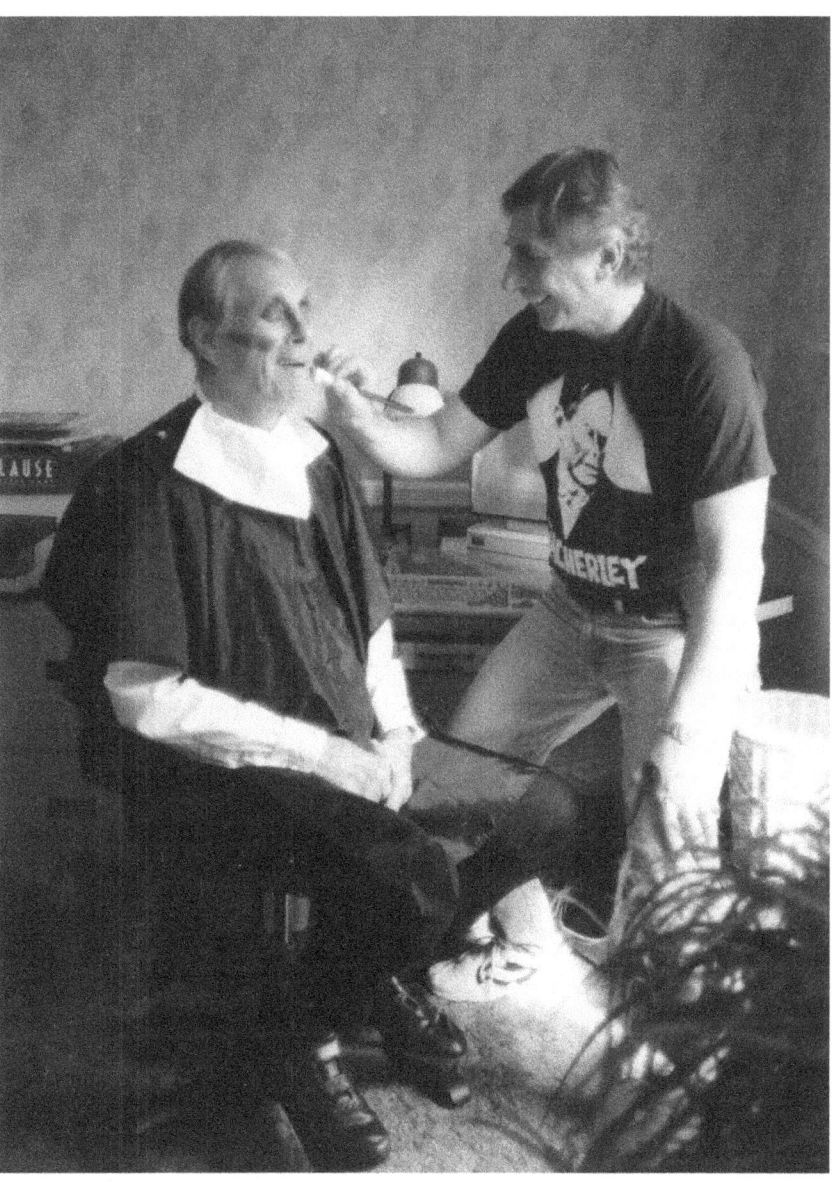

Mike Thomas applies Zach's makeup.

a musical play he did in 1962. I only found myself running into trouble in the second half-hour, when we had ten minutes left and I had at least 20 more questions to ask. I raced through the less important ones, basically touching on everything I had hoped, but forgot one important surprise we had planned for the very end: Mike and Christine had supplied a cassette of the song "Zacherley My Love," recorded almost 40 years previous by the Terry Sisters to a tune suspiciously similar to Frankie Avalon's 1959 hit "Venus." I was supposed to ask Zach if he could identify the song, but was so caught up in asking questions that I completely forgot. Luckily Paul, who was operating a camera, remembered and pressed the PLAY button within two minutes of the deadline. Zach did remember the song but was not positive at the time about who made the recording.

Excited about having Zach in the can for *Front Row*, we began the chore of dismantling the set and setting up for our second go at *The Zacherley Archives* intros. This time the lighting would be right on, having George Ann there to create the proper atmosphere and mood. While the technical work was going on in the basement "studio," I spent my time watching Mike Thomas work his makeup magic to turn John Zacherle into Zacherley once more. I had hung out quite a bit with Zach at Channel 47 during the *Disc-O-Teen* days, and more often than not he would still be chatting with people up in his office uncomfortably close to the start of the show. I wondered how he managed to get into his makeup and costume in time if this was the usual practice. I stopped wondering when I finally got to witness the ritual. Bing, bam, boom: After nine years of applying those famous shadows, he had streamlined it down to a routine that took all of two minutes. What amazed me was how effective and "symmetrical" the makeup still looked, even with that lightning-fast application. I had once asked him whether the character was sporting a small mustache, referring to the shadows under his nose, but he described those as "Atmosphere, my boy! Atmosphere!"

By 1966, he had lightened up the original concept a bit. Gone were the blackened insides of the ears, the gray at the temples and eyebrows and heavy black shadows around the eyes and bridge of the nose. He still looked ghoulish, but not quite as severe, and, of course, was totally recognizable as the character. Mike would have none of this. He was going to recreate the original visage of Zacherley, but with a more subtle use of shadow and light. Zach's makeup application that day had him in the chair for almost two hours. While Zach was sitting for the makeup and downing generous portions of burnt popcorn, I took the opportunity to dig up some old *TV Guide* clippings and force him to listen to some of the outlandish experiments he had done on *Shock Theater*. The two Mikes (Thomas and Brunas) were enjoying this Memory Lane trip, and so was Zach, often laughing and repeating, "Did I do *that*?" Zach couldn't remember doing most of the shows, but got a great kick out of the variety of ideas he had come up with over the years. As far as we were concerned, being able to reminisce with him about the old shows from our childhood was as good as it gets for a Zacherley fan.

George Ann carefully adjusted the lighting to create a more shadowy atmosphere, but it wasn't easy. What she had originally set up, while it would have been perfect for someone wearing straight makeup, cast garish shadows over Zach's now elaborate makeup, giving a raccoon-like look to his eyes. Mike carefully modified the white highlights at the top of Zach's cheekbones, George Ann further adjusted the lighting, and we had the look we were going for. Lighting is an art, and we would never have pulled off the effect we wanted without her expertise.

As Zach began speaking, 40 years melted away and his TV personality of the late '50s emerged. It was uncanny how effortlessly Zach could pull the character out of his hat, with an energy and wit so youthful that we had to remind ourselves that this was a man soon to turn 80. Mike Thomas and I sat next to each other on the floor, watching the whole surreal scene unfold. Appreciating for a minute what we were doing, I leaned over to him and whispered, "Do you believe all this?" It really was wonderful, being able to help create a Zacherley product and having a Cool Ghoul performance all to ourselves! This time we even had a second camera rolling so that Paul could cut away to a different angle from time to time if needed.

When the taping was concluded, it was evident that we had tired Zach out. We had accomplished a lot that day, and he had been before the cameras for a good part of it. Pictures were taken to document the event, and Zach even set up a tripod, attached a camera he had brought, and snapped off two pictures of all of us posing around the chair with him still in full makeup, looking very much like the patriarch of some bizarre family reunion.

Zach brought along with him some artifacts from the old TV shows. One was the liquid metal statuette that I had admired on a shelf in his apartment. Another was a beautiful oil painting of Zach, arms folded in his typical fashion. It was done in 1960 by Barbara McCormick, a fan of the classic character. (I once hung it on the wall of his *Disc-O-Teen* office.) Then there was something Mike Brunas and I unfolded on my living room carpet as if we were opening up the Dead Sea Scrolls, Ruth and Dona Steinman's fabulously detailed map of Transylvania, now almost 40 years old, still retaining its vivid colors. It was fragile and beginning to tear at the edges; I really felt it should be photographed and preserved. Having gawked at all the memorabilia, we ordered pizza and sat around the living room chatting for about half an hour. Zach thanked us all and headed back to Manhattan, tired but content that this time we had gotten our footage.

Now it was time to design a cover for the video. A friend of Paul's, Jeff Marshall of DePersico Designs in Havertown, Pennsylvania, was to do the honors, so a trip to the Havertown area seemed in order to iron out the details. Zach had come up with a simple design for the cover which consisted of a three-quarter profile WPIX publicity shot from 1963, in which he appeared to be "peeking around a corner." The graphics, which included things like **In glorious black and white** and **1958-1959 A.D.,** were Zach's idea, as well as the vertical title display seen on the spine of the box. As Zach reasoned, he wanted people in stores to be able to read the title easily, without having to crane their necks. We took a trip down to the Havertown area, which gave Zach a chance to show me his niece's house (no one was home, so he gave me a "tour" by peeking through the windows), which was notable for its model train layout that encircled the entire property, and then visit his older brother Bruce in a nearby nursing home.

The Zacherley Archives crew: Kneeling next to Zach, camera operator John Korkoutis; standing behind him: Paul Scrabo, George Ann Muller, me, Mike Thomas, Christine Domaniecki, the WereWolf of London and Mike Brunas.

Bruce was wheelchair-bound in the final stages of Alzheimer's, and Zach, the dutiful brother, visited him regularly, feeding him lunch and wheeling him back and forth to his room. He had also brought along some family videos to show Bruce in his room, which evoked smiles and recognition from him. It was a poignant visit, one I'll never forget.

We met Jeff, also a fan, for lunch at a roadside diner and discussed the cover design. Zach's major concerns were the size of the title (large enough so people could see it from across the store) and his face on the cover. I had always loved a photo I had first seen in an early issue of *Famous Monsters of Filmland*, originally taken at WOR, of Zach holding aloft a candelabra in a sort of celebratory pose. (The photo appears on page 34.) This I envisioned on the back of the box, along with notes I planned to write. Lunch was supposed to be devoted to talking about the video, but, as is the case with Zach, conversation turned to more of a personal nature, owing largely to Zach's short attention span when it comes to business talks. He'd much rather talk about the person he's meeting, their life and circumstances, than something as dry as designing a videotape box. Jeff left the diner an hour later with a few autographed photos and all the materials he needed to design a first-class cover.

About a week later, I received Jeff's design by fax, which showed a waist-to-head shot of the Cool Ghoul against a purple sky with a huge full moon overhead. I thought it looked beautiful and drove into New York to show Zach. He at first approved it, but later that day called me in a rather frustrated state expressing his disappointment that his face wasn't featured as prominently as he had indicated to Jeff. Also the lettering needed to be larger, and the spine lettering made vertical as he had asked. This was resolved rather quickly, and the new design passed muster. It was funny trying to fax the new design to Zach. He had recently been given a fax machine and hooked it up, but he had no idea how to use it. Over the phone, I walked him through it, told him how it worked, and that he should just ignore the ringing of the phone and wait for the fax to come through. Time after time it wouldn't work; everything was fine on my end, but for some reason the picture wouldn't materialize through Zach's machine. Becoming more and more frustrated, Zach took to picking up his receiver when it rang rather than waiting for the fax machine to do its thing. I could actually hear his voice coming through my fax machine at work, a distant "Hello! *Hello!*" as I tried again and again to send the picture. I called him: "Zach, don't answer the phone when it rings! Let the machine do what it's supposed to!" He complied and finally, only once, Zach's machine presented him with a fax. He never used it again.

The Zacherley Archives was finally unveiled at the Halloween 1998 Chiller convention in Secaucus, New Jersey. One thousand tapes were made, and fans bought them so furiously (in many cases multiple copies) that we soon ran off two more batches of 500 each. With an interest in the video manufacturing process, Zach made a trip with me to VideoLab Cassette in New Brunswick, New Jersey, to watch it happen. The manager, Tom Laverty, also a fan, was thrilled to have Zach as a client and wanted his picture taken with him. He of course got that and more, as Zach provided him with the usual autographed photos. Then from out of left field, Tom said that a "producer" friend of his had come up with an idea for a new Zacherley television show. I don't remember all the specifics, but I do recall a lab, a deformed assistant, and sundry other mad doctor details that would make up the basis for this new enterprise. As wacky as it all sounded, Tom was dead serious, and I looked over at Zach, politely nodding his head and listening to his every word. When asked if he would be interested, he responded simply, "Sure!" That made Tom happy. We were soon back in the car, where I couldn't resist asking Zach if he was serious about his response. His answer, which I should have figured out for myself, was, "You never say no. You can always say no later." It makes sense. There's something to be said for leaving the door open.

The Zacherley Archives *makes its debut!* Left to right, Paul Scrabo, me, Zach.

Chapter 17
Zacherley, Debbie Rochon and a Houseful of Idiots

During the early summer of 2001, Paul Scrabo and his wife George Ann approached Zach about appearing in a movie Paul was co-writing with B-movie actress Brinke Stevens. Paul is a gifted videotape editor with an incredible storehouse of energy and ambition which belies his mild-mannered appearance. He had been studying at various seminars in New York the business end of writing and producing low-budget movies. By the time he put the question to Zach, he had come up with a script (add writer to his list of talents) involving a half-dozen people involved in a sex therapy scam, in which Zach would play a straight character who once upon a time had a job introducing horror movies on television (a stretch?). The references to the ghoul character would be copious, but Zach would appear in straight make-up and play a wisecracking comedy role.

PAUL SCRABO: I didn't want him doing "Monster Mash," I wanted him doing something new, but I still wanted him to be "Zacherley." He was, I think to us, Groucho or W.C. Fields, and yet still original. I originally came up with the idea of a takeoff on those horror movies that play like an anthology. We could do the separate stories with separate weekend shoots and spend a week doing the wraparounds.

George Ann's many talents, chief among them lighting, made her invaluable to the project. I would serve as associate producer. On Tuesday, August 6, a very hot and humid evening, a dinner was arranged at a Chinese restaurant around the corner from Zach's place, attended by Zach (in shorts), Paul, George Ann, Mike Thomas, Christine Domaniecki and myself. Everyone at the table would have a part in the film, but the two with the lion's share of screen time would be Mike and Zach. Dinner was pleasant, Paul passed around a sample of the script, and by the end of the evening Zach had agreed to appear in *Dr. Horror's "Erotic" House of Idiots*. During our walk back to his apartment on West 96th Street, Zach stopped to chat with a doorman he apparently had known for years, exclaiming, "These are some friends of mine. We're gonna make a movie together!" It was a pleasant moment, everything on target and proceeding nicely toward the first day of production, September 10.

PAUL SCRABO: We had a lot of talented people, Mike Thomas could do a very good takeoff on Bela Lugosi, and so the original concept was called *Dr. Ygor's House of Idiots*. Zacherley would be Ygor's assistant or his butler. I didn't have to worry about writing anything that funny because just having Zacherley in the shot would make it funny. Just a look or just a reaction — funny. We changed everything around, we didn't want to use "Dr. Ygor" because Ygor's a kind of copyrighted character. The big deal for us was having Zach play an actual character. He would still be playing himself, but would be actually part of a repertoire company.

The next step was locking in the rest of the cast, at least the principal players. A real coup

From the set of 2004's Dr. Horror's "Erotic" House of Idiots: Left to right, me, with Mike Thomas' head apparently growing out of my shoulder, Debbie Rochon, Zach and writer-producer-director Paul Scrabo.

for Paul was obtaining the services of Debbie Rochon, a B-movie actress of note. Debbie had been working in the low-budget world for years, but had managed to secure roles in some "upper-tier" films as well, the most notable being *Abducted II* (1994), a "mountain-man/psycho/kidnapping" story shot on film in her native Canada, as well as British Columbia and Vancouver Island. *Abducted II* director Boon Collins was also able to secure the name-value acting services of drinking buddies Dan Haggerty and Jan-Michael Vincent, which gave the film an air of legitimacy. It was a decently made, entertaining 92 minutes, and a high-profile addition to Rochon's growing list of credits.

Paul was delighted with Debbie's enthusiasm, and after she read a sample of the script, she agreed to take the part. She was also thrilled to be appearing in a scene opposite Zacherley (it was obvious that she too was a big fan). She would play the lead role of Valerie Kenton, a slightly confused sex-therapy patient who visits the home and office of one Dr. Horace along with two other patients, played by actors Trent Haaga and Nate Sears. Makeup artist-turned-actor Michael R. Thomas was to play out-of-work writer Frank Mannering.

I'm not one who cares much for story rundowns, but to appreciate the sequence of events with Zach, I'll attempt a short one: Writer Frank Mannering (Thomas) hits up his old boss, local TV star Roland Andrews (Zach), for a loan, only to find that he is in no position to lend money. Roland is currently working as a groundskeeper for Dr. Horace, a "one-stop" sex therapist whose reputation attracts people hoping for a quick cure. Horace is out of town, but three desperate souls (Rochon, Haaga and Sears) come knocking at the doctor's door pleading for help. The most desperate is Ashley (Sears) who offers to pay as much as $5000 in cash for a speedy treatment. A light bulb goes on in Roland's brain as he sees a chance to procure the five grand, give 500 to Mannering and keep the rest for himself. All Mannering has to do is impersonate Dr. Horace (whom apparently none of the patients have seen), run three fake therapy sessions and hold his hand out for the money. That's the basic gist of the plot, and Paul wrote the part of the scammer for Zach, feeling he'd be great in it, drawing on the delivery and wit he made famous in his old *Shock Theater* days. The "therapy" sessions would be told via three separate fantasy sequences, the third of which would be largely penned by actress Brinke Stevens.

The concept was great in theory, but wound up stumbling in reality due to working with an 83-year-old John Zacherle.

> PAUL SCRABO: I always envisioned a number where Zach and Debbie were dancing, and done completely straight. I never did that, I guess it wasn't meant to happen, but I wanted a thing where it was centered on style and grace, and "Look at the two of them together."

Paul and George Ann had come up with an idea for a title song for the movie and had tapped out a basic melody and lyrics on a piano, handed me a tape and asked if my brother Doug (long out of Herald Square but still a working musician) and I could make a full-fledged production out of it. It was to be introduced about 20 minutes into the story and sung by Mike, Debbie and Zach. The lyrics sang the praises of the good doctor (now changed to Dr. Horror) by listing his genius-like abilities, while at the same time admonishing the three "idiot" patients of the potential dangers of their visit. It was really a clever composition, and between Doug and myself, it was developed into a tuneful song with an infectious beat. Now we had to get Zach, Mike and Debbie over to Doug's home studio to record it. The date was set for Thursday, August 30, another sweltering evening, at 7:00 p.m. at Doug's house in Saddle Brook, New Jersey. Zach's white Honda Civic pulled into my driveway right on time, followed by Mike Thomas, then Paul and George Ann. George Ann offered us a plate of homegrown cherry tomatoes, but Zach politely declined, saying, "I never eat anything before I'm going to sing." The caravan then took off for my brother's house. The session went smoothly enough, despite Debbie's inability to attend that evening (her vocals would be dubbed by George Ann, later to be perfectly lip-synched by Debbie), with Mike laying down his vocal in what was to be his Dr. Horror voice, a sort of "Ygor-lite," if that makes sense. Zach had a bit of trouble with the song's cadence, and took a few takes to nail it down, but we left that evening with the two vocals added and three left to go (Debbie's and a harmony part sung by two female characters; eventually, those two parts were performed by Doug's wife Joni and singer Laura Andresky). Zach, being the thoughtful man that he is, admired Kit, Doug and Joni's Sheba, a small orange dog resembling a fox, and sent them an issue of *The Smithsonian* which featured a fox on the cover.

Shortly after the recording session, I had a phone conversation with Zach during which he asked me when he could get a look at the script. Previous to this, he had told me that he had gone to an AFTRA representative to report that he was about to play a part in a small movie. This was unforeseen, although he had done the same while we were making *The Zacherley Archives*, advising them that he would be wearing a producer's hat for that project. There was a slight concern about the rights to the kinescope material we were compiling for the *Archives* video, but everyone he spoke to, including his lawyer, quelled any fears he might have had, citing the age of the clips and the relatively small amount of copies being manufactured. In short,

Zach poses with a machine-gun toy during a break.

the project was too small and the kinescopes too old. But by reporting his work on *Dr. Horror* to the union, and worrying that the movie was a non-union shoot, a chain of events started that snowballed into huge problems for Paul, eventually causing him to have to do a desperate, last-minute rewrite. From the beginning, Zach was a bit apprehensive about the size of his part, and had told me on a few occasions that he had never pursued acting aggressively after having created his TV persona because of his uneasiness about having to memorize a large amount of lines. He had built his career on his ability to ad-lib, and it was that talent which defined the public image of Roland-Zacherley. Now being faced with a part of unknown size, I had an uneasy feeling that Zach might be passive-aggressively sabotaging his part in the movie. Paul was taken by surprise (as we all were) by this turn of events, particularly by Zach getting the union involved, which would mean nothing but trouble.

The situation further deteriorated when I took it upon myself to print out the script (as it existed up to that point) and send it to Zach. I felt it was only fair to give him a chance to become acquainted with his role, and had told him what Paul had been telling me all along; Zach's part could and would be shot line by line to make it easier for him, and that there would be no need on his part to memorize pages of dialogue. As it turned out, when Zach got a look at the size of his part, he very gently freaked out, called me and announced that he was backing out of the movie. It wasn't easy for him to do this, but he admitted that he felt greatly relieved now that he had made the decision. This all happened before we shot the video portion of the song, so he felt that he would not be needed for that, but the musical sequence was to be an important part of Dr. Horror, and Paul wanted Zach in it at any cost. So he rewrote the concept of the sequence so that Zach would play a specialist brought in by Dr. Horror — Dr. Zacherley, and sing the song exactly as planned, as sort of a musical cameo. There was only one problem — the track had been recorded, but the scene, with everyone lip-synching to a playback had yet to be taped.

PAUL SCRABO: I think Zach freaked out a little bit thinking that he would let the project down, that he could not possibly memorize a whole script. In reality, he didn't have to memorize anything because it was done with that in mind. There were no big scenes where there was dialogue back and forth with Zach. We wanted to make it as easy for him as possible. So about three days before we were setting up the shoot, I got a call and Zach said, "I just can't do it." The script scared him off. It was the first time I ever heard John

Zach, Debbie Rochon and Mike Thomas.

Zacherle very concerned. He said, "No, Paul, Paul, I can't. I'm old now, Paul." He kept saying my name, and it was an interesting special moment of who he was as a man, as a human being. He was concerned about how he was going to come across. I had him on the phone and I knew that once I hung up that was it, so I said, "Do us one thing. You [recorded] the song, everybody's looking forward to working with you. Just come and do the song." He said, "All right, I'll do the song."

It wasn't as simple as it sounds getting Zach to even agree to do the song because having officially backed out of the movie itself, he just couldn't understand how it would work. We were all jumping through hoops in those weeks before shooting began trying to enlist Zach to do the song.

I told him that the number would now be more of a fantasy sequence, and that in a movie of this sort logic could very easily be stretched. He still had his reservations.

We had passed the hurdle of Zach's agreeing to appear in the musical portion of the movie, but still had union headaches ahead of us. It was decided that Paul and George Ann would make an appointment to meet with an AFTRA representative and try to get their official blessing. They might just as well have tried to arrange a softball game between the Israelis and Palestinians. They came away from the meeting having accomplished nothing, no surprise to Paul, but the attempt was made in deference to Zach, and on the one percent chance that something could be accomplished. To add insult to injury, the AFTRA representative had never even heard of John Zacherle. I spent some time beating myself up about all this, reasoning that if I hadn't spooked Zach by sending him the script, maybe it would all have worked out by the time shooting would begin. The truth is, it was better that this all happened shortly before the start of shooting while there was still a chance to regroup and find a suitable replacement for the part of Roland Andrews. There are some people who are just not replaceable, and are simply too original for anyone else to presume to take their place. John Zacherle is one of those talents. Paul had his work cut out for him to find someone for the vacated role, and he sure as hell wasn't going to find anyone who could come close to Zach. One thing we all agreed upon: We at least needed a name. If we couldn't have Zach, we had to have someone in the role whose name would be associated with the genre. Paul found the name, if not the talent: Conrad Brooks.

PAUL SCRABO: Everybody thought of Forrest Ackerman, and we did too. But we would have had the same situation; he's at least as old as Zacherle is, plus he's out in California, and I think people have an affection for Forry Ackerman but not in the same way. And it was too late to get him even if we had wanted to. Then all of a sudden the most obvious name that came around was Conrad Brooks, a person people also have affection for, but in a different way.

While it was painful to think of Conrad Brooks in the part originally written for Zach, wherein each line was tailored to the latter's particular style of delivery, there was, at this late date, really no choice. Paul had only Ackerman in mind for a replacement, and if he had been living on the East Coast instead of the Los Angeles area, he would most certainly have gotten a call. This, of course, was prior to Ackerman's latter-day medical problems. Conrad was available and happy to do it, and even though he was living in West Virginia, it turned out that he was planning to take part in a convention being held in New York City shortly after his part in Dr. Horror would finish. Paul had planned an intensive three-day shoot in Stockholm, New Jersey, where a friend's country bungalow would serve as the location for the doctor's home and office. My job was to pick up Conrad at Newark's Penn Station, drop him at the location, have dinner and become acquainted with the rest of the cast, then drive home and bring Zach to Stockholm the next day. Our fingers were crossed the whole time, hoping that Zach wouldn't change his mind again. If we didn't get the song shot the next day, we simply wouldn't have a song.

On the morning of September 10, 2001, at 9:15 a.m., Zach and I took off for Stockholm in my car. His intended part in the movie didn't involve him playing his television character, it just required a bit of straight makeup and casual clothes. Once he was no longer in the part, Paul and I thought it

Mike Thomas and Zach record Dr. Horror's *title tune.*

would be appropriate for him to appear as Zacherley in what would now be a true cameo. Neither of us had the nerve to ask him. To my surprise and delight, as he got out of his car in front of my house, Zach produced a small suitcase and opened it. Inside were the costume and a few props, one of them very familiar to me from old Channel 7 promotional photos: an oversized silver hypo. Any Zacherley fan would recognize it, it's the one shown in the publicity photo of the Cool Ghoul injecting a cauliflower brain. Zach explained to me that he felt his cameo would be more effective if he was dressed in the outfit and he were in character. Paul and I couldn't have agreed more!

When we arrived at the cabin on East Shore Road at 10:30 a.m., it was apparent that something was wrong. The song was scheduled to be shot first for Zach's convenience, and two young, buxom female dancers who were to be part of it hadn't shown up. To add to everyone's concerns, the weather was hot and muggy, with a storm clearly working its way toward us. It was vital that we get the song shot immediately, as there would be no time, with Paul's exhausting schedule, to re-shoot it. Zach sat inside with Conrad and enjoyed a bit of conversation while we waited for the dancers to arrive. When it was obvious that they were not going to show, it was decided to proceed without them. Zach was introduced to Debbie Rochon, cue cards were on hand to make things easier for him, and we were off and running. It didn't take long to shoot everything we could that didn't involve the dancers, and soon we found ourselves at the instrumental middle, the section for which they were needed. Not knowing exactly how to proceed, Zach came up with a solution: "The dancers aren't here? Well, let's do it ourselves!" What was intended as a show-stopping display featuring two sexy and provocatively dressed young ladies became a howlingly funny interlude, as Zach and Mike Thomas performed an impromptu dance on the streamer-bedecked set. We were all concerned for Zach, gyrating to the music with his famous "underarm" or, as Mike Gilks describes it, "monkey dance" steps, a terrific feat as the heat and humidity made it uncomfortable when we were simply just standing around. Here was Zach in his black undertaker costume (which was absorbing even more heat), frugging and hopping to the music, despite the pain he must have been enduring from the arthritis in his feet. At one point he feigned physical collapse and sank toward the ground as Mike, as Dr. Horror, tried to hold him upright. It was quite a moment, and can be seen in the movie.

MIKE THOMAS: I found myself dancing with the one, the only John Zacherle. As usual, Zach is one of the world's greatest ad-libbers, always has been, always will be. We had nothing planned, there was no pre-planned choreography whatsoever, and I just followed Zach's lead. The dancing girls didn't show up, and all of a sudden I wound up dancing with Zacherley. I just kind of put it into Zach's hands and followed his lead. On *Disc-O-Teen* he had the "armpit-punching" dance that he used to do every once in a while, so I think I either started punching my own armpits or I raised his elbow and started punching his armpit, but many armpits were punched that day, and I can say that no matter what happens, I will have danced with Zacherley in a movie!

During my conversations with moral support provider Mike Gilks, he suggested that, if Zach had a good time during the shoot, he might agree to stay and film a few choice lines that could be incorporated into the show. Fortunately for us, that is exactly what happened. Paul was able to shoot him doing what he was best known for on television: commenting on the action in the movie, peering through spyglasses and making comments like, "Boy, wasn't that sleazy!," and "Isn't that exciting — of course it is!" We no sooner came to the last sentence of Zach's performance when the sky opened up in the torrential downpour that had been threatening the entire day. Lights had to be quickly removed and brought inside for safety before the water did any damage. Zach was officially done for the day. Paul was happy — his footage was "in the can." It was time to drive Mr. Zacherle back to Bergenfield, where his car awaited him. We had gotten our footage and just in time; the next day was September 11, 2001.

PAUL SCRABO: When we shot those sequences, it was Monday, September 10, 2001, and Zach went home that night. The next day, of course, the world changed, and Zach could certainly not have come up or been in a condition to do a week's worth of shooting. Thank God I brought some provisions with us, and my laptop so we could communicate with people. Fortunately our close friends and loved ones were okay despite all the horrible things that were happening, and we, like everybody else around the world, had to continue to work. So in a way, we were very, very lucky, 'cause we certainly wouldn't have gotten Zach the rest of the week, and certainly wouldn't have gotten him happy or singing or dancing.

It's hard to forecast just what would have happened had Zach worked on the movie as originally intended, but my feeling is that his pulling out turned out to be an ironically fortunate thing. Knowing him as I do, my strong feeling is that the terrorist attack on September 11 would have upset him so much that he wouldn't have been able to (or had the interest in) continuing in the project. He probably would have been anxious to return to his Manhattan apartment, and if this had been the case, we would have had no chance to recast his part and keep to the shooting schedule to which so many were committed. As much as we would have loved to have had him in a larger and more important role, Providence wound up taking a hand in a way none of us could appreciate until time provided its perspective. As it turned out, with Paul's job in New York demanding most of his time, shooting for the rest of the movie proceeded at a slow pace, and in the waning months of the summer of 2003, Paul asked Zach if he would be kind enough to appear in a few more shots, one in which he would appear as a judge, and another that would take place on a spaceship set. The set had been painstakingly created by the multi-talented George Ann, and was carefully and tastefully painted and dressed to serve as a craft from a planet populated solely by women. Zach still felt uneasy with the union situation and politely declined. Another substitute was cast, "Uncle Floyd" Vivino, who essayed the roles of the judge and spaceship guest with highly amusing results, adding another name to the movie's rapidly growing cast. Then to add a touch of true surrealism to a production already steeped in it,

With TV's Floyd "Uncle Floyd" Vivino.

Zach, in an unexpected gesture of generosity, told me he'd like to finish up the few scenes in which Paul needed him! There was only one problem: the spaceship set had been shot with Floyd and dismantled. For a short time, maybe a couple of days, I had almost decided not even to mention it to Paul, fearing the frustration it might cause him. But in the spirit of professionalism, and more importantly the demand Paul had made on me that I share anything relevant to the production with him, I realized that he had to know.

> PAUL SCRABO: We had no time to be amazed, now we had to figure out what we had to do! There were some scenes that quite frankly needed help, so we just wrote things, filled things in and put some lines back that we originally took out because he wasn't around. So now it could appear that he was one of the ten major stars, which he was, because I gave the credits according to screen time, and he made the top ten. He made it incredibly magical, and gave the movie real personal value. He did the ending of the film where he wrapped up the story and then said, "Good night,

whatever you are," and ended the film. We all still can't believe that this guy we grew up with was part of our project. Maybe in a way, in the old days of the '50s, if some of the movies that he showed, a few of them weren't that great, and he "saved" them for you, in a way he kind of did that for *Dr. Horror*.

From start to finish, it took two years for *Dr. Horror* to become a reality. John Zacherle's part in it grew to not quite a supporting role, but much bigger than the originally envisioned cameo. A premiere was held at eight p.m. Tuesday, October 7, 2003, at Symphony Space's Leonard Nimoy Thalia, a small art theater on 95th Street and Broadway in New York City. The screening was attended by close to 100 people, including leading lady Debbie Rochon (with a bad case of the flu), Paul and George Ann Scrabo, myself, brother Doug and wife Joni, *Universal Horrors* authors and friends Mike Brunas and Tom Weaver, and Dr. Horror himself, Mike Thomas. The latter was accompanied by his fiancée Christine Domaniecki, who had played the part of Mike's wife in the movie. Zach had intended to make it, but was absent due to a broken shoulder he had suffered in a fall walking to Central Park some weeks earlier, the story of which reached the *New York Daily News*!

Dr. Horror's "Erotic" House of Idiots went on to accrue a few awards. Debbie Rochon and Trent Haaga won Best Actors in a Comedy Feature at Rapid City, South Dakota's Microcinema Fest in July 2004, and the film itself won Best Production at the 1st Annual Pittsburgh Film Workers Association Film Festival in June 2005. No less prestigious was coming in second place for Best Independent Film in the 2005 Rondo Awards. A DVD of the movie can be purchased at www.scrabo.com

Chapter 18
"Interment for Two"

On the morning of Friday, May 23, 2003, I awoke an hour and a half before the alarm which was set for 5 a.m. Trying to go back to sleep was fruitless, because I knew the pattern. The only times I've ever had any trouble sleeping were when I needed to be up early for an important day. Today I was going to pick Zach up at his apartment and drive him out to East Quogue, New York, to start work on his new CD, "Dead Man's Other Ball." The title, probably inspired by the Monty Python-Peter Cook movie *The Secret Policeman's Other Ball* (1982), had been suggested to Zach by Mike Thomas during Zach's *Front Row* taping in 1998. I left the house promptly at six a.m., got to West 96th Street and Zach's place by 6:20, and sat listening to Howard Stern. Zach came down, right on time, and we headed out across the Triboro Bridge on a cloudy and misty morning, the start of what was to be a very wet Memorial Day weekend.

Zach was in a good mood, the weather held and the rain was spotty at best, and since we had a two-hour ride ahead of us, I asked if he had brought along any tapes. "Oh, sure, sure I did," he quickly responded, digging out his sizable leather cassette carrying case. He fumbled among the dozen or so tapes, slipped one into my player, and, instead of the customary Pink Floyd or Neil Young, we were listening to audio from his 1959 New Year's Eve party on WABC-TV. This was the show wherein clips were shown from many of the classic horror films, with intros and cut-ins by Zach — sort of a review of what had been shown all year in 1958 on *Shock Theater*. On next week's show, the giant amoeba was introduced to the New York audience for the first time (he had already unveiled "Thelma" the amoeba in Philadelphia when he was Roland), and the movie being shown was the Boris Karloff mad doctor film *Before I Hang* (1940). I couldn't believe that he was interested in hearing these things, knowing how much he loved to listen to rock music in the car, and I assumed that he was playing them because of me. The last time this had happened was that first day I spent in his living room watching the kinescopes which would eventually become *The Zacherley Archives*. Zach got some genuine laughs out of some of his own comments, and of course I was thanking the fates for allowing me to share moments like this with my former television hero, now also my friend.

Despite the usual construction delays on the Long Island Expressway, the ride was uneventful and relatively quick, and we found ourselves at Mike and Ruth Gilks' house a little after nine. A quick jaunt over to Mike's brother Rich's house just down the street and we were inside his converted garage, now a fully functional recording studio. Present were myself, Mike, Ruth, Rich and Barry the engineer. Zach was anxious to get down to work, having reviewed the lyrics and music to the half-dozen songs (most of them written by Mike) they were hoping to commit to two-inch tape. I was there for two reasons: first to drive Zach out and back, and second to videotape the session for Mike's reference. Zach immediately sat down with Mike to go over some ideas he had for a couple of the songs, the most hilarious being a "hoedown" he would shout during the instrumental break of "Satan's Country Line Dance," a sequel of sorts to a number Zach loved from their previous collaboration, "Dead Man's Ball," in 1995.

The original song was "Eternal Polyester," a story about Zach's trip down a cavernous staircase straight to Hell, where he discovered that Disco music and polyester clothes were still in fashion. Zach loved "Polyester" so much that when he had just finished recording it, he called me to tell me about it, excitedly asking, "Do you want to hear it?" Before I could answer, he was trilling the tune in full voice into his telephone, with me at the other end wishing I had had enough warning so I could have taped it! The new song also took place in Hell (a place where it seems all forms of music Mike hates wind up) with its denizens zestfully indulging in the title's Satanic line dance. By the time Zach reached his "hoedown," none of us knew what to expect — then we heard: "Now all line up and growl at each other, grab some hair and give it to your mother! Kick your sweetie and knock down your brother, save a little moonshine, pour it on your father!"

Everyone broke up, but Mike and I were laughing so hard we had to be careful not to be picked up by the mike, as we were in the studio with Zach.

The session moved relatively quickly, with a few retakes (Zach is very good about redoing things, despite his penchant for doing it without rehearsal and moving on briskly to the next take) when Zach lost the rhythm and wound up a few beats behind. This, Mike told me, was common and happened a lot during the recording of "Dead Man's Ball." Breezing through "Zombie Zoo" (a Tom Petty cover that Zach requested), also "Frankenstein's Den" and Gilks' original "Interment for Two" (during which Zach contributed some great ad libs), a temporary time-out was called when it came time to work on Gilks' "Monster Blues," and the original track couldn't be located. While Rich and Barry searched the archives for the tape, Zach asked me, "Have you seen the pool and the house?" I hadn't, so we took a break and went out the small rear door of the studio which led into a charming back yard, a sizable pool still covered from the winter, and a private deck. Rich gave us a tour of the house, an old Victorian structure that had been cut in half and the two halves moved to the present site some years ago. The inside was filled with antiques, and once there you felt like you had left the 20th century behind. Zach loves houses with a history and was anxious to have me see it.

A tape with an alternate track of "Monster Blues" was located and it was back to work for Zach. Ruth had provided a nice array of liquid refreshment in a cooler and Rich was good enough to keep offering me coffee. Finally the vocal for "Monster Blues" was completed and all that was left were a few short tunes from old public domain songs that Zach had written new lyrics to and used on *Shock Theater* 44 years ago. One of them, sung to the tune of "Swanee River," was the official alma mater of Transylvania University, and started off with "Way down upon the dirty Danube, far, far away, there stands our golden Alma Mater sinking in the swampy clay." As the session was near an end and Zach was a bit tired, things started to get a bit loose: After singing the song

Recording "Interment for Two" with Mike Gilks. Zach won a Rondo for this CD.

normally, he hollered, "*Everybody!*" We didn't join in — I certainly didn't want to give in to a community sing atmosphere and have the others pissed at me for ruining a take, so Zach went through it alone. At the end, Zach sat back laughing and said, "Pretty sloppy!," then turned to Mike and asked, "Were you singing?" Mike, strumming along on a hollow-bodied guitar with a pickup, answered, "I was trying to get the chords, no, I started singing, but —" Zach added, "One more time. You should know it by now." Mike admitted, "I don't know the words." Zach would have none of it. "You just have to sound drunk, you don't have to know the words!" The next take Mike and I joined in — "Brain transplanting in the moonlight, making monsters too, oh how I wish that we were back at old Transylvania U.!" Zach yelled out, "Gimme a 'T'! Gimme an 'R'! Gimme an 'A'! Gimme an 'N'!" and so on, ending the sing-along with a cheer for the old college, and for a minute you could swear that the Cool Ghoul was a real person and had a genuine affection for his old school. I wondered if any of this stuff would be used, and if my voice could possibly wind up on a new Zacherley CD.

After a few more retakes for the bridge on "Zombie Zoo," it was nearly two p.m. and time to break up the session. Ruth offered lunch, but Zach had his mind on getting back to New York. Amenities were exchanged and we left, this time in a more substantial rainstorm. On the way back, Zach pulled some more rare recordings from his radio past and I got to listen to some side-splittingly funny commercials he wrote himself in the 1970s for a local clothes store named Adam Trent. These were, I believe, broadcast on WNEW-FM, and his delivery in them was at its most animated. A turn off the highway to stop for lunch as an intermission, and then he played the *pièce de résistance*: first, an old "opera" from his WOR-TV Channel 9 days in 1960, and a radio show hosted by Theodore Bikel from the same year, during which Zach got to sing three songs from his then-new "Spook Along with Zacherley" LP with Bikel fruitlessly trying to accompany him on guitar. Zach was in fine voice back then, but every time Bikel tried a flourish to back him up, it was off just enough to get a laugh. I asked Zach if I could please have a copy of the tape.

Another shot of the recording session at the Gilks home studio.

Sunday, March 21, 2004: A second road trip to visit the Gilks home, this time with my video camera to grab a few talking head shots of Mike describing his experiences recording with Zach. Paul Scrabo had asked me to get footage of Mike that he could use in the documentary extras for the *Dr. Horror's "Erotic" House of Idiots* DVD due out the following April. Zach coming along was an extra added bonus because any video footage of him is gold.

We arrived earlier than expected at the newly refurbished and extended Gilks home in East Quogue. Immediately Mike led us into the little studio in the backyard where he teaches guitar, the inside of which looked like the coolest clubhouse any kid who loves monsters could wish to own. Strewn from floor to ceiling with models, sheet music, toys, posters, banners and pennants, they shared the space with Mike's guitars and musical equipment. Zach asked Mike to help him attach his famous dickey with the large blue jewel in the center, changed into the Zacherley costume and sat down in a large wooden chair with carved lion's paw arms. I set up the camera and asked a nervous Mike questions about Zach, and he had to answer them with Zach sitting three feet to his right. It was a bit awkward and unsettling for Mike, but he got through it and immediately afterwards handed Zach a poem intended for the opening moments of the new CD, now titled "Interment for Two":

My Dear, as you lie napping and I stroke your matted hair,

I feel compelled to prove to you how much I really care.

I may not say "I love you" very often to your face,

but deep inside you know that you're my favorite basket case.

We share a certain chemistry and get along so well,

it makes me want to stay with you regardless of the smell.

They say the love you take is equal to the love you make,

but nothing says "I love you" like a hammer and a stake!

We packed up the equipment and went into the house when Zach whipped out a VHS tape and handed it to Mike. He loaded it up, we all sat on the sofa and were treated to a third generation dub of the only surviving episode of *Action in the Afternoon*. The "lecture track" was provided live by Zach himself, and we were regaled with inside stories about the cast members and production. Unfortunately, this episode was broadcast before Zach became a part of the cast, but you can't have everything. A quick brunch of pancakes and sausage prepared by Ruth, and at about one p.m. Zach was ready to go. We passed the time going back to Manhattan listening to a CD of one of Zach's K-Rock Halloween shows from 1992. I dropped him off and, despite the great day, spent the rest of the ride home beating myself up over not having asked him a thing on video about *Dr. Horror*. The following Saturday, March 27, I was up early setting up my camera equipment. Zach was on the road again, on his way out here for a brief taping. He was nice enough, as expected, to agree to this session after I called him and explained my dilemma over not getting any comments from him on camera last week at the Gilks place. I offered to drive over to his apartment where we could with very little effort shoot him answering a few questions about his appearance in Dr. Horror. I couldn't believe that he suggested coming out to Jersey to do it. I was beginning to think he liked my house. Again he had brought his suitcase with the costume and we set up to shoot in the living room. Zach knew exactly what he wanted to do, and the idea of a straight question-and-answer session went out the window. The thing with Zach was, if he wanted to "perform," it was best to let him go his own way — the results were always better and funnier than sitting him in a chair answering some dry questions. "Now, you said you have the 'Spook Along' album?" he asked me. "Yes, it's on the CD player now," I said. "Well, start up the song 'Frank and Drac Are Back,'" he continued, and his soft-shoe act and plugs for *Dr. Horror* that followed were far more entertaining than any interview we could have done.

It was a wrap, but not before I screwed up again by not pushing the **RECORD** button when I thought I did, causing one whole take to be for naught. When we did it a second time and got a good one, Zach insisted on looking at it and suggested we do it a third time just to be sure. I wasn't asking, but I wasn't passing up the opportunity either. We were both happy with the last take, Zach packed up his costume and we headed out on a cloudy morning for a short ride. I wanted to at least treat him to lunch for having gone to this trouble, so we drove up through Piermont, New York, and then to Nyack. Zach suggested we drop in on an old friend of his named Susan Reed, a former folk singer from the '50s who had been running a unique clothes shop on Nyack's Broadway since the early '70s. The former wife of Zach's friend, actor friend James (*Poltergeist*) Karen, Susan dealt in jewelry, clothing and art from all over the world, and, sadly, had just begun the process of selling the business. She apparently hadn't seen Zach for a long time and was thrilled that he had dropped in. I enjoyed watching these two old friends reminisce, but also found her stories about friends Pete Seeger and Tom Chapin (among others) quite enthralling. We excused ourselves after about an hour and drove back to Piermont's Sidewalk Cafe, where, in the outside rear garden, the clouds began to part and the sun streamed down on what felt like a perfect Spring day. I ordered a crock of French onion soup and Zach dined on a lunch of shrimp and rice. For his health, he had also cut back on his alcohol intake and ordered a non-alcoholic beer. I felt thankful for being able to spend some more quality time with him.

Chapter 19
The Grand Reunion

September 19, 2003, a Friday, still carried the remaining traces of Hurricane Isabel, which had traveled up the East Coast causing havoc in North Carolina, Virginia and western Pennsylvania. Clouds still frowned from the sky and spits of rain sprinkled against the windshield, but the full fury of the storm had missed the New York-New Jersey area and had moved to the northwest, now a mere tropical storm. The windshield in question was not my own, because I was driving Zach's Honda Civic into the city to pick him up for a milestone event in his life, a reunion of the Stagecrafters, a community theater group he had joined back in the early 1950s.

This group had been responsible for jump-starting his acting career, eventually turning the mild-mannered Philadelphian into the surly and legendary Roland in October 1957. Why was I driving Zach's car? Because on the previous Monday he had taken a stroll from his West 96th Street apartment up to Central Park to see a fireworks display, lost his balance on one of those corner slopes meant for wheelchairs, and taken a tumble that resulted in the dislocation of his right shoulder. A day in the hospital and Zach left sporting a sling, bruises and a puffy shoulder. So now I was driving the little Honda Civic down the West Side Highway and up 96th Street for a journey out to the affluent Chestnut Hill area of Philadelphia and a visit to Zach's past. I was armed with a video camera, 35mm camera and tape recorder just in case.

Zach emerged from his apartment building wearing blue jeans, a long-sleeved pale blue shirt and white walking shoes — his standard casual dress. With a little difficulty he worked his way into the passenger seat and we were off. Even at 85, Zach was still a rock'n'roll devotee, and we traveled the tedious stretches of the New Jersey Turnpike with the Rolling Stones blaring from the speakers, both of us singing along like kids, and Zach (to my amusement) at the top of his lungs with that familiar operatic vibrato he always brought to his records and *Shock Theater* operettas. I laughed inside as I listened to him singing "She's a Rai-i-n-bow-w-w" in that voice. Keeping time with his hands and tapping his feet, it seemed impossible that this wasn't a much younger man, someone who was a kid when these songs were first played on the radio.

When we reached the Philadelphia area, we spent some time at one of the beautiful parks in Zach's old stomping grounds, and also an ancient boathouse within which canoes were stored for rides taken with friends in his youth on the Wissahickon Creek. It was obvious that Zach loved his home town and its surroundings. At one point, a profusion of ducks caught his eye, particularly three or four white ones which stood out. "You know," Zach mused, "it's entirely possible that one of those ducks is a descendent of the old duck from *Disc-O-Teen*. I let him go upstream from here in this very creek. Except it wasn't a him, it was a her!"

The Stagecrafters is a still-functioning community theater located on Germantown Avenue in exclusive Chestnut Hill. I had known about the group for years; after all, it has been a part of Zacher-lore for any true fan. It is historic for Zach, and I could see that it was very important to him that he attend this reunion. He spent many happy years there in the early '50s building scenery, painting and doing any odd jobs needed by the group, including, of course, acting. Zach was "knocking around" after getting out of the Army (Zach served in North Africa and Italy during World War II), and his cousin suggested that he join this local acting group.

Germantown Avenue is like a combination of an old New England hamlet and the main drag in Piermont, New York. Piermont was the location used in the Woody Allen movie *The Purple Rose of Cairo* (1985); watch the film and you will see the village with its storefronts rebuilt to recreate the look of a Depression-era town. Its cousin, Germantown Avenue, elegant, illuminated by the golden glow of globe-capped streetlights, is a home to small shops and artists' studios. An oldfashioned oval sign, **Stagecrafters**, hangs over the sidewalk on the east side inviting you to visit. There, set back about 100 feet to the rear of the adjacent building, is what Zach described as an "old barn," looking as if it had perched there for 200 years, sturdy, built of the same rock as many of the historical houses in the area, with a timber upper section above a pair of wooden doors, upon which hangs a sign in tasteful, scrolled, rust-colored lettering bearing the theater's name. As Zach explained, the doors opened to permit scenery to be brought in, which, when put in place, left little or no room for movement behind the set. Upon entering the theater itself, I was impressed at the modernity of its facilities — new seats, air conditioning — and a look of comfort, while still managing to evoke the feeling of days long gone.

Zach was immediately greeted by his old friend Jack Matlack, white-haired, with an infectious smile and laughing eyes, surprisingly young-looking for a man of 83 years, who included me in the conversation and made me feel welcome right away. I was saddened when it was revealed that this gregarious gentleman was suffering from emphysema and cancer brought on by years of smoking, but it was heartwarming to see the strong affection the two men had for each other. I was here, sharing a very personal piece of Zach's past with him, meeting people

Zach with his friend Jack Matlack, a Stagecrafters alumnus.

from his youth, and enjoying the privilege of a glimpse into the birth of his career. One by one the elder attendees became aware of Zach's presence and showed obvious delight at seeing him again. A middle-aged, stout woman with short, dark hair and a cherubic face introduced herself as the current president of the group and immediately announced that there would be some special presentations made just before the show. Conversation flowed, Zach's slinged arm prompting his story of his fall in Manhattan, but it wasn't long before the adoring fans, the older members of the group, started talking about their fond memories of Roland. Zach obviously expected that, and I feel he enjoyed the recognition, but part of him was observably and understandably more interested in talking about the old theater days.

Jack took me aside at one point and told me a story I couldn't believe. "I was on his last Roland show, you know." "Oh, really?" I asked, wondering how and why. "Yeah, one of the actors who was supposed to appear couldn't, so I was enlisted." "To do what?" I continued. "I was a man in a white coat who came to take him away," said Jack. I was dumbfounded. To any Zacherley or Roland fan, this was a revelation. Zach appeared in New York on two different local stations — WABC Channel 7 during the 1958-59 season, and on WOR Channel 9 the following year. On the last installment of both shows, a man in a white coat came in (supposedly from Bellevue Hospital) to "return him to the nuthouse" from which he had apparently escaped. On WABC the part of Dr. Bellevue had been played by hefty sound effects man Bob Prescott, on WOR by a cherubic man of similar bulky appearance. Never had I heard that the same had been done on WCAU in Philly, but here was the man who had allegedly played the part telling me about it! I looked over my left shoulder at Zach, who was gesturing and wrinkling his nose into a puzzled expression, apparently having overheard Jack's story. I excused myself and asked Zach what was going on. He whispered, "I don't know what he's talking about. I don't remember doing that on the Philadelphia show." We dropped it for the moment, but for the rest of the evening I wondered whether the story was true or just a figment of an old man's imagination.

Approaching Zach was a nicely dressed old lady, slim, with white hair and carrying a cane. She looked to be about 90 years old. One of the older members had told Zach she was there and wanted to reunite him with her. Before she was within earshot, Zach held his free hand up to his mouth and whispered in my ear, "Excuse me, I have to pretend I know this lady." I tried hard to stifle a laugh, turning away so she wouldn't notice. As she extended her hand, Zach's face simulated a look of recognition and delight: "My gosh, how are you? It's so good to see you again!" It turned out that the lady was the oldest member of the group, at 94 still active and well. I don't think Zach ever did remember who she was.

Parked on a wooden bench in a tree-shaded yard adjacent to the theater, Zach, Jack and I chatted pleasantly about the past. We were regularly visited by theater members, many of whom wanted to get a picture of the man they remembered from those late-night horror shows of old. Flashbulbs popped. Cute teenage girls from a local deli named Bruno's circulated with large plates of the most delicious hors d'oeuvres ever, the wine flowed freely, as did the old stories and shared memories. Across the yard stood a tall stockade fence in need of repair, the tops of antique houses looking down over it onto a crowd that was rapidly growing. There were now about 200 people milling around as a warm autumn breeze kept us all comfortable. Zach, about to pop a cherry tomato into his mouth, looked up at me and shouted, "Food — G-O-O-O-D!" A rare monster-related joke coming from him.

It was nearing eight p.m., at which time the Stagecrafters were planning the presentations to take place on the stage, and then the old chestnut *Arsenic and Old Lace* was to be performed. Zach had never planned on staying for the show, and began making the rounds to say his goodbyes to old friends. I shook hands one last time with Jack, feeling a warmth colored by the melancholy of knowing that his condition would probably grant him only a few more years of life. I had written down his name and address, promising to send him a copy of *The Zacherley Archives*, in which he could see Bob Prescott (whom he said he had known) playing the white-jacketed part at the end of Zach's last WABC show. With that, Zach and I headed out toward the street where his car was parked. I was so pleased that I was there to share some memories of his younger days and get a look into a part of his life that I had only read about, never thinking that I'd one day be sharing it with him.

The Stones again blasted from the car speakers as we sped down the Pennsylvania Turnpike at nine p.m. "You know, Zach," I said, turning down the music for a minute, "I've been thinking about Jack's claim that he played the part of the guy in the white coat on your last Roland show, and it comes to this: You yourself told me that the man has an uncanny memory, and how could he make up something like that? If he hadn't done it, he would have had to have seen your New York show to have even known about the Dr. Bellevue bit. So how could he retain that memory unless he actually played it as he said?" Also, truth be told, by his own admission, Zach's memory could be notoriously spotty, so I felt that it would be better to default to Jack's. Zach agreed; perhaps Jack had played the part. But unless some lost kinescope miraculously comes to light or someone else's memory of that last Roland show surfaces, we'll never know for sure.

RICH: How did you enjoy the reunion?

ZACH: Oh, I thought it was great! My big regret was that when the lady who we first met when we went in there had asked me before I left, "Did you get here for the 50th?" And of course, I said, "No, I don't even remember that it happened." It may have been that I was, like I told you earlier, working in New York. If anybody did ask me to come down, I didn't even know about it. I wish I had, because the people that I knew when I was there would have still been alive. But there were very few of them there on Friday.

RICH: How many people did you meet from the old days besides Jack?

ZACH: I guess maybe ... I had to fake it, I can't remember between faking it and ... but of people who actually were there a long time, I guess a couple dozen, I don't know. But I didn't actually remember them. Then there were the people who just knew me from television, knew me from being Roland, who were not members way back then. But it's too bad, really, there were so many people that were active. I think that they and all these little groups must be in trouble now, there's so much going on in the world in the way of what do you do with your spare time? They say it's just tough getting people interested to come out and be in plays. And Jack said that the audiences are not very good any more. That's something else, you know — do you want to go to the theater or do you want to watch football on TV or whatever?

RICH: It may come back.

ZACH: Well, it may, it may, but you know, there are so many other things that people will do, go home and play with their computer at night or whatever. Regional theater just has to compete against too many things. It's a shame, because there is nothing like live theater.

As a fitting postscript to the experience, as promised I sent a copy of *The Zacherley Archives* to old Jack with a few words attached telling him how nice it was to meet him. Within a week, I received a short note:

SEPT. 30, 2003

RICH:

THANKS FOR SENDING ME THE KINESCOPE OF ZACH. IT'S AMAZING. IN OUR DISCUSSION OF THE "SHOCK THEATRE" (WITH ZACK) [SIC] AT CBS CH. 10 IN PHILA., I WASN'T ON THE SET AS LONG AS BOB PRESCOTT. HE MUST HAVE BEEN ON AT LEAST 10 MINUTES.

THANKS AGAIN

JACK MATLACK

The next time I spoke to Zach, I read him the note. The mystery seemed to be solving itself. With customary good humor he seemed to accept the fact that his old friend most likely did indeed play the Philadelphia equivalent of Dr.

Bellevue, the cameo that grew into a featured part for sound effects man Bob Prescott and for his successor when Zach moved to WOR Channel 9 in New York. Yes, there was a Dr. Bellevue on the last show there also. His identity remains a mystery to me, my only memory being that he was large and round (like Prescott) and had a baby face. Zach didn't remember that either, but I was watching and I remember. That's good enough for me.

In June 2005, while finishing the last chapters of this book, Zach called me with the sad news that he had a funeral to attend. Jack Matlack had passed away.

Chapter 20
Excursions

Tuesday morning, December 9, 2003, a brisk winter's day. Snow and ice from a recent storm still covered the city streets, and I headed along with Zach to the Boathouse, one of his favorite eateries in Central Park. He had invited me, rather cryptically, into the city today and told me to expect to spend the day here. When I asked him what he had planned, he simply said, "Oh, just a fun day in New York City!" After a guided tour in and around the park, the Boathouse was our first stop at around 11 a.m., a place Zach likes to hang out when he has to move his car for the sanitation workers to clean the streets. Dressed in jeans and a blue winter coat and sporting a cane for relief from the arthritis in his feet, he led me into the dimly lit building over to a series of tables looking out through huge glass windows upon a small lake. The scene was sheer postcard stuff, a blanket of snow covering everything in sight, including overturned aluminum boats stacked up on the shore and, in the near distance, the New York skyline. It's easy to see why Zach likes to kill time here. Over coffee and bran muffins we discussed people we know in common and went over plans for the DVD release of *The Zacherley Archives*. It became apparent that Zach had a case of cabin fever and needed desperately to get out of his small apartment, and I appreciated the fact that he chose to spend an entire day with me.

The cabin fever had its origin in his accident the previous autumn. Now that he was wearing a sling and unable to drive, I drove into Manhattan with my friend Mike Brunas and brought Zach's car back to my place where, as I mentioned earlier, it would remain garaged in my backyard for the next two months. Worse news followed: It turned out that Zach's shoulder was not just dislocated, but broken, and a piece of bone had snapped off and lodged within some muscle tissue. An operation had followed at Lennox Hill Hospital on September 26 (Zach's 85th birthday), the whole experience, according to Zach, the most painful thing he had ever been through in his life. He was also less than pleased at the hospital's initial treatment of him, causing him to lie there in excruciating pain, buzzing for a nurse and being for the most part ignored. After several sessions of (also painful) physical therapy, he was on the mend, and even dispensed with the sling in time for the October

Zach atop Perkins Drive at Bear Mountain, New York.

Chiller Theatre expo, where he sang and danced on stage for the midnight show as if nothing had ever happened.

By early afternoon we were on our way to the Museum of Natural History and Planetarium to catch a few exhibits and see the sky show. Making our way through the spacious hallways, we found ourselves staring through the glass at a diorama recreating a meeting between the Hackensack Indians and Peter Stuyvesant commemorating the birth of Manhattan. The chief was walking peacefully toward the white men, hand outstretched in a gesture of obvious good will. I said, "Look, it's the Hackensack Indians." Zach returned, quickly and quietly, "Yeah, on their way to gettin' fucked." It's these moments, understated and unexpected, that make the private John Zacherle such a funny man. I knew exactly what he meant, but it's the offhand manner in which he tossed it off that had me breaking up. I couldn't help myself, I just turned to him and said, "You really don't know how funny you are, do you?" His response was to continue on about how the white man royally screwed the Native Americans by paying them that paltry $24 worth of trinkets and junk. Zach, if you haven't guessed by now, was a tried-and-true liberal.

After viewing a new exhibit, "Petra, the Lost City of Stone," we took in the sky show, always wondrous and even more so in its new refurbished format. During the narrator's hypnotic description of the awesome size of the universe, I caught Zach out of the corner of my eye staring upward and lost in thought, a man with an endearingly childlike sense of wonder; a man in awe of science and history. We left the museum at midafternoon, thinking I'd be dropping him off for the day. Instead he asked me to come up for awhile and help him sort through more pictures he had uncovered. Again I sat on the floor and arranged the pile into sections to be filed into the appropriate careerphase envelopes, a task I thoroughly enjoyed, being probably the first one in years other than Zach himself to look upon some of these treasures. The picture-sorting took enough time to allow us to run out to Acqua for a quick Italian dinner. Then it was back home for Zach and back to New Jersey for me.

While the city outing was new for me, I had been, in the last couple of years, company for Zach on what is his prime passion — taking long rides in the country. I wasn't the only friend to join him for these trips; best friend Jeff Samuels had been his country companion for many years, and Zach told me that he was always hijacking someone to join him on the rides. I had enjoyed this pastime by myself many years ago, but stopped during the energy crisis of the early '70s to avoid those long lines at the gas station becoming more than a once-a-week event. However for the past two years or so I would find myself sitting next to Mr. Zacherle in his Civic as we whizzed up and down the mountain roads of Harriman Park and Bear Mountain, his favorite afternoon activity. He always brought along a cache of cassettes with his favorite music, usually careful to somewhat tailor it to my (and, I assume, whoever would be his traveling companion) taste so that we could both enjoy it. I have always held that Zach had a lot of little boy in him) and this would come out whenever we reached a certain spot on the ride, where he would put the car in neutral and see how far it would coast down the hillside, the goal being to beat his last record for distance. During the summer of 2001, when my friend Paul was gearing up to film *Dr. Horror*, he needed the entrance to a cave as a setting for one of the stories, and Zach said he knew the perfect spot; not actual caves, but huge openings in the rocks that you could actually walk into. Somewhere I have a video of Zach, attired in T-shirt and shorts, leering and ducking in and out of one of these locations.

The mountain jaunts happened so frequently (and still do to this day) that they took on a definite pattern: Zach would pull up to my house somewhere between 10 and 11 o'clock in the morning (I had recently retired from my job at NBC Television in New York, and was available at almost any time for these travels), get out and carefully Windex the windows, front and back. Then it would be off to either the Palisade Interstate or Route 17 north to the Bear Mountain area. During a few rides, I had the satisfaction of suggesting we retrace the ride my father always took, the back roads through Washington Township and luxurious and affluent Upper Saddle River, with its castle-like houses and garishly luxurious properties. A short cut through a private development called Powderhorn Estates was always on the route. Zach loved it, and always bristled at the showy excess of the expansive estates, but his appreciation of the beauty of the countryside was very much like my father's. He would always traverse the scenic Seven Lakes Drive, and during the fall take in the eye-popping foliage through the twists and turns of Harriman Park. Once when I was along, he provided tinted glasses for both of us to bring out the color of the autumn mountains more vividly. He loved Harriman so dearly that at times, when he couldn't sleep due to a noisy upstairs neighbor, he would drive up there the next day and doze off in a favorite spot under a tree. He even went so far as to mention, during a conversation about death, that when his time came, he would like to be cremated and have his ashes spread around his beloved Harriman Park.

The high point of our rides was always the search for a place to eat lunch. I had never eaten in the Bear Mountain Inn, with its long history and massive wooden rooms and great fireplace, until Zach took me there, incredulous that it was my first time inside the place. Another of his favorite places was Greenwood Lake, a summer vacation resort on the New York-New Jersey border. Long winding roads up into the hills surround the lake; there are hundreds of cabins and bungalows, each with its own unique charm. Zach enjoyed picking out the ones he'd like to own, expressing his desire to move out of the city to a small property with a garden, trees and the chirping of birds. His dream would remain a dream when he'd realize that he could never bring himself to give up his rent-controlled apartment, something he would always be chained to due to its extreme affordability. I always thought Zach was at heart a city dweller, but he seemed genuinely frustrated that he'd probably never know the pleasures of living in the country. His favorite lunch stop along the lake was the Breezy Point Inn, a place right on the water where you could sit out on a huge deck, nurse a drink and watch the boats go by in the shadows of the surrounding mountains. More often than not, though, lunchtime would fall at a

ings of many American folk singers including the Kingston Trio, Bob Dylan, Joan Baez, Judy Collins and many more. He had gotten it for being a member of PBS Broadcasting, listened to it once and decided to make a present of it. I have played and enjoyed it many times since. We headed up to the usual mountains, west through Harriman, and stopped for lunch at the South Street Restaurant on Route 17 in Tuxedo, New York. The thing I remember most about this stop: the restaurant's other patrons, only four people, all obese. Zach

Zach at his favorite destination, the Breezy Point Inn, with me and Marsha, Disc-O-Teen's "flower child."

time when there was nothing more available than the old reliable country diner, where Zach generally ordered a grilled cheese and tomato sandwich.

On Friday, January 24, 2003, a very cold day, Zach popped over at 9:30 AM, bearing gifts: a book and video devoted to the life story of one of his favorite scientists, Nikola Tesla, a man who popular legend has it would have taken American technology ahead through quantum leaps with his theories about solar power and other alternative energy sources. Another gift, one I treasure, was a ten CD set called "This Land Is Your Land—The Folk Years," featuring the record-

murmured, shaking his head, "About four other people here and they're all overweight." He has never had much tolerance for corpulence, not due to any particular prejudice, but more because of overweight people's apparent disregard for their health.

Winter didn't put a damper on the ritual; one morning I got a call asking me if I had my video camera handy so that I could tape the spectacle of snow clinging to the northern pines and covering the mountains in the distance. I have a video of the view out the window of Zach's car during two of these rides, but for me the novelty of a record of the event (with shots of Zach at the wheel singing along to his tapes) eclipses the rather unspectacular footage. The most memorable of these winter rides by far was the time we were combining business with pleasure, enjoying another snowy jaunt in the hills while conducting an interview for this book. With my portable cassette recorder running, Zach rattled off story after priceless story about his years at *Disc-O-Teen*, when I realized, with my consummate professionalism, that in the recorder was my only blank tape, with only about 30 minutes of recording time left. Zach suggested we pull into a huge mall in the area called Woodbury Commons where I could buy some blank cassettes. It then dawned on me that we were in the vicinity of my brother Steve's cabin in Monroe, New York, a place I had described many times to Zach, and which he had expressed a desire to see. I thought, "Why not now?" Zach agreed, and after buying the tapes we headed up into the mountains toward the cabin. Steve had purchased the small bungalow to live in during the summer months, while spending the winter in his primary house in Naples, Florida. My brother Doug and I would sometimes alternate in riding up there, usually in the Spring, to check on the condition of the place. I had never gone up those steep, winding roads in the wintertime — most of it was unpaved and rocky, and regular snowplowing was the responsibility of the local residents. Slowly Zach's little white Civic crept up the mountain until the cabin came into view. Even though the going was slow, the slippery, twisty road up to that point was passable. As soon as we reached the cabin, we could see that the road ahead was a cascading sheet of ice. A few feet more to afford us a view of the property and it would be time to turn around. Then, immediately and without warning we heard a loud "thump!" and the right side of the car slumped down into a ditch deep enough that the right front wheel was in a free spin. I thought it was extractable, but Zach knew we were screwed. "Oh, that's it, this is bad, we're stuck!" he said calmly. He was right. The ditch was deep enough so that the entire body of the car rested on the icy road surface. "Shit!" I thought. Here I

Zach with my brother Steve at Steve's cabin in Monroe, New York.

bring Zach out of his way on an Arctic expedition that could have waited for better weather and I've stranded us and maybe damaged his car. Damn! On top of that, it was mid-afternoon and it got dark around four o'clock. Zach, gentleman that he is, tried to calm me by insisting that he wasn't upset, but all I could think of was that I was responsible for stranding his car, and that being stuck in the cold on top of a mountain in the snow with a man in his eighties was not going to be fun. "Listen, we've eaten, it's not that cold, and we don't have to pee. It could be a lot worse," was Zach's attitude.

I knocked on the door of my brother's neighbor Leroy's house, who, to our good fortune, had just winterized his cabin and was now living there year-round. Smiling and helpful, out he came, looking like a combination of Grizzly Adams and Haystacks Calhoun, took one look at the situation and told us the good news: There wasn't anything he could do to help! But he did give me the number of a local towing service, and within a half hour Zach's car was being slowly dragged out of its icy prison via hydraulics and a hefty hook and chain. We bade goodbye to Leroy, headed down the mountain and back home. Zach's take on it? "Hey, we had an adventure!"

An excerpt from a July 2004 phone message from Zach:

> Maybe next week we can do this: My plan would be for you to come in here someday like Tuesday or Wednesday and come inside and we'll get everything out and see what's here. Then we'll program it so we won't be saying, "Shall we do this, shall we do that?" when the time comes, and we'll hang pictures on the wall, the big pictures that have to hang, actually — the framed pictures, so that they're ready to go at a moment's notice, and we can plan the thing and then any other afternoon come in again and we can start right off. I'll get dressed up and do the whole schtick, and we should probably test the smoke bombs, well, we'll talk that over ahead of time, see how much of the ingredients of a smoke bomb we need, and the lighting and all that stuff, so that we just spend one afternoon shooting it. I think it'll be easy, and I'll do the whole act and we'll show everything and we'll get it organized ahead of time.

Thus the seeds of bonus material for the DVD release of *The Zacherley Archives* were planted one hot July afternoon with a declaration of Zach's intentions for the unveiling of his fabled closet — the holding room for an untold amount of career-oriented paraphernalia, posters, paintings, letters, sculptures, records, scripts and *objets d'art* — you name it. Just when I thought I had seen everything possible Zacherley-wise, the contents of The Closet, "King Tut's tomb" to Cool Ghoul fans, were about to be shown to the fans, and I would have a front row seat.

Phase 1 of "Project Closet" was comprised of unloading everything we could find within. A large white door opened into a walk-in about 8' x 5' x 6' in area, not overly huge, but the high ceiling made way for a series of shelves upon which many rolled-up posters, wooden boxes (they caught my eye!) and pieces of luggage were stacked. On the floor were more boxes, framed pictures and what looked like an old black leather doctor's bag. "We have to take everything out, and I can't reach the shelves very easily these days," Zach said. I immediately reassured him that it was my immense pleasure to help in this endeavor. "I want to hang a few pictures too," came next, and I soon found myself on a stepladder doing my best to straighten out Barbara McCormick's large oil portrait of Zach, and a nicely impressionistic representation of the Grim Reaper ("Father Time without any skin," as Zach described it). When the pictures were hung and the closet for the most part emptied, I was able to begin appreciating some of the treasures I was holding: Zach's original frock coat, worn when he was Roland in 1957, through the *Shock Theater* New York years, and abandoned after the demise of *Disc-O-Teen*, a pair of gray Roland spats, and the orange and black-striped Gay Nineties–style bathing suit he occasionally wore on the air.

Phase 2 was to lay everything out in some kind of order so we could videotape Zach reminiscing about the items and giving credit to any fans whose names were affixed to the various artifacts. Zach always appreciated when people took the time to create original works of art, and if they were clever enough he would keep them. I was impressed with the array of sculptures, done mostly by females (the surfeit of creations sent in by teenaged girls caused Zach to reflect with amusement, "I was hot and I didn't know it!").

The largest, about two and a half feet tall, was fan Gretchen Sharpless' version of Gasport, sitting in his burlap bag, the upper third of his body exposed, looking like a moaning dwarf monk. An attached card read **Season's Greetings to Lost Souls Everywhere.**

Gretchen had also contributed a small white bust of Zach in caricature, totally impressionistic in concept, and a large Christmas card showing a Gothic mansion. When you opened the cutout flaps of the dozen-plus window shutters, a different monster appeared. I could go on forever describing the huge assortment of art, but most of it took the form of handmade cards, charcoal sketches, and in one case a beautiful life-size Zacherley wax head done by Rosemary Schroeder. All these items and more can be seen in the bonus section of the *Zacherley Archives* DVD.

Once everything was laid out, I began taping with my hand-held Panasonic mini-digital camera. We started with Zach emerging from the closet, upon the door of which he had smeared a generous helping of mud for "atmosphere." Coughing and acting like the air inside had turned foul from years of disuse, Zach commanded his audience to retreat to "the parlor" while he unloaded the closet. Joining us inside the parlor, the tour through the many years of his career began. Rosemary's huge color portraits of Zach and his family were first, followed by Ms. Sharpless' work, some twistedly gruesome and detailed black-and-white pen-and-ink creature drawings by Philadelphia fan Anne "Roland" Ambirge, and finally an impressive collection of fine creations by mother-and-daughter team Ruth and Dona Steinman. Ruth and Dona had at one point met up with New York fan Anne Di Dio (whose written recollections provided some very welcome notes for this book's appendix) and between the three of them contributed some of the finest and most detailed work of all of Zach's TV career. Among the most impressive items were a 1961 Zacherley calendar with fine artwork for all 12 months, a book of grisly nursery rhymes titled "A Child's Garden of Curses," a handmade cushion containing Zacherley images in beautiful stitch work, a beanbag fish and snake (both used on the air), a small collection of homemade Zach dolls, *The Transylvanian Times* (a full newspaper with different sections) and, of course, the official full color Transylvania map, too large to photograph except in sections.

Another segment of the taping was devoted to the contents of the doctor's bag, containing a pile of ancient medical tools including the familiar oversized silver hypo with which Zach injected the cauliflower brains and amoebas. Various leg and arm bones emerged from the bag also, along with (as we found out later) a gizmo used for spreading the rib cage during open heart surgery (ouch!). Most if not all of these were provided by Zach's older brother George, who was a doctor. Next were two collector's items which would probably snag a small fortune today on eBay: an original poster used on Philadelphia buses to promote *The Saturday Evening Post* issue featuring the first ever article on the Roland *Shock Theater* show, and the original six-foot poster of Zach once advertised in *Famous Monsters of Filmland*—in near-mint condition! Many more items were put on display, too many to list here, but we finally, after a full afternoon's work, ended on a shot of an ingenious mobile made up of arms, legs, a bat, mace, a tana leaf jug and a coffin, "swinging around in the warm, fetid air" of the Zacherle apartment.

The entire project took two full days to realize. The first was devoted to sorting and laying out the items in different categories, the second, July 2, 2004, to the taping itself. Zach had turned off his air conditioner during the taping because of the noise it added to the audio, and the summer heat made for a sweaty and uncomfortable shoot in Zach's small apartment. We had only one more thing to tape, an ending with Zach in the basement of my house, sitting bathing-suit–clad in the chair he had given me, having a "cookout" of sorts by heating up hot dogs and marshmallows in the electrical arc of his Zap Machine. His idea. When the time came, my camera inconveniently developed a problem and became useless, to my utter embarrassment (Zach had already gotten into makeup), so the "addendum" to the closet tape had to be postponed, causing me to call on George Ann to help us finish it. No big deal; the major portion of "Project Closet" was in the can.

Was it? You'd think I'd learn. Another Zach phone message:

> This was a great "dress rehearsal," the whole thing. I think I looked terrible and I sounded terrible on the tapes, now that I think about it, and I will organize it much better next time, all we need is a good camera that goes in and out, and if we have to rent one we'll rent one, whatever, but I think we can do it if we got a … you and I are both retired and we can do this and do it better. I just didn't like the way things were laid out and my scrambling around to do things. Now we know what it looks like — it's a great dress rehearsal, no kidding. And I will use makeup next time — I looked like a dead person who died maybe 20 years ago! I sounded that way too. I've gotta pick my voice up and be a little bit more cheerful. But organization is what it needs. So we'll do it, and maybe we can do that thing with the Transylvania map with George Ann, as you said she's willing to do that. We could do that and get that out of the way, that'd be okay. But we still need a good camera, we really do. You broke your … neck, I was gonna say your ass, but your ass is already broken. You did a great job, but we still need a camera that works and doesn't frustrate you to death."

At this point I was getting used to redoing projects with Zach, and was fortunate enough to have good friends like Paul and George Ann who have always risen to the occasion whenever a situation of this sort arises. Much more than I, they are consummate professionals and always get the job done right and on time. That is exactly what happened, because on Friday, July 16, George Ann and I returned to West 96th Street, had breakfast at the Boathouse with Zach while waiting for a place to park in the neighborhood, then trekked up to the apartment and finished the job with which Zach was originally displeased. Six days later, in my basement (which now housed the needed Zap Machine), we had the pleasure of a private Zacherley show in the grand old tradition as he "electrocuted" a series of small windup toys and roasted marshmallows at his "indoor barbecue." This time George Ann made it a two-camera shoot so that we could get close-ups of the toys waddling through the blue lightning of the Zap Machine, some of them catching fire halfway through. Manning the close-up camera, I saw the show through eyes full of tears, laughing so hard it hurt. It reminded me of those midnight evenings of long ago sitting in front of the TV console, the same emotions, the same laughing, a joy the Cool Ghoul gave all of us that I could never seem to get him to fully appreciate. When he had given me the machine, I had told him it was a sad occasion; I felt that he never planned to use it again. But never say never, right? We were finally finished, but Zach took the time to pose in costume and makeup for a few photos with the neighbors next door, older than I, but fans from their college days.

The next step was to edit the footage into an entertaining package and design a modified cover for the DVD. This, I hate to say, became a minor roadblock to the project and a major headache for me. Unbeknownst to us, Zach had cobbled together a cover design by taking the old VHS cover, flattening it out and cutting and pasting new information over old. For example, wherever it said "video" on the box he would literally paste a strip of paper that read "DVD" over it. He also added a cartoon-style balloon to his face on the back of the box that had him shouting "DVD!" That plus some other hand-drawn material gave the new design a kind of *Monty Python* look" that unfortunately Paul, George Ann and I didn't care for. Repeated attempts to explain why we couldn't send the Kinko's-reproduced artwork to the DVD people proved frustratingly fruitless,

A Zach phone message from October 23, 2004:

> I forgot to mention yesterday that I do this radio show on Monday, I don't know if you're able to go along to see it or be in it maybe even, because if you did want to go, I could get you "on the panel" or whatever the heck this is ... get you in there and talk about the book that you're writing and all that stuff, and the *Archives* DVD. I want to get a DVD anyway to take along with me and get to talk about that on the radio. I'm gonna take a CD along too, Mike's Gilks' first CD, which has a lot of stuff from the old *Shock Theater* show on it, you know, between the songs there's some audio from the early days of (loud, spooky voice) — ZACHERLEY — on television.

The radio show in question was to be taped on Monday, October 25 at Q104.3, the classic rock station in midtown Manhattan. As I listened to Zach's phone message, I couldn't believe what I was hearing; was I really going to be on a radio show with him and actually get to plug this book?

Zach had a relative with a vineyard in California. (Photo courtesy Tom Weaver.)

but I have to admit that Zach's original intent was to save us work by designing the new cover himself. The problem was resolved by Paul rescanning the original box and reproducing Zach's pop-art package as closely as possible. Once this was finished and the "closet show" polished up a bit, we added a few extra surprises and sent the results to the Florida-based DVD replication company. The new and improved *Zacherley Archives* would be debuting at the October 2004 Chiller Theatre Expo.

Almost as quickly as the thought came into my head, I told myself, "Don't get too excited about this, it may not happen the way Zach described it." At any rate, on a brisk sunny Monday afternoon at one p.m. I found myself in a cab with him headed downtown to the corner of West 46th Street and Sixth Avenue for our radio adventure. After another escapade, losing Zach on one of the new post-9/11 security elevators, we regrouped and entered the studio waiting room where we met Mike Furno, a video cameraman who had worked on the recently finished documentary *Unconventional*, a look at Kevin Clement's Chiller Theatre convention. We were soon ushered into a small studio where Zach introduced me to disc jockeys Maria Milito, Pat St. John (a former colleague of Zach's from his WPLJ days) and the man who was running the show that afternoon, Zach Martin. It was immediately apparent that my dream of speaking about this book on the air was, as I had warned myself, in the toilet, as we found out that Zach would be replacing the recently deceased Scott Muni as host of the station's Halloween special. Oh well, at least I had the privilege of sitting in on the show and helping Zach out if necessary. Deejay Martin went over the songs he wanted to play, giving Zach lots of leeway to choose cuts from the "Dead Man's Ball" CD as well as some vintage "Spook Along" songs.

I will say that the show, taped in advance with just Zach's intros and outros, was an absolute hoot. Martin went over the station's number, Q104.3, and reminded Zach to open with a mention of it. The tape rolled. Try as he might, Zach's memory would not serve him well, and he went through at least a half-dozen variations — "This is Q107.2 — no? 103.4?" and so on. All of us, including Mike Furno, who was videotaping the show from the sidelines, were in stitches. Zach was the most hysterical of all, laughing up a storm, tears glistening from the corners of his eyes, able to enjoy the irony of the fact that the man struggling in vain to get out this one bit of information had spent almost half his career as a deejay! As of this writing, I have no idea if that portion of the show was edited to remove the confusion, or more appropriately, left alone as a classic Zacherley moment. A few minutes later, Zach topped himself by describing how an installment of a live cable TV show he was doing years ago was taken off the air as he cavorted with a naked female rubber sex doll with a ping-pong ball in its mouth! It was more innocent than it sounds, but as he described it, he and the rest of us lost control again, Zach so much that he genuinely couldn't continue speaking! The breaking point came after his attempt to describe the action for a PG radio audience: "You see, the mouth was shaped to fit a ping-pong ball..." It was all over after that.

The show aired the evening of Friday, October 29, the opening night of the Chiller convention. Some months later, I helped Zach videotape a special message for his old friend Dick Clark who had recently suffered a pair of strokes. Zach sat in his old chair once more and introduced the video of our wild afternoon at Q104.3 which we edited to the end of his intro. Zach had it transferred to DVD, mailed it, and weeks later received this message from Clark:

MARCH 22, 2005

I CAN'T TELL YOU, JOHN, HOW MUCH I APPRECIATE YOUR STREAM OF MAGNIFICENT DIALOGUE FILLED WITH MEMORIES AND GOOD WISHES. THE DVD WAS REMARKABLE! YOU ARE TRULY OUTSTANDING AND AMAZING.

I CAN'T TELL YOU HOW MUCH YOUR WORDS MEANT TO ME. I ASSUMED YOUR DVD WAS SOME PROMOTIONAL TOOL FOR AN UPCOMING PRODUCTION. LITTLE DID I REALIZE, IT WAS SO PERSONALIZED AND INTIMATE.

MY BEST WISHES TO YOU, "THE COOL GHOUL." MAY YOU REIGN SUPREME FOR MANY MORE YEARS!

SINCERELY,

DICK CLARK

In the early days of a bitterly cold February in 2005, Zach made the trip to my house once more, this time bringing with him two large boxes the size of milk crates. I knew that he had been working on straightening up his apartment ever since we had strewn the contents of his closet all over his living room during the making of the "Zach's Closet" portion of the *Zacherley Archives* DVD. To try and prevent him from struggling with his ever-present hand truck, I hurried out to his car and grabbed one of the boxes which was fairly heavy. We got them both inside and Zach plopped himself onto the ottoman, myself in an easy chair facing him, the boxes between us. A piece of cardboard hid the contents of the first box. He removed it, and instantly I knew what he was going to leave with me. There they all were; the past lying before me in black vinyl. All the 45s that we danced to on *Disc-O-Teen* some 39 years ago were now lying at my feet. Zach had put together a collection of them on cassette some years ago and sent copies to a bunch of us, but now here was the real thing. As we started going through them, recollections came flooding back, images of the good times hanging out in Zach and Barry's office in the summer of 1966. Some singles forgotten, some probably never used on the air, but most were familiar — "Summertime," Billy Stewart's fabulous jazzy take on the George Gershwin tune; "Rescue Me" by Fontella Bass, a staple of the show in the fall of 1965; Gerry and the Pacemakers' beautiful ballad "Girl on a Swing" from 1967, where Zach would feature a different "Disc" regular riding on a swing in the studio every time he played the song (I can still see a lovely young Wende Sasse swinging herself high over the cameras during one show); "Good Lovin'" by the Rascals, "Uptight" by Stevie Wonder, "Expressway to Your Heart" by the Soul Survivors (not a favorite of mine, but so identified with the show it could almost have been its theme song), Los Bravos' "Black Is Black," the Capitols' "Cool Jerk" and many other priceless pieces of the past. Each were marked with a large "X" on the "A" side to denote which song was to be used on the show.

It's very strange: While *Disc-O-Teen* was happening, I felt I was not a participant but a gatecrasher, a kid watching from the sidelines, an observer seeing it through a pane of one-way glass. I had my camera to hide behind which gave me a feeling of legitimacy, but I never really felt I had a function there, just that I had to be there as surely as I had to be at school or at my job. Then during the planning for 1991's reunion, a role started to materialize for me. I realized I was playing

Wende Sasse and Zach reunite after 38 years at the April 2005 Chiller convention.

a sort of "historian," a keeper of memories. I had catalogued hundreds of Polaroid snapshots into six albums, and under each picture entered the names of some of the bands, the kids, dates and even times the show was taped for Saturday's broadcast. These photos helped give some structure to the two-and-a-half-year run of the show and aided me immeasurably in reconstructing the timeline for the story told in this book. I would often be asked questions by Zach ("Did we have a live band every day?") and was very happy to have an answer for him more often than not. I was gradually discovering that I was more a participant in the show than I had ever imagined; it was my show as much as it belonged to the people who worked on it and the kids who danced on it. But perhaps most significantly, it was an opening chapter to a much larger story.

On Sunday, September 11, 2005, the *Newark Star Ledger* "Spotlight" featured a story in their Sunday "Spotlight" section honoring the 40th anniversary of the Rolling Stones' 1965 Mosque Theater appearance. The article had included details of the concert related by Zach and my brother Doug. On November 7, Zach, my friend Tom Weaver, three ex-Herald Square members (Dave and Kurt Meyers and Doug Scrivani) and I stood on the Symphony Hall stage where the concert had taken place 40 years ago to the day. At Kurt's request, *Star Ledger* reporter Guy Sterling had arranged for the people in charge of the building to give this "tour," and brought along a photographer to boot. After being shown plans for the theater's complete restoration, we rode upstairs in the still-working, clattering elevator and stepped out into what used to be Channel 47's Studio "A" — the home of *Disc-O-Teen*. The huge, aging facility was empty now, painted black and dimly lit. A set of bleachers, also painted black, occupied the center of what used to be the dance floor. Zach chatted with the people who now ran the place, enjoyed seeing the studio again, and was visibly animated by memories of his old program. Roaming the halls, I was able to locate the room that had once been his and Barry's office. It was bare and freshly painted. I walked inside one last time with the man who had hosted the show, the man who was *Disc-O-Teen*. His only comments during the few seconds in which he revisited "the scene of the crime": "I forgot how tiny this place was," and "It's much too tidy now for my taste!"

It has been said that everything happens for a reason. Nothing has made that philosophy ring truer for me than things that have come to pass since *Disc-O-Teen*'s 39-year gestation period. In the intervening years, I would revisit my photo albums, and wonder: The experience was unique, the memories so luminous and strong, but — what was it all about? Why was it so important in my life? Did it just end there? I could never have imagined that it would all return to play out in a far more grand manner, almost as a symphony, with the original show serving as the first movement. The reunion offered a second chance to form adult friendships with kids I knew only fleetingly during the whirlwind of the mid-60s that, for us, manifested for "one brief shining moment" as *Disc-O-Teen*. For two of these "kids," Christine Domaniecki and Mike Thomas, it was even more vital; their long-standing relationship following the reunion eventually culminated in marriage. As for me, aside from getting to know these people again, the ensuing years yielded the gift of a treasured friendship with John Zacherle, the man who started it all. This is not unique to me, because for everyone life brings with it a touch of magic. Call it providence, destiny, fate or whatever you are comfortable with, all experiences are intertwined. One simply has to take the time to stop, look around and see.

It's a warm autumn afternoon in 1967. Another visit to *Disc-O-Teen* is coming to a close. There's a touch of melancholy in the air, but I can't put my finger on why. Zach has closed up the office and left the building; the last few kids are still hanging out near the elevators, but I don't recognize them. I don't seem to recognize anyone any more; most of the regulars have grown up and gone on to other things. As special as it has been these last two years, something has begun to dull the luster that seemed to hover over these corridors.

I pack up my camera, walk slowly down the marble stairway with its wrought-iron banister and into the poster-lined vestibule. As I head toward the brass doors that open onto Newark's Broad Street, I can make out Zach's tan Ford Falcon station wagon parked in front. Through the twilight, I see a half-dozen teenage girls sprawled over the hood, dry markers in hand, scribbling casually, some intently concentrating, others giggling. The car is being covered with graffiti. I want to tell these kids to stop until I see Zach and John the Cop standing off to the side, both of them cheerfully enjoying the spectacle, Zach actually cheering them on! I recognize two of the girls: June and Marsha Conner, regulars for the second year of the show's run — June, the quiet one, Marsha,

Three shots of Zach's graffiti-covered car.

Disc-O-Teen's beautiful "flower girl," often seen on camera sporting a radiant smile, either dancing with a small handful of posies or revealing a tiny one painted onto one of her cheeks. She seems to be having the most fun now as she adds huge yellow daisies to the psychedelic mural, below them the words **Love**, **Doughboys** and **Crunch**, among others.

I stop long enough to snap a few shots of this imaginative desecration, and Zach strikes a mock angry pose for the camera, as if to say, "What are you kids doing to my car?!" I wave goodbye and head down Broad Avenue toward Kinney Street and the parking lot where my Chevy awaits. But this time I sense a change in the surroundings. The "automobile artwork" seems strangely symbolic to me, like a line of demarcation between two different times. I didn't know it then, but the relatively simple years that characterized *Disc-O-Teen* were giving way to a new era of myriad colors; artistic and musical expression, experimentation, loss of innocence, and, with the increasing popularity of recreational drug taking, a touch of tragedy. I was leaving that innocent world behind as I walked away from the Mosque Theater that day.

Late March, 2005. This year's winter has been long and brutal; every time the weather seems to warm up and promise to erase the last traces of ever present snow, the skies cloud up again, the temperature plunges, and the countryside is once more coated with another three to six inches of the white stuff. Today it's about 60 degrees and Zach and I decide to take advantage

Another road trip: Enjoying the spring thaw in upstate New York, March 2003.

of this weather reprieve with another drive in the country. My newly acquired Toyota Prius bearing Zach and myself is heading further north this time, up the Thruway and into the Catskill Mountains. We stop for lunch at a small restaurant in the cozy little town of Phoenecia, New York. I wanted to show Zach where friends and I used to go tubing in the Esopus Creek, a substantial and beautiful waterway that winds through a mountain pass and along Phoenecia's outskirts. During lunch we pore through some contact sheets I found in my closet with small but outstanding photos of Zach in makeup from his Channel 9 and *Disc-O-Teen* days, hoping that he might be able to have them enlarged to 8x10 prints. He loves the shots and says he'll have a photographer friend check them out to see if they'll be usable for sale at the next Chiller convention. After lunch we wend our way through and over the mountains on what turns out to be the most awesome ride we have taken yet. The day is bright and warm, but snow is still plentiful in the hills; half-frozen waterfalls gleam in the sunlight and streams gurgle through the woods, swollen from the first stirrings of a spring thaw. On the return trip, Zach repeatedly thanks me for the ride and for driving, little knowing how lucky I feel being able to share these journeys with him. As we near my house, the afternoon still blue-skied and warm, Zach is inspired to sing a familiar tune: "When the fungus starts in spreadin', and the werewolves start their sheddin', it's a sure sign of spring!" I struggle to remember the lyrics, and join in:

> When each little girl amoeba acts like she's the Queen of Sheba, It's a sure sign of spring!
>
> When the ghosts close up their cupboards and move out to the suburbs, It can only mean one thing ...
>
> It's a sure, sure sign of spring!

"You know," Zach laughs, "we oughta call in to a radio station and request that they play this one today!"

We struggle on with the song, screwing up the words magnificently, on into the long shadows of the afternoon.

Afterword

John Zacherle today is, at 87, still active, vital and in demand. His major physical complaint remains the arthritis in his feet and ankles, which makes long walks difficult for him, and in recent years has taken to walking with the aid of a cane. His right shoulder has healed, but the doctors had told him that unless he went through one more operation to remove that piece of bone and muscle that had broken off in his fall, he would never regain complete mobility on that side. He has chosen to live with it the way it is. Though it's inconvenient at times, he has enough movement there for his needs, and has no intention of experiencing another excruciating operation.

Currently living in Los Angeles is a special lady, someone Zach has been romantically involved with for many years, the dazzlingly attractive Perri Chasin. Although the relationship is a long-distance one, he still makes the trip west from time to time to see her, and she comes east and stays with him at his apartment just as often. Zach's best friend Jeff Samuels has said that whenever Perri is in town, Zach gives her all the time at his disposal, causing him to do sort of a disappearing act for awhile. I have tried to get Zach to convince Perri to come in during the Halloween season so she can attend the Chiller convention and see how popular and adored he is with the fans. So far that hasn't happened. Her job as a teacher may limit her ability to take time off during that period. Long-distance relationships notwithstanding, the two have been together and very close for a long time, and I'm hoping that at some point I'll get to meet his better half. When it comes to that part of his life, Zach is extremely private, so I have asked very little about his relationship with Perri.

Being that Zach never seemed to take the significance of his calling very seriously (he once referred to it as "my so-called career"), I gave up trying to get him to give me a perspective on his life as a wrap-up for this book. I've decided to pinch hit for him:

If I were John Zacherle, I would be pleased about the world I created for my fans and elated that my years on the air meant so much to so many; that I created something original and uplifting, and through that character, beyond the makeup and the shadows, people could see the sensitive and kind man beneath, within reach, accessible, smiling at them. I would be grateful that my popularity did not fade, and my generosity of spirit so touched those who met me that many were still a part of my life a generation later. I would have appreciated that some people felt that the world was a better place for my presence. I would reflect on these thoughts during my quiet times, and I think it would have made me very happy.

At the October 2004 Chiller Theatre convention, PS Productions debuted the DVD version of *The Zacherley Archives*, a project that Paul, George Ann and myself considered a labor of love and of which we were honored to be a part. PS Productions has also released *Dr. Horror's "Erotic"*

> *When this book was originally published in 2006, it was capped by this afterword. I am retaining it in this volume even though it refers to Zach in the present tense and talks about his future plans.*
> *– Rich Scrivani*

House of Idiots on DVD, another treat for Zach's legion of fans. Mike Gilks' second Zacherley CD, "Interment for Two," was released in October 2005, and debuted to excited fans at Kevin Clement's Halloween Chiller Theatre expo. Zach continued to appear at Chiller, soon to be expanded to three shows a year, still attracting more fans to his table than most of the other celebrities there. He was also asked to be a guest at Lead East, an automobile expo held in Parsippany, New Jersey every Labor Day weekend. Uneasy at appearing there ("Who's gonna know me at a car show?"), he twice became the hit of the event. His table was constantly busy, so much so that Mike Thomas and I decided to stay with him and give him a hand for the rest of the weekend. So popular was Zach there that they drove him around in an open car on Saturday evening as he lip-synched "Dinner with Drac" to a very appreciative crowd! In the spring of 2000, Zach and Soupy Sales were the guests of honor at the "Doo Dah" Parade in Ocean City, New Jersey, and Zach was asked to appear again in 2004.

He was busier than ever.

Zach at Chiller with Billy Mumy of TV's Lost in Space.

Zach at Chiller with Elvira, "who had two things I never had," to quote Zach.

With Ray Manzarak of The Doors at Chiller (Photo courtesy John Zacherle.)

Zach with friend James Karen at Chiller.

Zach's Final Years

Another highly regarded although smaller expo, created by a fan of the Golden Age horror films, premiered at the Days Inn in the small town of Butler, Pennsylvania, in the summer of 1997. With a family-friendly approach and an emphasis on horror, sci-fi and fantasy fare from the 1930s through the 1950s, Ron Adams' Monster Bash was born. I first ran into Ron and his dad when they were vendors at Chiller, and Ron told me how much it would mean to him to have Zach appear at the Bash. I wished him good luck and told him that Zach never traveled that kind of distance (a seven-hour-plus trip by car) to attend *any* convention. He was devoted to Kevin Clement and generally limited his convention appearances to twice a year at New Jersey's Chiller Theatre. Ron didn't give up easily, and finally got Zach to agree to a three-day Monster Bash appearance in June 2006.

My journey to Butler that summer was honored by the presence in my car of Zach and Richard Gordon (producer of *The Haunted Strangler*, *Fiend Without a Face* and many more). Writer Tom Weaver, was along also. Speeding along on Route 80, I had to swerve to avoid a car coming at us from the right lane. I was a little rattled, but the only thing Tom seemed concerned about was that, if there *had* been a collision and we'd all perished, a headline in the next day's paper would read,

JOHN ZACHERLE, LEGENDARY TV HORROR HOST, 3 OTHERS, **DIE IN CRASH.**

The weekend turned out to be very enjoyable. I spent most of my time at Zach's table, handling the money as fans paid for autographed photos. I had done this a few times before, but this was usually Zach's friend Jeff Samuels' job at Zach's Chiller appearances. Guest Yvette Vickers, popular for playing sexy roles in *Attack of the 50 Foot Woman* and *Attack of the Giant Leeches*, was new to Monster Bash and looking for someone to hang out with, took to Zach right away and became his dinner partner for most of the weekend.

Zach at Monster Bash with artist Basil Gogos.

The Monster Bash visit wasn't the only occasion on which Zach suspended his policy on extended traveling. In the summer of 2007, Tom and I found ourselves accompanying Zach on a plane ride to Louisville, Kentucky's WonderFest, a convention with an emphasis on movie special effects guests and model contests for sci-fi, horror and comics-related subjects. On this trip, Zach used a wheelchair to ease the everpresent pain of arthritis which by now caused extreme swelling in his ankles. I again assisted at Zach's table. Just for fun, he brought along a pair of deformed false teeth that created the goofy effect of a huge overbite. The first day at his table, he had just slipped them on when we noticed that the young man next in line had teeth almost identical to the fake ones in Zach's mouth. I'd never seen Zach move so fast: He removed the offending attachment quickly enough to avoid what could have been a very embarrassing moment.

With Forry Ackerman at the 2007 Monster Bash.

I was surprised by the number of Zacherley fans there; I had to revise my opinion that his popularity was limited largely to the New York and Philadelphia markets. A number of attendees even asked permission to push Zach around the hotel in his wheelchair.

The morning after the end of the convention, the WonderFest staff treated us to a visit to the Louisville Zoo. It was a very hot day and at one point Zach wanted to stop for a drink. A crowd was lined up to enter the aviary and we joined them thinking we might be able to buy something to drink there.

Zach at Monster Bash with (standing) John Clymer, Tim Lucas, David Colton and (sitting) Eileen Colton.

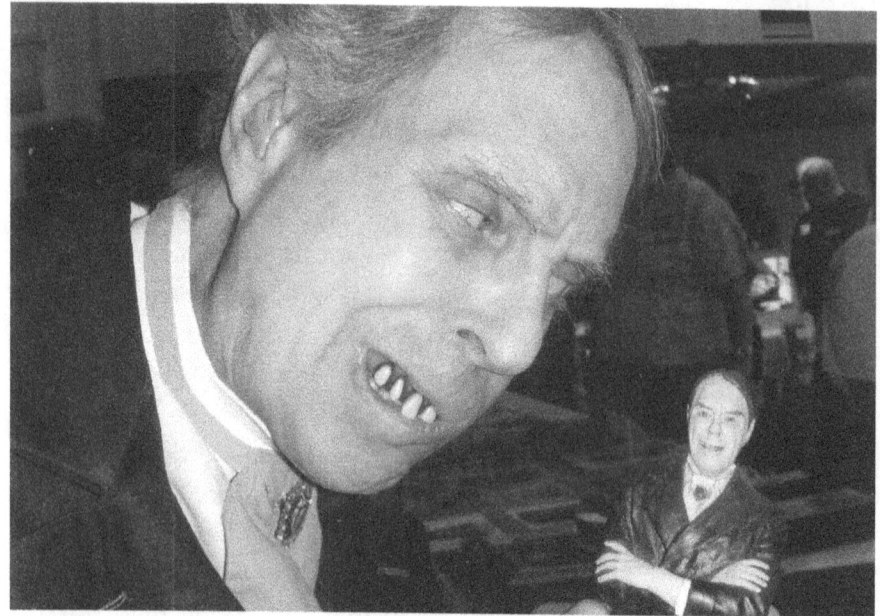
Zach with his goofy fake teeth at WonderFest.

Zach meets a young fan.

Each visitor to the aviary was handed a very small paper cup of liquid to feed to the tropical birds. Zach, thinking it was for the patrons, downed his right away, causing a wave of laughter. When he was told what he'd swallowed, he began to worry about getting ill, at first not knowing he had merely drank what was basically sugar water. Even the next day, on the flight home, he seemed concerned that he might start growing a beak and feathers.

One of the activities I enjoyed the most was continuing our drives through Harriman Park, stopping by "Zach's Bench"—a hand-hewn park bench donated to the park by Sharon Shaw, a fan from Miami. It was complete with an inscribed brass plaque (see photos on next page). After that, it was off to lunch at the Breezy Point Inn on Greenwood Lake. We'd sit on the large deck overlooking the activity on the water: jet skiers, swimmers and vintage motorboats. On one occasion, Zach noticed a classic old boat made of wood rather than the more prevalent Fiberglas. Remembering the 8mm horror movie my friends and I shot back in the mid-1960s, I told Zach how we filmed a sequence in the ruins of a chapel on a small island across the lake (appropriately named Chapel Island). Suddenly a voice called over from the next table: "Hey, I *live* on Chapel Island!" Our conversation had been overheard by this man, who turned out to be the owner of the wooden boat; he also told us that he had recognized Zach's voice. Then this very friendly guy, Victor, offered Zach and me a ride around the lake *if* we came back the following Saturday when he would be participating in a boat show. Of course we returned a week later. By that time, a few local fans had gathered and Zach signed photos for them. Someone handed Zach a straw hat to wear on the boat, which he used to wave to the crowd as he enjoyed being part of the show. Then Victor veered off for our trip around the lake. Victor had had a unique house built when he purchased Chapel Island and after our ride gave us a tour of it. It was equipped with an elevator, a large bank of solar panels and a wraparound deck.

We visited Victor on one more occasion, this time accompanied by Rosemary Schroeder DiPietra and Marsha (Conner) Silvestri, friends from the *Disc-O-Teen* days. As a gift for Victor, I had brought along a copy of my then-new book *The Z Files*, which featured a collection of rare newspaper articles, vintage photos, scripts and handwritten notes from Zach's horror-hosting days. Victor was happy to see us, especially with two beautiful women along. Another tour of the house followed, for the benefit of Rosemary and Marsha, and we all signed the book as we left the house.

Since 1990, Zach had looked forward to his Chiller Theatre appearances and remained loyal to its creator Kevin Clement. His table, manned by Jeff Samuels and Jeff's friend Arnie DeGaetano, never failed to draw large crowds. In the line waiting to meet Zach, there were often celebrities. Just a small sample: Pee-wee Herman, KISS drummer Peter Criss, Doors keyboardist Ray Manzarek, Alice Cooper and actress Valerie Harper. One year the table next to Zach was occupied by Bobby "Boris" Pickett of "Monster Mash" fame (Zach had covered the 1962 hit on his second LP "Monster Mash," also released in 1962). Pickett was selling his own self-published autobiography and I was sitting next to him selling the first printing

Zach at the Louisville Zoo with feathered fans.

Zach's bench in Harriman State Park, New York.

With Chiller guest Pee-wee Herman.

The Zach Pack: Zach's convention table aides Arnie DeGaetano and Jeff Samuels.

After one particularly busy Chiller weekend, Zach, well into his eighties, realized he was too exhausted to drive home to his Manhattan apartment and booked his room for one more night. He wasn't about to risk falling asleep behind the wheel. In a crowded elevator, he expressed astonishment about all the attention he was still getting at the convention. Someone responded with the compliment, "But Zach—you're a famous man!" Zach shot back, with a straight face, "Yeah, I'd be even more famous if I'd tried to drive home today!"

In 2012, Zach's health began to decline. When he felt up to it, he appeared at Chiller, but he had stopped performing on stage due to a lack of energy—a shame, since he had only just turned 96! As much as he enjoyed meeting his fans, each successive Chiller event had become harder on him. On one occasion, Zach exited Jeff's car and passed out in the hotel parking lot. When he revived shortly afterward, he complained about losing the vision in his right eye. A doctor was summoned and his sight soon returned, but after that, his Chiller visits ended. Eventually Zach's memory degraded so badly that he actually forgot that the convention itself even existed. Zach's last Chiller appearance took place in October 2015.

When Zach reached his mid-90s, some of us thought it was possible for him to hit the century mark, but we were also prepared for the alternative. On July 13, 2014, Zach was stricken with severe stomach pains and admitted by his lawyer-friend

of this book, and I enjoyed comparing notes with Bobby on getting a book published. I asked if he had made a tidy profit, and I got a good laugh out of his response: He shot back a sarcastic "Are you *kidding*?" Zach and Pickett performed "Monster Mash" together at Chiller's Saturday night party, backed by the Dead Elvi, with Mike Gilks joining in on guitar. Less than a year later, April 25, 2007, Bobby Pickett died of leukemia at the age of 69.

Dave Chidekel to St. Luke's Hospital in Manhattan. During his stay there, Jeff, Arnie, Dave and Paul Russak straightened up and cleaned Zach's apartment. Shortly after that, there was talk of moving Zach into the Actors Fund Home in Englewood, New Jersey; it was clear at this point that Zach should not be living by himself. He had taken a few falls in the apartment and had recently been provided with a Life Alert monitor. Since moving into Assisted Living was exactly what Zach did *not* want, it was instead arranged for nurses to care for him around the clock at his apartment. One nurse grew fond of Zach and often took him by wheelchair to Central Park, a few blocks east, to watch the tennis matches, a routine Zach especially enjoyed.

Posing with one of Zach's undertaker coats at Chiller: Mike Gilks, Zach, Arnie DeGaetano and Ruth Gilks.

On September 18, 2016, he was taken to Mt. Sinai Hospital with intestinal and leg pains, and then on September 23 to Isabella Geriatric Center. He returned home in October and died peacefully in his own bed on October 27, the way he would have wanted it. John Karsten Zacherle had turned 98 on September 26.

Of all the phone conversation I'd had with John Zacherle, there's one that will always haunt me. Zach wasn't well in the last year of his life, and he was very low-key on this particular day. At one point he said softly, "You know, I think back on all the crazy things I've done in my life—the TV shows, the experiments, radio, the conventions and all the people I've met and how I've been so lucky to have all this craziness happen. [*Pause*] And now—it's over. [*Pause*] It's all over." His tone was so subdued; I couldn't remember another moment like it in all the years I'd known him. This was a very personal moment and I was sharing it with him. And all I could think was, "Not yet, Zach. Not yet."

As long as there are video and audio players, in whatever forms they take in this mega-technical age of ours and in the future, John Zacherle will always be with us. Mike Gilks and I have taped hours upon hours of Zach's talks and performances at Chiller, plus videos of Mike's private recording

sessions with him. Many others have done the same with their own recording equipment. And that's only the tip of the iceberg. There exists on video a treasury of guest appearances on television. Just a few examples: *What's My Line*, *The Mike Douglas Show*, *Tomorrow with Tom Snyder*, MTV Halloween specials, hosting the 3-D film *Gorilla at Large* (1954) and two TV pilots, *Z-TV* and *Don Kirshner's Crazy Nights* (featuring Zach, Vincent Price and John Carradine).

What is truly irreplaceable for me, and always will be, is the privilege of enjoying his quiet presence during those peaceful long rides through Zach's beloved Harriman State Park … sharing laughs and stories while sitting on his bench at Seven Lakes Drive … lunches at the Bear Mountain Inn and Greenwood Lake's Breezy Point. I consider those years a great gift and incomparable blessing in my life.

John Zacherle's presence in this world touched thousands of people and influenced the professional choices of many of them. Some became actors, some makeup artists, at least one a scientist. Maybe those of us who loved him will be fortunate enough to experience him again, maybe (as he often said) in the next world.

John Zacherle's Memorial Service

A story on John Zacherle's memorial service appeared in the magazine *Monster Bash Special #3*; it began with this intro:

John Zacherle died a few days before Halloween 2016, and 18 days later there was a memorial service. At a community chapel on Manhattan's Amsterdam Avenue, approximately 125 friends and family members crowded a room for this celebration of his life. Several speakers, including his niece Diane Hanson and girlfriend Perri Chasin, described him in glowing terms that would have made the ashen-faced Zacherley blush. Several storytellers mentioned his yellow

Volkswagen convertible, which he drove with the top down, sometimes even during snowfalls, the wind in his face and hair and Pink Floyd playing as nature lover Zach soaked up the sights and sounds of his favorite places, among them New York's Bear Mountain and, on the New York-New Jersey border, Greenwood Lake.

Turns out the Cool Ghoul was even cooler than we thought. Way cooler.

R.I.P., John Zacherle.

John Zacherle
1918 to 2016

Forever in our hearts

Good night, whatever you are.

Welcome, Opening Remarks:	Jeff Samuels
Remembrances:	David Chidekel
	Gene Dunham
	Steve Olsen
	Diane Hanson
Reading:	Perri Chasin

In Memoriam A. H. H. 116
BY
Lord Alfred Tennyson

Is it, then, regret for buried time
That keenlier in sweet April wakes,
And meets the year, and gives and takes
The colours of the crescent prime?
Not all: the songs, the stirring air,
The life re-orient out of dust,
Cry thro' the sense to hearten trust
In that which made the world so fair.
Not all regret: the face will shine
Upon me, while I muse alone;
And that dear voice, I once have known,
Still speak to me of me and mine:

Yet less of sorrow lives in me
For days of happy commune dead;
Less yearning for the friendship fled,
Than some strong bond which is to be.

Appendix 1

The following is a record of the films hosted by Zacherley in New York City from Monday September 22, 1958, when he debuted on WABC Channel 7's *Shock Theater*, through his WOR Channel 9 season of 1959-60 (*Zacherley at 12:00*), and ending with his half-season on WPIX Channel 11's *Chiller Theatre* in the Spring of 1964. I'd like to call it a complete listing, but due to the fact that the films shown on WOR were never listed (*TV Guide*'s listings only say, **ZACHERLEY — Mystery**), the compilation of titles there is incomplete. Where possible, I've included a brief synopsis of what Zach did on a particular evening, from *TV Guide* descriptions and, more significantly, from the very valuable and complete notes of devoted Zacherley fan Anne Di Dio, who, sad to say, is no longer with us. Anne could never have foreseen that her dedicated accounts of shows both from WABC and WOR would some day find their way into a book, and I am grateful to her for her priceless contribution to a portion of television history which could very easily have been lost forever.

John Zacherle's first year in Philadelphia as Roland was documented in John Skerchock's *Zacherley Scrapbook* (Dark Dungeon Enterprises, 2002).

Shock Theater (WABC-TV Channel 7)

MONDAY, SEPTEMBER 22, 1958: *Mystery of Edwin Drood* (1935)
TV Guide: Beginning tonight the ghoul Zacherle [sic] will inhabit *Shock Theater*'s subterranean laboratory every Mon. and Fri. nights [sic].
FRIDAY, SEPTEMBER 26, 1958: *Man Made Monster* (1941)
TV Guide: The ghoul Zacherle is host on Friday and Monday nights.

Anne Di Dio: Zach demonstrates "how to wrap a mummy" (a doll which cried throughout the procedure).
MONDAY, SEPTEMBER 29, 1958: *The Invisible Ray* (1936)
Anne Di Dio: Zach has a cosmic ray explosion.
FRIDAY, OCTOBER 3, 1958: *Night of Terror* (1933)
Anne Di Dio: Zach cleans up the crypt following a cosmic ray explosion (which occurred on his Monday night show). He tosses well-deserved insults at the horrible film throughout the night.
MONDAY, OCTOBER 6, 1958: *The Mummy's Hand* (1940)

FRIDAY, OCTOBER 10, 1958: *The Black Room* (1935)

Anne Di Dio: Zach presents a lecture on the Transylvanian language. Isobel and Gasport "speak" in Transylvanian while Zach translates. Isobel babbles things like, "Who was that creature I saw you with last night?" Gasport, offering no cooperation, tosses some arms, legs and other wildly assorted junk at Zach from the ceiling.

MONDAY, OCTOBER 13, 1958: *Son of Dracula* (1943)

FRIDAY, OCTOBER 17, 1958: *House of Frankenstein* (1944)

Anne Di Dio: Zach dissects a brain.

MONDAY, OCTOBER 20, 1958: *Mystery of Marie Roget* (1942)

TV Guide: Zacherley has a party for Isobel tonight, at which he plays "Pin the fang on the Vampire."

FRIDAY, OCTOBER 24, 1958: *The Witness Vanishes* (1939)

TV Guide: Zacherley makes Spider Soup tonight.

Anne Di Dio: Zach concocts spider soup. Some Rutgers boys send him a banana!

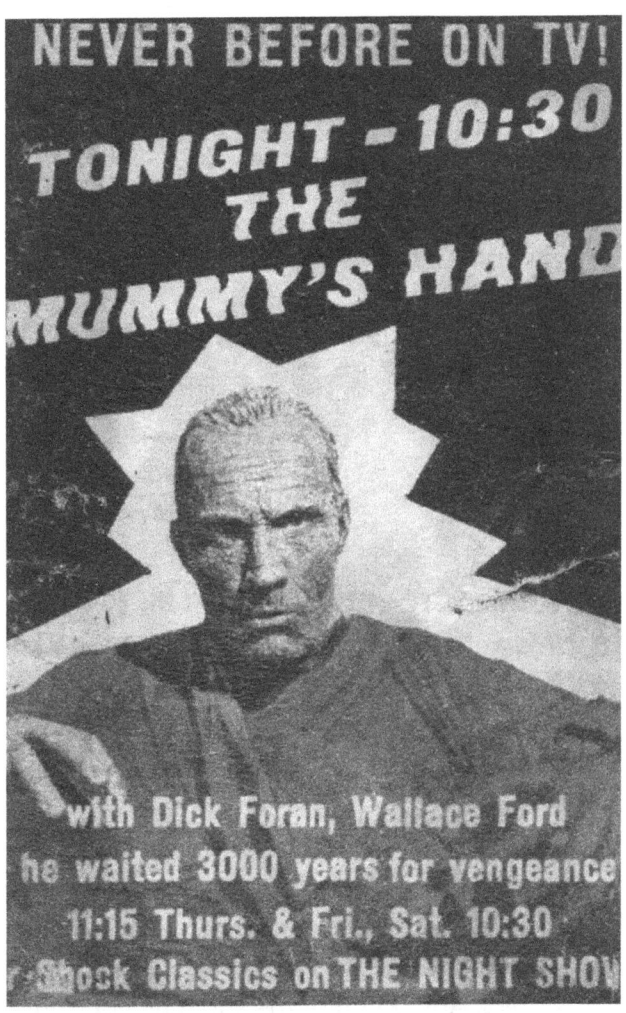

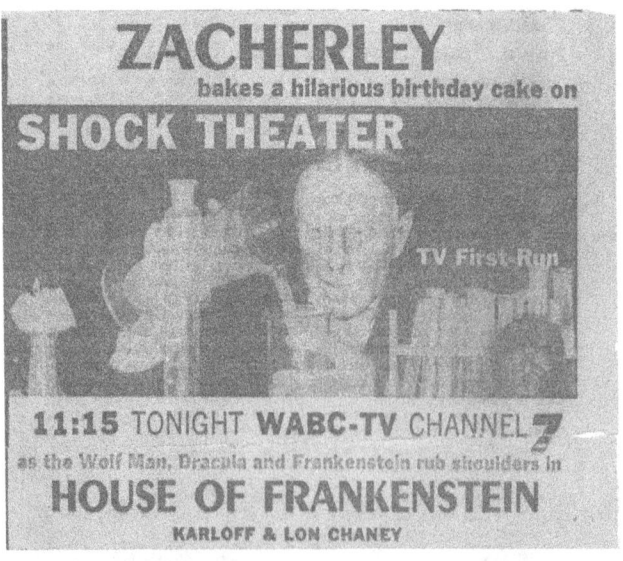

MONDAY, OCTOBER 27, 1958: *The Mad Doctor of Market Street* (1942)
TV Guide: Zacherley redecorates Isobel's resting place with fresh dirt.
FRIDAY, OCTOBER 31, 1958: *The Invisible Man's Revenge* (1944)
TV Guide: Zacherley is host. Gasport gets a medical checkup.
Anne Di Dio: Zach feeds Isobel some invisible chicken soup; she makes quite a mess of the feathers. At the end of the show, he goes out "trick or treating."
MONDAY, NOVEMBER 3, 1958: *The Mummy's Ghost* (1944)
TV Guide: Zacherley and his friends dress up for a costume ball in honor of "Mummy's Day."
Anne Di Dio: Zach campaigns for President of Transylvania. He stands up and salutes when "The Count" phones to wish him well.
FRIDAY, NOVEMBER 7, 1958: *House of Dracula* (1945)
TV Guide: Zacherley is busy making a werewolf mold culture tonight.
MONDAY, NOVEMBER 10, 1958: *Frankenstein Meets the Wolf Man* (1943)
TV Guide: Zacherley discusses the workings of the "nervous system."
FRIDAY, NOVEMBER 14, 1958: *Secret of the Blue Room* (1933)
TV Guide: Zacherley is host. Gasport gets a medical checkup.
Anne Di Dio: Zach attempts to cure Gasport of some illness, first by jumping on top of him to administer artificial respiration, then by making up a giant pill and trying to force Gasport to swallow it. Cutting into the film, Zach chimes in with the (dreary) characters as they continuously bid "'Good night, Irene" to the heroine. Zach ends the show Ben Hecht-style by standing in front of a door sign which reads, "Irene—Off the Air."
(*TV Guide* ran my favorite promo line with their picture of Zach this week: "Zacherley keeps quiet in six languages on *Shock Theater*.")
MONDAY, NOVEMBER 17, 1958: *Murders in the Rue Morgue* (1932)
TV Guide: Zacherley cures Isobel of insomnia.
FRIDAY, NOVEMBER 21, 1958: *Captive Wild Woman* (1943)
TV Guide: Zacherley tries to cure Isobel of her falling hair.
Anne Di Dio: Zach cures Isobel of falling hair by giving her shock treatments to restore hair growth. She loses dark hair and grows back white hair. Zach exclaims: "Isobel, you've been disillusioning me! I thought you said you weren't dying your hair!"
MONDAY, NOVEMBER 24, 1958: *Pillow of Death* (1945)
TV Guide: Zacherley hosts tonight, when Gasport has nightmares.
FRIDAY, NOVEMBER 28, 1958: *Black Friday* (1940)
TV Guide: Zacherley plays Transylvanian folk music.
Anne Di Dio: Zach presents a hysterical demonstration of Transylvanian folk music. He sings and dances (with tambourine) while Isobel plays the piano.
MONDAY, DECEMBER 1, 1958: *WereWolf of London* (1935)
FRIDAY, DECEMBER 5, 1958: *Bride of Frankenstein* (1935)
Anne Di Dio: Zach reads his mail, including a letter "from home" (Transylvania). He draws a map of Transylvania and practices a little

brain surgery to round out the evening. At the end of the show, he and Isobel depart for Transylvania to participate in the Annual Brain Transplant Contest. He promises to whip up a bride for Gasport when they return.

MONDAY, DECEMBER 8, 1958: *The Strange Case of Doctor Rx* (1942)
TV Guide: Zacherley looks on while Gasport starts looking for a bride.

FRIDAY, DECEMBER 12, 1958: *The Invisible Man Returns* (1940)
Anne Di Dio: As promised, Zach whips up a bride for Gasport ... a doll named Melanie. One look at her and Gasport protests by leaping off the table.

MONDAY, DECEMBER 16, 1958: *The Raven* (1935)
TV Guide: Zacherley is host to an invisible Gasport.

FRIDAY, DECEMBER 19, 1958: *The Devil Commands* (1941)
TV Guide: Zacherley holds a banquet for trustees.
Anne Di Dio: Zach prepares a dinner for his "trustees" at ABC. He announces that he'll be presenting an opera, "Il Draculare."

MONDAY, DECEMBER 22, 1958: *The Frozen Ghost* (1945)
TV Guide: Zacherley visits a termite factory.

FRIDAY, DECEMBER 26, 1958: *Horror Island* (1941)
TV Guide: Zacherley and his friends perform in the opera *El Draculare* [sic].
Anne Di Dio: Isobel provides piano accompaniment.

MONDAY, DECEMBER 29, 1958: *Son of Frankenstein* (1939)
TV Guide: Zacherley prepares a hot toady tonight.

[Author's note: This was the evening of Zach's gala New Year's Eve party. Clips from a number of Universal horror films were shown.]
Anne Di Dio: In a poignant moment, Zach serenades Isobel with a sensitive rendition of "My Funny Valentine."

MONDAY, FEBRUARY 16, 1959: *The Spider Woman Strikes Back* (1946)
TV Guide: Zacherley celebrates Gasport's birthday.

FRIDAY, FEBRUARY 20, 1959: *The Soul of a Monster* (1944)
TV Guide: Musical works will be played on this, the closing night of the opera in Transylvania.
Anne Di Dio: Zach performs another opera, "Dr. Frankenstein Meets Faust." The show is plagued with technical problems ... microphone and camera mix-ups!

MONDAY, FEBRUARY 23, 1959: *Night Monster* (1942)
TV Guide: Zacherley practices demoralization of mind over matter tonight.

FRIDAY, FEBRUARY 27, 1959: *The Man They Could Not Hang* (1939)
TV Guide: Zacherley experiments with cross-breeding of amoebas.
Anne Di Dio: Zach conducts an experiment in breeding slobbus amoebae ... all of which end in happy chaos with little amoebae jumping around and Zach tossing them at someone off-camera. One fan sends in a very nice antique telephone for Zach to use; another (female) fan sends him a hilariously mushy mash letter.

MONDAY, MARCH 2, 1959: *Dracula* (1931)
FRIDAY, MARCH 6, 1959: *The Mummy* (1932)
Anne Di Dio: Today is Gasport's second semi-annual birthday (the first was February 16).

Zach celebrates by joining Gasport in a potato sack race.

MONDAY, MARCH 9, 1959: *House of Horrors* (1946)

TV Guide: Zacherley gives a lesson in sculpting.

FRIDAY, MARCH 13, 1959: *She-Wolf of London* (1946)

TV Guide: Zacherley celebrates the winter grape-squashing festival.

Anne Di Dio: Zach squashes some grapes Transylvania-style ... barefooted. He mentions that good ole "Alvin" Freed had been on his Monday night show.

MONDAY, MARCH 16, 1959: *Man Made Monster* (1941)

TV Guide: Zacherley gives his wife Isobell [sic] her yearly diathermy treatment.

FRIDAY, MARCH 20, 1959: *The Jungle Captive* (1945)

Anne Di Dio: Zach entertains his old fiancée ... an ape!

MONDAY, MARCH 23, 1959: *Weird Woman* (1944)

FRIDAY, MARCH 27, 1959: *The Black Cat* (1934)

Anne Di Dio: Zach revamps the "nervous system" of "Alvin" Freed and Roger Shope. He also experiments with the "brains" of Freed and Ben Gross. In honor of the film, he has a cute "two-tone job" Siamese cat with him.

FRIDAY, APRIL 3, 1959 (the first *Zacherley at Large* episode): *Danger Woman* (1946)

TV Guide: Zacherley discusses the hypothesis: "One of our nervous systems is missing."

Anne Di Dio: Zach's show has a new title: *Zacherley at Large*. Now live on Fridays and Saturdays rather than Fridays and Mondays. Zach spends the evening fishing for Alan Freed's "nervous system."

SATURDAY, APRIL 4, 1959: *Behind the Mask* (1932)

FRIDAY, APRIL 10, 1959: *House of Dracula* (1945)

TV Guide: Zacherley presents an original operetta, *The Student Monster, Opus 3*.

SATURDAY, APRIL 11, 1959: *Frankenstein* (1931)

FRIDAY, APRIL 17, 1959: *The Mummy's Hand* (1940)

Anne Di Dio: Zach conducts a head-shrinking experiment.

SATURDAY, APRIL 18, 1959: *Son of Dracula* (1943)

Anne Di Dio: Zach presents a swimming demonstration. The coffin is filled with water. Zach swims and splashes around wearing an old-fashioned bathing suit (with his dickey!) and stages a fight with an underwater monster (a large paper fish), then finds an enormous boot in the water. Throughout these little adventures, Zach demonstrates various "diving tricks."

FRIDAY, APRIL 24, 1959: *Captive Wild Woman* (1943)

Anne Di Dio: Zach operates on Gasport until Gasport finally explodes!

SATURDAY, APRIL 25, 1959: *Pillow of Death* (1945)

FRIDAY, MAY 1, 1959: *WereWolf of London* (1935)

TV Guide: Zacherley conducts a special May Day program.

Anne Di Dio: Zach celebrates May Day (Night) with songs, dinosaur eggnog, a May Pole, an art exhibit and the crowning of Isobel as May Queen.

SATURDAY, MAY 2, 1959: *The Man Who Lived Twice* (1936)

Anne Di Dio: Zach explores the core of the Earth; he blasts a hole through the coffin and sends Gasport down to observe the earth's interior!

FRIDAY, MAY 8, 1959: *The Invisible Man's Revenge* (1944)

Anne Di Dio: Zach performs a brain transplant between Gasport and Isobel.

SATURDAY, MAY 9, 1959: *The Invisible Ray* (1936)

TV Guide: Zacherley presents an original musical comedy: "Kharis the Mummy in Cairo."

FRIDAY, MAY 15, 1959: *Frankenstein Meets the Wolf Man* (1943)

Anne Di Dio: Zach constructs a monster to celebrate National Monster Week.

SATURDAY, MAY 16, 1959: *House of Frankenstein* (1944)

TV Guide: In commemoration of International Monster Week, Zacherley will show audiences how to construct your own monster at home.

FRIDAY, MAY 22, 1959: *The Raven* (1935)

TV Guide: Zacherley holds a testimonial dinner in honor of Edgar Allan Poe.

Anne Di Dio: Zach prepares a Transylvanian cookout.

SATURDAY, MAY 23, 1959: *The Frozen Ghost* (1945)

TV Guide: Zacherley takes his viewers on a tour of Zach's Wax Works.

FRIDAY, MAY 29, 1959: *Son of Frankenstein* (1939)

Anne Di Dio: Zach announces that someone has stolen his clothing from his car and he fears he will have to drive home in his Transylvanian garb! He prepares to shoot Gasport and himself into outer space "to clean up all the junk those silly nations have been shooting up to impress each other."

SATURDAY, MAY 30, 1959: *Dracula's Daughter* (1936)

Anne Di Dio: Zach continues his space shot … without success. All ends with Gasport, the rocket, and Zach's trousers leaving the ground, leaving Zach behind.

FRIDAY, JUNE 5, 1959: *The Mad Ghoul* (1943)

Anne Di Dio: Zach experiments with "brains." A couple of fans send him donations of clothing!

SATURDAY, JUNE 6, 1959: *The Devil Commands* (1941)

FRIDAY, JUNE 12, 1959: *The Mummy's Tomb* (1942)

Anne Di Dio: Zach features his Gypsy Marching Band once again; four live musicians. They accompany him as he sings several Transylvanian songs.

SATURDAY, JUNE 13, 1959: *The Cat Creeps* (1946)

Anne Di Dio: Zach lectures on travel in Transylvania.

FRIDAY, JUNE 19, 1959: *The Spider Woman Strikes Back* (1946)

Anne Di Dio: Zach packs for his trip home to Transylvania.

SATURDAY, JUNE 20, 1959: *Weird Woman* (1944)

TV Guide: Zacherley starts his summer vacation tonight. He will return in September.

Anne Di Dio: At the close of this last show of the season, Zach (*sans* makeup) says farewell to his audience.

Appendix 2

Zacherley at 12:00 (WOR-TV Channel 9)

Each episode of this taped show was run three times, on Friday, Saturday and Sunday.

FRIDAY, OCTOBER 9, 1959: *Zombies on Broadway* (1945)
Zacherley returns to television. According to a listing compiled by Channel 9's Chris Steinbrunner, "Zacherley stumbles down into the crypt under Times Square and decides to make it his home at Channel 9."

FRIDAY, OCTOBER 16, 1959: *Before Dawn* (1933)
Anne Di Dio: Zach is reunited with dear Isobel.
Chris Steinbrunner: Zacherley anxiously awaits the arrival of his wife Isobel, mailed in a packing case from his old channel.

FRIDAY, OCTOBER 23, 1959: *You'll Find Out* (1940)
Anne Di Dio: Zach tries to contact Dracula's spirit through Isobel but doesn't quite make it. He does, however, manage to contact Larry Talbot, Frankenstein and himself!
Chris Steinbrunner: Using Isobel as a trance medium, Zacherley communicates with the beyond … and some very active ectoplasm.

FRIDAY, OCTOBER 30, 1959: *The Return of the Vampire* (1943)
Anne Di Dio: Zach celebrates Halloween with a giant pumpkin. He concocts atomic jelly apples which he then tosses at trick-or-treaters.
Chris Steinbrunner: Zacherley celebrates that holiday of holidays, All Hallows Eve, with a special radio address by Count Dracula in Transylvania. A pumpkin explodes.

FRIDAY, NOVEMBER 6, 1959: *Murder on a Honeymoon* (1935)
TV Guide: After introducing the film, Zacherley tangles with a spinster as he and Isobel prepare for a second honeymoon.
Anne Di Dio: Zach builds a brain … made up of little brains.
Chris Steinbrunner: Zacherley decides to put together a brain for the Cardiff Giant, but over-achieves the parts.

FRIDAY, NOVEMBER 13, 1959: *Red Morning* (1934)
TV Guide: Zacherley presents tonight's film and investigates head-shrinking recipes.
Anne Di Dio: Zach shrinks some ape heads and then winds up growing hair all over himself and his laboratory.

FRIDAY, NOVEMBER 20, 1959: *Cry of the Werewolf* (1944)
TV Guide: Zacherley introduces tonight's film, uses magic to make Isobel disappear.
Anne Di Dio: Zach celebrates National Gypsy Week by preparing Transylvania goulash. For the occasion he wears a single earring!
Chris Steinbrunner: Zacherley campaigns to be chosen leader of the Transylvania gypsies, and is miffed when Isobel is selected Queen of the tribe instead.

FRIDAY, NOVEMBER 27, 1959: *Bluebeard* (1944)
TV Guide: Zacherley introduces tonight's film and decides the world is ready for another Cardiff giant.
Chris Steinbrunner: Zacherley tries to force Isobel to abdicate from gypsy royalty by means of a love potion. When that fails, explosions follow.

FRIDAY, DECEMBER 4, 1959: *One Body Too Many* (1944)

TV Guide: Zacherley recruits civic-minded citizens for his Society for the Preservation of Dark Old Mansions.

Chris Steinbrunner: Zacherley builds a telescope just in time to do battle with some spores from outer space.

FRIDAY, DECEMBER 11, 1959: *The Mask of Diijon* (1946)

TV Guide: Zacherley reminisces about the good old days at Transylvania University.

Anne Di Dio: As a grand finale to his experiment of the evening, Zach ends the show by pouring a sloppy flour and water mixture over himself. The mixture clogs his microphone and drives someone off-camera to shout, "Wipe it off, you idiot!"

Chris Steinbrunner: Zacherley puts on a magic show, climaxing it by sawing Isobel in half.

FRIDAY, DECEMBER 18, 1959: *The Woman Who Came Back* (1945)

TV Guide: Zacherley is official fog-maker for the state [*sic*] of Transylvania.

Anne Di Dio: Zach grows a giant protoplasm — a blob of dough!

Chris Steinbrunner: Zacherley reminisces about prehistoric times with a pasty-faced Glob that dates far, far back.

FRIDAY, DECEMBER 25, 1959: *Avalanche* (1946)

Anne Di Dio: Zach and Isobel celebrate the return of their son from Transylvania University ... after 45 years as a freshman!

Chris Steinbrunner: Zacherley welcomes his always-failing son home from Transylvania University for the Christmas holidays and opens some rather unusual gifts.

FRIDAY, JANUARY 1, 1960: *White Pongo* (1945)

Anne Di Dio: Zach reads "Isn't It Grand?" from Ruth Steinman's and Anne Di Dio's "A Child's Garden of Curses."

FRIDAY, JANUARY 8, 1960: *Love from a Stranger* (1947)

Anne Di Dio: Zach presents the winners of the Isobel Art Contest.

FRIDAY, JANUARY 15, 1960: *Unknown Island* (1948)

FRIDAY, JANUARY 22, 1960

Anne Di Dio: Zach presents another grand opera featuring the aria "You Drank More Beer, Dear, Than I, Dear."

FRIDAY, JANUARY 29, 1960: *Two Lost Worlds* (1950)

Anne Di Dio: Zach experiments with brain surgery and does a dance to Bobby Darin's record "Mack the Knife." He listens to a radio broadcast of a "unique medical demonstration" by Gypsy Rose Lee. He tunes in on sexy striptease music followed by wild clapping and then a police raid. Says Zach, "She's obviously showing slides!"

FRIDAY, FEBRUARY 5, 1960

Anne Di Dio: Zach gives a mummy-wrapping demonstration.

FRIDAY, FEBRUARY 12, 1960

Anne Di Dio: Zach gives Isobel a bubble bath.

FRIDAY, FEBRUARY 19, 1960: *The Body Snatcher* (1945]

Anne Di Dio: Zach sings "Vampire Bite Me," by Anne Di Dio and Betty Valenza. His experiment involves testing men for travel in outer space.

FRIDAY, FEBRUARY 26, 1960

Anne Di Dio: Zach campaigns for the Presidency of the U. S.!

FRIDAY, MARCH 4, 1960: *Cat People* (1942)

Anne Di Dio: Zach presents some of his fans and their pet cats ... in his search for a "vampire cat."

FRIDAY, MARCH 11, 1960: *Mighty Joe Young* (1949)

Anne Di Dio: Zach performs an operation on Joe, Jr., to remove a soccer ball Joe had somehow managed to swallow.

FRIDAY, MARCH 18, 1960

Anne Di Dio: Zach contacts the spirit of Isobel's old nanny who materialized as a charming bone with a hank of hair on top.

FRIDAY, MARCH 25, 1960: a Zasu Pitts film

Anne Di Dio: Zach discovers the "missing link" in the New Jersey swamps ... a swampus amoebus! The friendly amoeba sings with Zach.

FRIDAY, APRIL 1, 1960
(Starting with this entry, some installments present disparities between *TV Guide* and Anne Di Dio — choose your favorite. For accuracy, my money is on Anne!)
TV Guide: Zacherley performs an operation on an injured member of the Transylvanian Olympic soccer team.
Anne Di Dio: Zach presents another opera, "Un Forzo del Banco."

FRIDAY, APRIL 8, 1960
TV Guide: Zacherley mixes zombie gumbo.
Anne Di Dio: Zach tries to revive a mummy.

FRIDAY, APRIL 15, 1960
TV Guide: The spirit world is heard from.
Anne Di Dio: Zach presents a circus, garbed in Bermuda shorts; he performs various crazy antics while swinging from a trapeze!

FRIDAY, APRIL 22, 1960: a Saint film
TV Guide: The Transylvania Light opera Company comes to town, with Zacherley conducting.
Anne Di Dio: Zach explores the weather in his own weather balloon, and discovers an "outer space female" (a floating piece of netting).

FRIDAY, APRIL 29, 1960: *The Seventh Victim* (1943)
TV Guide: Zacherley relates the adventures of his latest trip to the Valley of the Nile.
Anne Di Dio: Zach, Isobel, Gasport and Joe, Jr., go to Central Park for a midnight picnic.

FRIDAY, MAY 6, 1960
TV Guide: The Transylvanian Giant Monster Circus makes its first appearance in the U.S.
Anne Di Dio: Zach gives a tour of Transylvania, performs an Apache dance, and sings with dummy Paula Dupree. He also bakes a cake for Princess Margaret's wedding.

FRIDAY, MAY 13, 1960: *Emergency Call* (1933)
TV Guide: Zacherley's off in a weather balloon.
Anne Di Dio: Zach builds a "Cardiff Giant" (about seven feet tall) which turns out to be a baby giant ... Bawling and wanting to be rocked!

FRIDAY, MAY 20, 1960: *Roar of the Dragon* (1932)
TV Guide: Zacherley selects a queen for the Transylvania Embassy Ball.
Anne Di Dio: Zach digs a tunnel to Transylvania in honor of (what else?) National Tunnel Week.

FRIDAY, MAY 27, 1960
TV Guide: Zacherley starts blasting a tunnel through to Transylvania.
Anne Di Dio: Zach presents a Transylvanian County Fair.

FRIDAY, JUNE 3, 1960
TV Guide: Zacherley builds a merry-go-round, Transylvania style.
Anne Di Dio: Zach gives one of his inimitable swimming and diving demonstrations.

FRIDAY, JUNE 10, 1960: *The Return of the Vampire* (1943)
TV Guide: Zacherley joins in the festivities at a transplanted Transylvania carnival.
Anne Di Dio: Final show of the season; taped reruns will continue through the summer. Zach is joined by Dr. Bellevue who finally leads him away in a strait-jacket. Dr. Bellevue made his first appearance on last season's final show.

FRIDAY, JUNE 17, 1960
TV Guide: Four volunteer apes try out Zacherley's new head-shrinking formula.

FRIDAY, JUNE 24, 1960
TV Guide: Conducting an advanced seminar in the wrapping of mummies, Zacherley is caught in his mummy-wrapping machine.

FRIDAY, JULY 1, 1960
TV Guide: Zacherley undertakes to give Isobel her semi-annual bath.

FRIDAY, JULY 8, 1960
TV Guide: While building a brain for the Cardiff Giant, Zacherley accidentally over-activates the parts.

FRIDAY, JULY 15, 1960
TV Guide: Four "volunteer" spacemen run through a series of Zacherley's readiness tests.

FRIDAY, JULY 22, 1960

TV Guide: Zacherley runs for President with the motto: "Put a Vampire in the White House."

FRIDAY, JULY 29, 1960
TV Guide: Zacherley describes how Transylvania is a summer festival.

FRIDAY, AUGUST 5, 1960
TV Guide: Nanny Bones, Isobel's old nurse, stirs up a batch of voodoo gumbo, with Zacherley's assistance.

FRIDAY, AUGUST 12, 1960
TV Guide: Zacherley sings a duet with an amoeba who hails from the New Jersey swamps.

FRIDAY, AUGUST 19, 1960
TV Guide: Zacherley tries to revive life in a mummy from the Valley of the Nile.

FRIDAY, AUGUST 26, 1960
TV Guide: Ascending into the stratosphere in a weather balloon, Zacherley encounters some strange space creatures.

FRIDAY, SEPTEMBER 2, 1960
TV Guide: Zacherley operates on Olympic star Mighty Joe Young, Jr., who appears to have swallowed a soccer ball.

FRIDAY, SEPTEMBER 9, 1960
TV Guide: Zacherley stirs up trouble with a Cardiff Giant of his own design atop the Empire State Building.

FRIDAY, SEPTEMBER 16, 1960
TV Guide: While building a tunnel to Transylvania, Zacherley gets somewhat off-course and has some strange adventures.

FRIDAY, SEPTEMBER 23, 1960
TV Guide: Zacherley tries out a head-shrinking on four "volunteer" apes.

FRIDAY, SEPTEMBER 30, 1960
TV Guide: Isobel gets her scheduled bath while Zacherley gets one unexpectedly.

FRIDAY, OCTOBER 7, 1960
TV Guide: Zacherley runs tests on spacemen.

FRIDAY, OCTOBER 14, 1960
TV Guide: Zacherley's slogan is "Put a Vampire in the White House!"

FRIDAY, OCTOBER 21, 1960
TV Guide: Zacherley salutes the Transylvania Tourist Bureau.

FRIDAY, OCTOBER 28, 1960
TV Guide: Zacherley and Nanny Bones whip up a batch of voodoo gumbo, a dish which interests a number of culinary experts as well as the Board of Health.

FRIDAY, NOVEMBER 4, 1960
TV Guide: Zacherley croons a duet with a floppy, tenor-voiced amoeba rescued from the Jersey swamps.

FRIDAY, NOVEMBER 11, 1960
TV Guide: Zacherley illustrates a lecture on ancient history with a mummy "borrowed" from the museum.

FRIDAY, NOVEMBER 18, 1960
TV Guide: Zacherley boards a weather balloon and begins an ascent into the stratosphere.

FRIDAY, NOVEMBER 25, 1960
TV Guide: Mighty Joe Young, Jr., the star member of Transylvania's Olympic Team, has swallowed a soccer ball and Zacherley must operate at once.

FRIDAY, DECEMBER 2, 1960
TV Guide: Zacherley builds a Cardiff Giant and takes him up to the top of the Empire State Building for his first thunderstorm.

FRIDAY, DECEMBER 9, 1960
TV Guide: Zacherley begins building a trans-Atlantic tunnel to Transylvania.

Despite my efforts to match the movies with their broadcast dates, the information has remained frustratingly elusive due to a complete absence of such records in any local listings from 1959 and '60. Luckily enough, while helping go through piles of paper stored for decades in his notorious "closet" (in preparation for taping bonus material for the DVD version of *The Zacherley Archives*), we came upon Zach's own handwritten records from the WOR period. From these I was able to compile a nearly complete list of the additional Channel 9 films he hosted. Actually, when I do the math, there seem to be too many titles listed below, but it's hard to argue with the original notes written by Zach himself!

The Gay Diplomat (1931)
Repeat Performance (1947)
Crime Ring (1938)
Lady Scarface (1941)
Forty Naughty Girls (1937)
I Walked with a Zombie (1943)
Super-Sleuth (1937)
Desert Passage (1952)
Step by Step (1946)
Roadhouse Murder (1932)
Two in the Dark (1936)
Mummy's Boys (1936)
Their Big Moment (1934)
Conspiracy (1930)
A Date with the Falcon (1942)
You Can't Buy Luck (1937)
Ladies of the Jury (1932)
Isle of the Dead (1945)
The Saint's Double Trouble (1940)
Blind Ambition (1933)
The Saint in London (1939)
Highways by Night (1942)
Star of Midnight (1935)
Murder on a Bridle Path (1936)
Lightning Strikes Twice (1934)
The Sin Ship (1931)
The Saint in New York (1938)
Passport to Destiny (1944)
The Penguin Pool Murder (1932)
Genius at Work (1946)
The Great Flamarion (1945)

Appendix 3

Chiller Theatre (WPIX-TV Channel 11)

7:30 Saturday evenings

Unfortunately, I could find no record of Zach's experiments from this season.

FEBRUARY 1, 1964: *Monster from the Ocean Floor* (1954)
FEBRUARY 8, 1964: *The Creeping Unknown* (1956)
FEBRUARY 15, 1964: *The Neanderthal Man* (1953)
FEBRUARY 22, 1964: *Frankenstein's Daughter* (1959)
FEBRUARY 29, 1964: *Killers from Space* (1954)
MARCH 7, 1964: *Attack of the 50 Foot Woman* (1958)
MARCH 14, 1964: *She Demons* (1959)
MARCH 21, 1964: *Plan 9 from Outer Space* (1959)
MARCH 28, 1964: *Pharaoh's Curse* (1957)
APRIL 4, 1964: *Daughter of Dr. Jekyll* (1957)
APRIL 11, 1964: *Return of the Terror* (1934)
APRIL 18, 1964: *Curse of the Faceless Man* (1958)
APRIL 25, 1964: *Revenge of the Zombies* (1943)
MAY 2, 1964: *Indestructible Man* (1956)
MAY 9, 1964: *The Walking Dead* (1936)
MAY 16, 1964: *The Four Skulls of Jonathan Drake* (1959)
MAY 23, 1964: *Mark of the Vampire* (aka *The Vampire*) (1957)

Zacherle's last-ever TV gig was an October 25, 2008, return to WPIX to host a prime-time *Chiller Theatre* showing of the 1955 giant-spider movie *Tarantula*. Because of a doctor's appointment, I couldn't accompany Zach to WPIX on October 7 (when his intro and some bumpers were recorded) but Tom Weaver did, and wrote about the experience at some length in the *Tarantula* chapter of his 2017 McFarland book *Universal Terrors*. Part of his writeup:

> [The two ladies in charge] had certain expectations of what a 90-year-old would be able to do—and then in walked the spry, ever-youthful Zach, who wanted to open the show by lying on the floor on top of a six-foot poster of himself from the old days, so that as he sat up, he'd reveal the "young" Zach beneath. His idea was accepted, the camera guys re-adjusted, Zach got down on the floor atop the poster—and one lady whispered to the other, "We *shoulda* got the coffin! We *shoulda* got the coffin!"—apparently they'd had some grand ideas but didn't know if a 90-year-old would be "up" to doing the things they concocted.

(Photo courtesy John Zacherle.)

www.ingramcontent.com/pod-product-compliance
Lightning Source LLC
Chambersburg PA
CBHW081222170426
43198CB00017B/2683